ZERO BASE™ PRICING

PRICING

ACHIEVING WORLD CLASS COMPETITIVENESS

THROUGH

REDUCED ALL-IN-COSTS

A Proactive Handbook for General Managers, Program Managers and Procurement Professionals

David N. Burt
Warren E. Norquist
Jimmy Anklesaria

BYLINE XY PUBLISHING

Library of Congress Cataloging-in-Publication Data

Burt, David N.
    Zero base pricing : achieving world class competitiveness through reduced all-in-costs : a proactive handbook for general managers, program managers, and procurement professionals / David N. Burt, Warren E. Norquist, Jimmy Anklesaria.
        p.   cm.
    Includes index.
    ISBN 1-55738-132-1:$79.95
    1. Industrial procurement—Cost effectiveness.   2. Industrial procurement—Cost control.   I. Norquist, Warren E.   II. Anklesaria, Jimmy.   III. Title.
HD39.5.B86 1990
658.8'16—dc20
                                                                  90-9008
                                                                  CIP

Printed in Malaysia

        19   18   17   16

This book is dedicated to our wives
who contributed to it in so many ways.

Sharon Burt
Carol Norquist
Jennifer Anklesaria

Table of Contents

Preface

A revolution in purchasing is in progress: we are redirecting your attention from seeking the lowest price for supplier-furnished materials and services to obtaining the lowest all-in-cost. All-in-cost is the acquisition price plus all in-house costs required to convert a specific purchased material into the end product. All-in-cost includes any costs resulting from the end product's failure to function in the field due to a defect in the specific purchased material. The principle of all-in-cost also applies to the procurement of equipment, plant, and services.

A second revolution has taken place in what is obtained from outside suppliers and how purchasing managers obtain these supplies and services. No longer do manufacturers limit themselves to the buying of materials and components. Now they also purchase many more complete assemblies. Over the past 50 years, the value of purchased materials and services has grown from 20 percent to 56 percent of the selling price of finished goods.[1] A similar change has occurred in the supplies and services purchased by nonmanufacturing organizations such as banks, hospitals, and governments. Purchasing professionals are their companies' managers of its "hidden factories"—the facilities and expertise available at supplier firms.

---

1. *Annual Survey of Manufacturers: 1985* (Washington, DC: U.S. Bureau of the Census, Government Printing Office, 1987), 1-8.

A third revolution is taking place in the relations with outside suppliers. No longer are suppliers seen as "the enemy" or "necessary evils." At several progressive firms, suppliers are seen as "Partners in Progress." These partners bring technology, design and manufacturing expertise, and managerial skills to the partnerships. They are involved during the design and modification of products. Frequently, they become a single source of supply for the life of the product.

Zero Base Pricing™[2] addresses the development of requirements in three settings: (1) designing and manufacturing products, (2) acquiring capital equipment and plant, and (3) procuring services. The requirements determination process plays a key role in our efforts to obtain the lowest all-in-cost. Not matching the design to the final process and specifying needlessly expensive materials and processes are examples of a requirements process *not* oriented to the lowest all-in-cost.

Historically, buyers have been "price takers," or bid receivers, largely relying on competitive market forces to help them obtain a "fair and reasonable" price. But the application of new price and cost analysis techniques, new questions to ask suppliers, new sources of information, new approaches to what is a fair and reasonable profit, new methods of structuring the pricing of contracts, and new principles and techniques of negotiating combine to allow the professional buyer to adopt a much more proactive approach to obtaining the "right" price.

The professional buyer's responsibilities have grown far beyond that of obtaining the right price. Quality, timeliness, service, technology flow, and purchase of the right material or service are all responsibilities of modern-day procurement professionals and their fellow members of the procurement system. Many of these responsibilities affect the firm's in-house costs.

In-house costs include incoming transportation; incoming inspection and testing; storage; production; warranty, service, and field failure; returns; and lost sales. Each of these in-house costs has two components: (1) an unavoidable element which cannot be further re-

---

2. Zero Base Pricing™ is a registered trademark of the Polaroid Corporation and is used by permission.

duced with the existing state of the firm's resources and (2) an avoidable component. This avoidable component can be reduced or eliminated, provided that the firm's procurement system operates effectively. Zero Base Pricing describes the procurement professional's role in reducing or eliminating avoidable costs.

The quality of purchased materials affects the success and viability of the firm. Defect-free incoming material is a prerequisite to just-in-time manufacturing. Defect-free incoming material results in increased productivity by avoiding production disruptions, scrap, and rework. And defect-free incoming material results in higher quality end products. Zero Base Pricing introduces management principles which greatly reduce the number of defects in incoming materials.

Global competition requires that buyers adopt a proactive philosophy and embrace modern pricing techniques. In 1982, procurement professionals in Polaroid began applying some of these principles under the banner of Zero Base Pricing (ZBP). Using ZBP, Polaroid was able to buy comparable items for significantly less in 1985 than in 1982. Additionally, by focusing on all-in-cost instead of purchase price, Polaroid procurement helped the company gain many additional cost reductions and cost avoidances. In recognition of the critical role played by Polaroid purchasing, the function became seen by top management as a major contributor to the corporation's success in the areas of profits, product quality, reduced cycle time, and the early introduction of reliable new products. Chris Ingraham, at the time a Vice President of Polaroid Corporation, made the following statement recognizing purchasing's contribution: "Today, there is no single group in the corporation with more direct influence on the bottom line than the purchasing organization."

While Polaroid's program may be one of the most dramatic ones on the scene, other organizations have used similar techniques to aid in their efforts to obtain the "right" all-in-cost. Several divisions of The Ford Motor Company and of General Motors, Xerox, General Electric, and the Tennant Company also have achieved great success applying many of these or related techniques. The United States Air Force is the source of many of the techniques of analyzing indirect costs described in Chapter 11, the weighted guidelines approach to profit described in Chapter 12, the sophisticated methods of compensation described in Chapter 13, and the recommendations for documentation of negotiations advanced in Chapter 14.

This book represents the collaboration of three professionals. When the authors began working together in 1986, Mr. Norquist, who is currently Vice President of the Purchasing and Material Management Division at Polaroid, had created Zero Base Pricing and had four years of experience developing it. He had been writing about and teaching the use of ZBP. Articles discussing ZBP have appeared in professional magazines and *The Wall Street Journal, Fortune,* and the *New York Times.* Portions of the present book draw on papers Mr. Norquist presented at the 69th, 71st, 73rd, and 75th Annual International Conferences of the National Association of Purchasing Management. Mr. Norquist was Division Vice President and Corporate Director of Quality and Reliability at Polaroid before he moved to Purchasing in 1981. In 1989, Mr. Norquist received the highly coveted Edwards Medal from the American Society for Quality Control for his work in quality.

Mr. Burt, an authority in the field of procurement, had developed a manuscript dealing with price and cost analysis which drew on state-of-the-art commercial and Department of Defense pricing techniques. In his capacity as Professor of Procurement at the University of San Diego, Mr. Burt had been conducting research on purchasing's role in new product development and had written extensively on this subject. In addition, he had begun research on the procurement system's role in obtaining defect-free material. Portions of the present book draw on Mr. Burt's earlier book, *Proactive Procurement: The Key to Increased Profits, Productivity, and Quality,* published in 1984 by Prentice-Hall. Mr. Burt is coauthor with Donald W. Dobler and Lamar Lee, Jr., of the leading text, *Purchasing and Materials Management: Text and Cases* (McGraw-Hill Book Company, 1990).

Mr. Anklesaria, a chartered accountant and visiting professor of finance and procurement at the University of San Diego, brought accounting, financial, and international expertise to the partnership. He has been teaching and conducting seminars on Zero Base Pricing around the world. Mr. Anklesaria has presented some of these concepts at the 75th Annual International Conference of the National Association of Purchasing Management. Relevant books and articles by the authors are listed in Appendix A.

It is our hope and belief that the concepts, principles, and techniques described in this book will help procurement professionals obtain the lowest "all-in-cost" that is both fair and reasonable under virtually all market conditions.

David N. Burt
Cardiff-by-the-Sea, California

Warren E. Norquist
Weston, Massachusetts

Jimmy Anklesaria
San Diego, California

Chapter 1

Zero Base Pricing™

During a 1982 sales call on a buyer at Polaroid, a supplier's sales representative drew the cost/price scenario depicted in Figure 1.1 on the buyer's chalkboard.

"Now you can see why my company needs a substantial price increase," said the rep. "We've been absorbing rising costs against our profit margin to comply with your hold-the-line pricing. Our company needs to regain its margin. The margin's eroding while we hold our pricing to you stable."

The buyer, who had been trained in Zero Base Pricing™, began to explore this argument by inquiring into the supplier's actions during the period of cost absorption. "How are you fighting inflation? Are you working to resist and change the forces that led to increases in cost?" asked the buyer. "What is your company's strategy for handling price increase requests from your own material suppliers? You even show the future cost as a solid line, not a dotted one! How can we afford to do business with a company that projects costs increasing indefinitely?"

"When your labor rates went up last quarter, were they offset by improved productivity? Hasn't the recent emphasis on reducing scrap and rework reduced both your material and labor costs?" the buyer continued. "This product is now mature and you've had plenty

---

Zero Base Pricing™ is a registered trademark of the Polaroid Corporation and is used by permission.

Figure 1.1 Supplier's Drawing

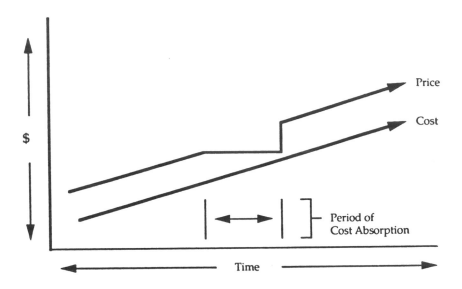

---

of time to recover your initial research and development investment. Besides, a mature product demands less of your general and administrative budget. What else are you doing to reduce your material costs? Have you applied Value Analysis to your product? What is *your* purchasing doing to reduce the cost of *your* materials?"

The buyer drew up a mental cost model: fully recovered research costs, labor and materials cost reduced by learning, less scrap and rework, lower break-even points as a result of diminished G&A and factory overhead expenses. The buyer then stated, "An increase in one or two cost elements doesn't justify a price increase without reviewing *all* of the cost elements."

During this fact-finding period, it became evident that the sales representative lacked a clear understanding of the elements of his company's costs and possessed no tangible examples of having resisted or influenced inflationary cost factors. The sales representative was asked to go back with a points-of-difference summary and do his homework by collaborating with his cost accounting, design, and manufacturing departments. He was asked to review all his costs and develop a list of proposed cost reduction alternatives for consideration at the next session.

Simplified Description

A simplified description of the acquisition price component of Zero Base Pricing (ZBP) was developed to help buyers explain the program to suppliers and salespeople who call on Polaroid. The five cost elements are material, labor, factory overhead, general and administrative costs, and supplier's profit. These are shown in Figure 1.2. Suggestions, more fully developed later in the book, are now presented for each element:

- Material cost—the ZBP approach is to *not* accept material costs from suppliers without supporting evidence. Alternate sources as well as make/buy decisions are considered. Suppliers are questioned on their use of process control techniques and their efforts to reduce material usage. Suppliers are asked: What are you doing to eliminate scrap? Do you have an active Value Engineering/Value Analysis program? What can we together do to reduce packaging, transportation, and storage costs?

- Labor—under ZBP, buyers do not accept labor cost increases from suppliers without supporting evidence. Supplier's wage increases must be absorbed through productivity improvement, or they become a source of inflation and make the manufacturer less competitive in a global market. Emphasis is placed on application of the learning or improvement curve. The supplier's attention to the quality of its purchased materials and its production processes should result in labor savings associated with the "right material," "defect-free incoming material," and "making it right the first time." The professional buyer also recognizes that direct labor costs commonly are the basis for allocating indirect costs and thereby can have a multiplier effect.

Figure 1.2   The Philosophy of Zero Base Pricing: Acquisition Price

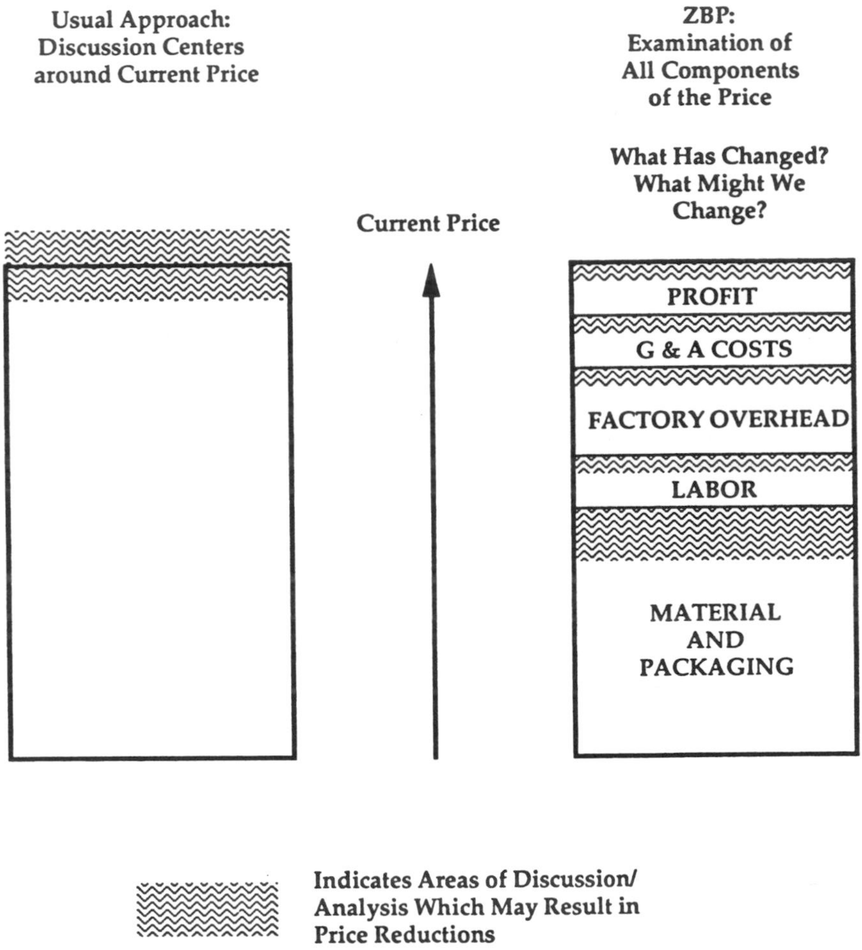

Usual Approach:
Discussion Centers
around Current Price

ZBP:
Examination of
All Components
of the Price

What Has Changed?
What Might We
Change?

Current Price

PROFIT

G & A COSTS

FACTORY OVERHEAD

LABOR

MATERIAL
AND
PACKAGING

Indicates Areas of Discussion/
Analysis Which May Result in
Price Reductions

Copyright © 1990, Burt, Norquist, and Anklesaria.

- Factory overhead—the buyer looks for outdated factory overhead allocations. Mature products take less management effort and incur low or no development costs. Overhead should not be increasing when there are reductions in break-even points associated with streamlined management structures.

- General and administration costs—the buyer questions these from a variety of perspectives. For example, when a purchased item matures, the account costs less to service, it requires less corporate research allocation, and receives less corporate management attention.

- Profit—*profits are not an entitlement.* Profits must be *earned* by performance based on assumption of risk, quality, cost, delivery, and service. The professional buyer varies the profit objective with the situation.

THE EVOLUTION OF ZERO BASE PRICING

Zero Base Pricing was developed by Polaroid purchasing as a means of fighting inflation and controlling price increases during the inflationary days of the early 1980's. Initially, buyers using Zero Base Pricing treated their suppliers more as adversaries than partners. As Zero Base Pricing evolved, a significant change took place in how Polaroid and other professional buyers and their suppliers view one another. The adversarial relations of the early 1980's are being replaced by a collaborative approach between the buyer and seller.

The professional buyer's responsibilities have grown to include: (1) ensuring that the right material or service is purchased, (2) the quality and timely availability of the purchased material, and (3) the supplier's service and technological support. Many of these responsibilities affect the firm's in-house costs including the following: incoming transportation; incoming inspection and testing; storage; production; warranty, service, and field failures; returns; and lost sales. These in-house costs have two components: an unavoidable element which cannot be eliminated at the present state of the firm's personnel, processes, and equipment resources and an avoidable component. We define this avoidable component to be one which can be reduced or eliminated if the firm's procurement system operates effectively. Zero Base Pricing describes the procurement professional's role in reducing or eliminating avoidable costs.

Avoidable in-house costs are all of those costs which are over and above the current day's optimal base cost which results from getting a material or component into the finished product. Included are any costs resulting from the end product's failure to function in the field as a result of incorporation of defective purchased material.

Avoidable in-house costs include the following:

- *Avoidable incoming transportation costs.* Selection of the wrong carrier or route and failure to negotiate a reasonable rate are examples of *avoidable* incoming transportation costs.

- *Avoidable inspection and testing costs.* Failure to select suppliers whose production processes are stable, who demonstrate the capability of meeting the buyer's quality needs, and who are certifiable results in *avoidable* incoming inspection and testing costs.

- *Avoidable storage costs.* The selection of remote and/or less than 100 percent dependable suppliers results in the incurrence of *avoidable* storage costs.

- *Avoidable production costs.* In the area of purchased materials, there are four significant contributors to avoidable production costs. (1) Delivery was not on time or the material was not of usable quality. (2) The wrong material may have been specified. For example, brass is more easily machined than steel. The purchase of steel instead of brass for some processes results in the incurrence of *avoidable* production costs. (3) Use of the wrong tolerances can result in the incurrence of *avoidable* production costs. (4) Avoidable production costs result when incoming defect rates are above the current state-of-the-art optimal base rate. For example, if it is possible to purchase a material at a defect rate of 50 parts per million (50 ppm) and the firm purchases it at an acceptable quality level (A.Q.L.) of 1 percent (10,000 defective ppm), then a significant *avoidable* production cost will be incurred. These avoidable costs will be in one or more of the following areas:
    - ➤ A general degradation of productivity

➤ Rework
➤ Process yield loss
➤ Scrap

- *Avoidable warranty, service, and field failure costs.* Such costs result from the use of inappropriate materials, materials with suboptimal reliability, and from defective purchased materials which pass through production.
- *Avoidable customer returns and lost sales.* The cost of customer returns and the opportunity cost of lost sales resulting from the use of the wrong materials, materials with suboptimal reliability, and from defective purchased materials which pass through the production process are *avoidable.*

Figure 1.3 depicts in-house costs, with emphasis on their avoidable components. Both the acquisition price and in-house costs are significantly affected during the design and development of the products incorporating the purchased materials. These factors are depicted in Figure 1.4.

ZERO BASE PRICING TODAY

Zero Base Pricing is a proven process based on reviewing all the cost elements and working with internal customers and with suppliers to reduce the all-in-cost of purchased materials, equipment, and services. Figure 1.5 shows the interdependent components of Zero Base Pricing.

ZBP and Other Purchasing Trends

Zero Base Pricing fits into today's purchasing environment. Companies *are reducing* their supplier base and establishing *closer, long-term ties* with preferred, certified suppliers. A *mutual understanding of cost* can help build the trust required for the fewer, longer-term relationships.

"Life of the product" relationships now bring suppliers in during the design phase. This trend leads to early supplier involvement, more just-in-time delivery, 100 percent fit-for-use materials, and consideration of all-in-costs.

Figure 1.3   The Philosophy of Zero Base Pricing: In-House Costs

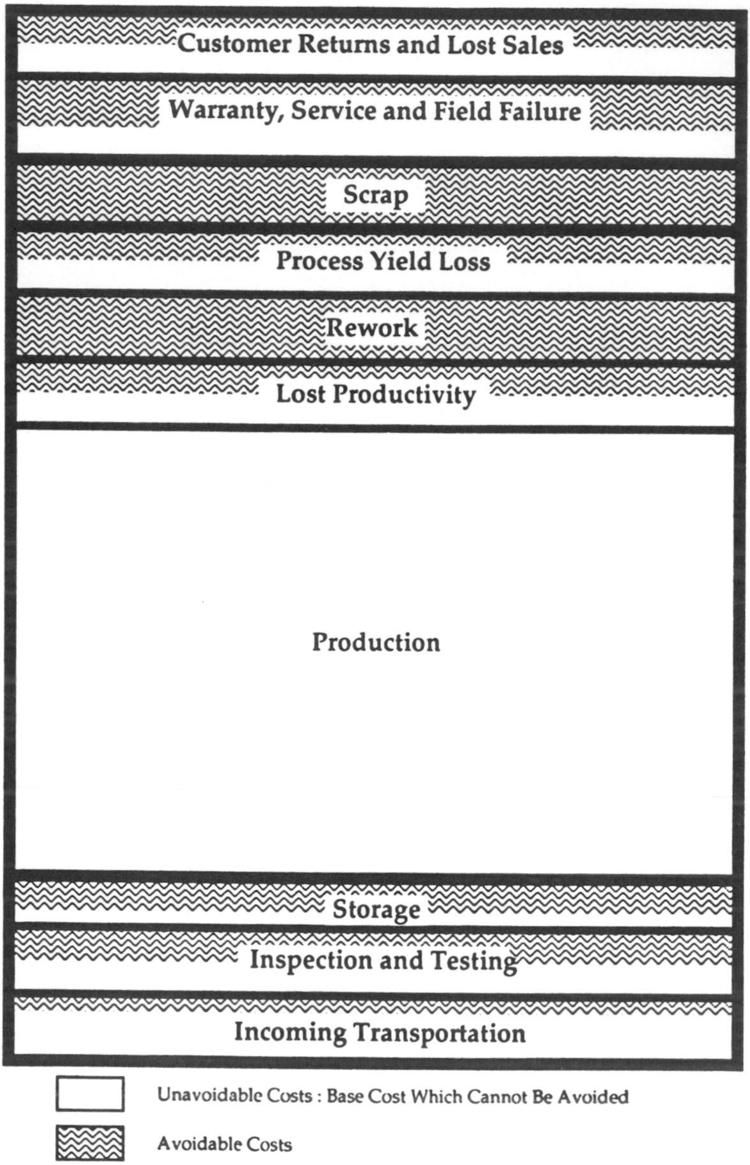

Customer Returns and Lost Sales

Warranty, Service and Field Failure

Scrap

Process Yield Loss

Rework

Lost Productivity

Production

Storage

Inspection and Testing

Incoming Transportation

☐ Unavoidable Costs : Base Cost Which Cannot Be Avoided

▨ Avoidable Costs

Figure 1.4   The Philosophy of Zero Base Pricing: Cost and Quality Drivers

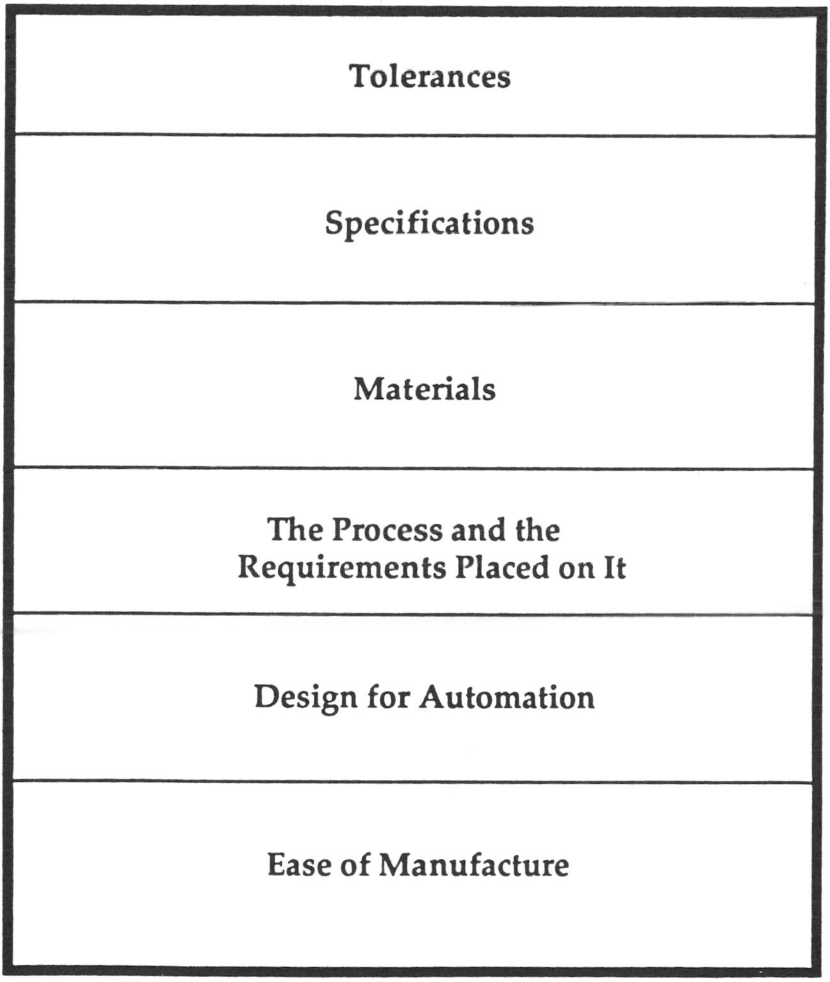

Tolerances
Specifications
Materials
The Process and the Requirements Placed on It
Design for Automation
Ease of Manufacture

Copyright © 1990, Burt, Norquist, and Anklesaria.

Figure 1.5   All-in-Cost

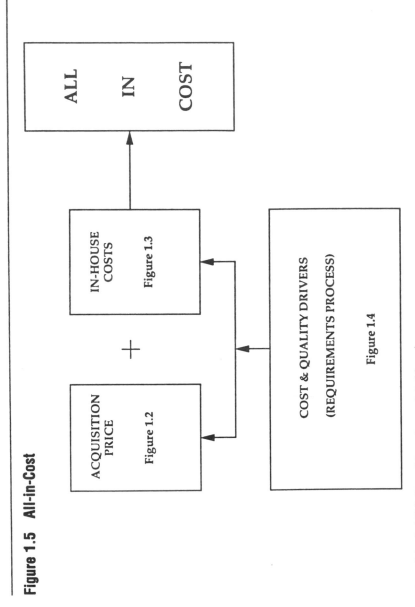

ZBP's approach to opening up cost data is consistent with today's buyer/seller relationships. Well-developed cost models can help identify the major cost components and allow a variety of comparisons. A series of "what if's" can be examined quickly with cost models through the use of a personal computer. As "targets of opportunity" are identified, they can be addressed early and examined for potential cost avoidance/cost reductions which would benefit both the buyer and seller.

As companies emphasize quality in an effort to become or remain competitive in the world marketplace, *purchasing professionals no longer focus on just the low price.* Rather, they are more interested in the all-in-costs achievable by inspection-free, 100 percent fit-for-use materials that run trouble-free through automated equipment and ultimately result in customer satisfaction. Additional factors in all-in-cost are incremental costs in such areas as supplier packaging, transportation, storage, unpackaging, and even disposal of yield losses and incoming packaging. All-in-cost is the meaningful criterion, not the initial price!

Specification and performance requirements should be matched to supplier process compatibility early when changes are easy and inexpensive to implement. When a tool and die maker lacks the opportunity to contribute to the design, the problems encountered during prototyping generally require many costly changes that make cost control difficult.

All-in-Cost: Acquisition Price is <u>Not</u> the Cost That Matters

The "all-in-cost" approach requires help from the buyer's entire design and manufacturing organizations. Where significant, the costs of lost productivity and added inspection, rework, scrap, production disruptions, customer returns, and lost sales should be measured or estimated and provided to the buyer. The buyer must have a "meaningful measure" of quality if quality is to be a deciding point in selecting potential suppliers.

Unless quality performance is solidly documented, it may slip off the scale when the other "available" facts are weighed. Too often, unwarranted optimism plays the part illustrated by the following statements: "Now that 'that mistake' has been made, it won't happen again," or, "The quality is bound to be better in the future so let's stay with the current supplier."

The professional buyer should be in the forefront of demanding clear, realistic, and appropriate specifications from his or her internal customer; be involved in how the supplier controls quality; emphasize the all-in-cost to support a balanced perspective; and involve the supplier early enough to allow supplier innovation and insure cost-effective lead times.

Purchasing Contributes to the Bottom Line

It is the belief of many experts in the field that use of the principles and techniques of Zero Base Pricing can reduce a firm's expenditures both for and related to purchased material, equipment, plant, and services by 10 to 15 percent. Many savings result from refining the requirements process and from improved cooperation on the part of all who are involved in the procurement process. Many of these savings are difficult, but not impossible, to document. They show up in lower production and overhead costs and as a lower cost of goods sold.

Equally important, implementing the principles described in this book will significantly reduce in-house costs. Selecting the "right" material or equipment, establishing sound specifications, selecting suppliers carefully, involving suppliers early in the development process, establishing realistic prices, and managing the supplier relationship during production combine to produce greatly improved internal productivity and product quality and reduce in-house costs. One high-tech firm reports a 90 percent reduction in incoming defects, while another reports a 95 percent reduction. The reader can easily anticipate how these will improve the manufacturer's productivity and product quality.

Return on investment (ROI) will improve by the action of two forces: reduced material costs, and processing the right purchased materials at the required level of quality. Reduced material costs and increased productivity combine to reduce the cost of sales. Material costs, inventory carrying costs, and conversion costs all will be reduced as a result of buying the right material at the lowest all-in-cost. Productivity will increase since higher quality incoming materials will reduce the time spent on test, rework, and scrapped items. Improved product quality will result in increased sales. Figure 1.6 shows the impact of reduced material expenditures, productivity improvements (resulting from reduced incoming defects), reduced overhead, and inventories on ROI. **In this example, ROI increases by over 200 percent.** The improvement on ROI is even greater if the effect of reduced incoming defects on product quality and market share is considered.

Purchasing must get recognition for its contribution to lower material, supply, and services costs and the improved quality of incoming materials if it wants increased management support. The first step is to establish and obtain acceptance of a set of standardized rules for determining savings and quality improvements. Cost reductions and quality improvement reports should be initiated by purchasing, if they currently are not documented. Recognition for their contribution should be given to all members of each procurement team. A cost reduction and cost avoidance program and a quality improvement program listing projects and goals by manager, with very specific rules for calculating savings, and quarterly progress reports, generates a strong image of purchasing as a contributor to the bottom line.

Creditability is a major problem in any reporting system. From the first year, Polaroid purchasing obtained confidence in the savings calculations on hundreds of projects. Purchasing management did this by conducting reviews for top management using random sampling to pick out the projects to be explained in detail. Momentum and enthusiasm are developed by accumulating and publicizing a succession of buyer/customer collaboration success stories emphasizing the dollar savings to the corporation. The ground rules used to report cost reductions, cost avoidances, and quality improvement are discussed in Chapter 16 and Appendix I.

Figure 1.6 Zero Base Pricing's Impact on ROI

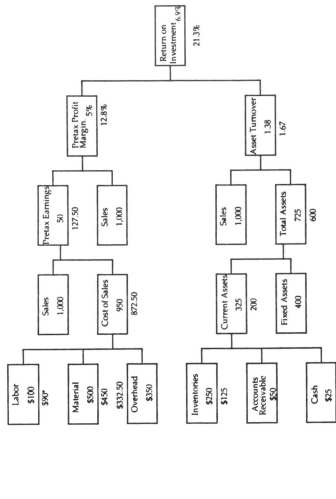

All figures in $ millions.

*Assumes purchase price down 10%, incoming defects down 50%, inventory down 50%, productivity up 10%, overhead down 5%.

ZBP AND THE BUYER

When should ZBP be used?

- Early in the design stage
- Before negotiation with internal customers
- Before negotiation with managers
- Before normal price review dates
- At the time a price increase is requested
- During contract performance
- Continuously during the procurement cycle

The key ingredient in "WHEN" is the word *before*—which stresses the importance of doing homework *before* negotiation sessions. This preparation is especially helpful in dealing with internal customers, who are often the toughest with whom to negotiate. When conducting prenegotiation research, a buyer may find that a different order quantity or delivery schedule will yield a more effective purchase. The buyer should take this information back to the internal customer and stress the possible savings.

Buyers need to be involved from the ground floor even during the design stage and to sell the advantages of early supplier involvement. For instance, simpler tools can be developed and changes made when they are inexpensive to implement if supplier suggestions are asked for as components are being designed. Higher quality at lower cost results.

With whom can ZBP be used?

- With distributors
- With manufacturer's reps
- With suppliers' salespeople
- With the manufacturer's top management
- With internal customers

The "WITH WHOM" of ZBP strategy points out that ZBP is a portable skill.

How should ZBP strategy be employed?

- To develop the "right" requirement
- To develop and review internal cost models
- To set price goals
- To educate the salesperson
- To involve the supplier's upper management
- To manage the supplier relationship to get the "right" quality on time
- To establish the power of legitimacy
- To lower supplier expectations
- To project future costs
- To learn more about supplier's cost
- To motivate the buyer to rehearse and to develop enthusiasm and conviction for his or her own strategy

ZBP Results

Buyers have reported the following results from the ZBP program.

- *Changes focus* from price to all-in-cost
- Dramatically improves *incoming quality*
- Assists in obtaining *the "right" requirement*
- *Emphasizes preparation*
- Pinpoints arbitrary and inequitable *overhead allocations*
- Turns up *cost reductions* not shared with the customer
- Generates proposals for cost reductions and *quality improvements*
- Lowers cost through *improved forecasts*
- Focuses both buyer and seller on progress along the *learning curve*
- Presents *one corporate position*
- *Makes negotiations easier* in multibuyer/single-supplier situations
- Lowers price *expectations*
- Highlights the need for *specification reviews*
- Fits well with supplier quality *certification*
- Identifies supplier/process mismatches and causes *resourcing at lower cost and higher quality*

- Causes announced price *increases to be withdrawn*
- Helps supplier *increase profits by lowering costs*

THE PROFESSIONAL BUYER'S TOOL KIT

We emphasize the following principles, tools, and techniques to support buyers in implementing Zero Base Pricing:

- Maximizing Value Internally
- Value Engineering and Value Analysis
- Early Purchasing Involvement in Capital Expenditures
- Early Purchasing Involvement in Procurement of Services
- Price Theory and Competitive Pricing
- Price Analysis
- Competitive Price Quotations
- Historic Price Comparisons
- Price Index Numbers
- Independent Cost Estimates
- Cost Analysis
- Supplier Partnerships and the Staircase of Knowledge
- Cost Models
- Cost-Volume-Profit Analysis
- Direct Cost Analysis
- Learning Curves
- Indirect Cost Analysis
- Profit Analysis
- Contract Compensation Arrangements
- Economic Price Adjustment Clauses
- Negotiation
- Purchasing Research
- On-Line Data Bases
- Purchasing/Quality Teamwork
- Proactive Procurement
- Procurement System Review
- Documenting Cost Reductions and Quality Improvements

Maximizing Value Internally. Purchasing must work with each internal customer to clarify what is really needed from the supplier. If we are to obtain the lowest all-in-cost, the buyer must be involved early in the process of determining what is required and how the requirement is described. This is true for production requirements, for plant and equipment requirements, and for services.

Buyers also must be salespeople and convince their "customers" (the requisitioners) to be willing to try alternate, lower cost methods to meet their needs. The buyer often must prove that brand preference and value are not related.

Value Engineering and Value Analysis. The fundamental approach of V.E. and V.A. is that nothing is taken for granted. Everything about a product, including the necessity for the item itself, is questioned. V.E. should be used before the design is released to manufacturing and purchasing. V.A. should be used during the manufacture of the product. A savings of $20 for every $1 invested in V.E. and V.A. is common.

Early Purchasing Involvement in Capital Expenditures. The professional buyer must be involved early in the procurement of equipment and plant facilities.

Early Purchasing Involvement in the Procurement of Services. The keys to successful service procurement are the buyer's knowledge of the service, a sound statement of work, selection of the right source, development of a fair and reasonable price, and aggressive management of the contract.

Price Theory and Competitive Pricing. Price theory ties actual practice to economic conditions.

Price Analysis. Price analysis is the evaluation and review of the total price of an item without regard to cost or profit.

Competitive Price Quotations. Once the buyer has determined that effective price competition exists, he or she can accept the lowest responsible and responsive quote.

Historic Price Comparisons. The professional buyer can perform price analysis by comparing a proposed price with historic quotes or prices for the same or similar item. In these comparisons, it is vital to ensure that the base price is fair and reasonable, a valid standard against which to measure the offered price.

Price Index Numbers. Price index numbers are used to (1) deflate or inflate prices for comparison analysis, (2) to project price or cost escalation in contracts, and (3) to inflate and deflate costs for trend analysis.

Independent Cost Estimates. When other techniques of price analysis can't be used, the buyer often can have a company cost engineer develop an independent cost estimate. This estimate becomes the base for comparisons. This comparison allows the buyer to decide if the price is fair and reasonable.

Cost Analysis. Cost analysis provides a technique to evaluate a price by analyzing the individual elements of cost such as material, labor, indirect cost, and profit. Cost analysis is a prime way to assure value. The reader will be shown when cost analysis is warranted, how to do it, and what to guard against.

Supplier Partnerships and the Staircase of Knowledge. The development of supplier partnerships may be viewed as a series of steps which ultimately results in open cost negotiations.

Cost Models. With such models, the buyer can show the effect of a change in material or processes on cost (the dependent variable). A cost model becomes more valuable as it increases in definition, accuracy, and detail. Industrial and process engineering should be invited to help develop such models and to help purchasing fit the pieces whenever there is a cost/price puzzle.

Cost-Volume-Profit Analysis. How does increased or decreased volume affect the supplier's total and unit costs? How should an option to buy more affect the unit price?

Direct Cost Analysis. Direct cost analysis reviews and evaluates the supplier's direct cost data and other factors used in estimating the direct costs.

Learning Curves. Knowledge of learning curve theory allows the buyer to predict direct labor hours, and units of material required, as well as the dollar cost of subcontracted items for recurring operations when requirements are known for the first unit of production.

Indirect Cost Analysis. Indirect cost analysis reviews and evaluates the supplier's indirect cost data and judgmental factors applied in projecting and allocating from the data (or cost model data) to the estimated indirect costs.

Profit Analysis. Profit analysis should reward good suppliers and result in effective and economical contract performance.

Contract Compensation Arrangements. A wide selection of contract compensation arrangements is necessary to provide the flexibility needed when buying a variety of supplies and services under varying conditions of risk.

Economic Price Adjustment Clauses. The buyer recognizes that the supplier's material and labor unit costs may go up or down over time. A well-constructed economic price adjustment clause eliminates the contingencies in prices resulting from the supplier's uncertainty about cost increases. Such a clause also ensures that any decreases in the price of significant inputs are passed on to the purchaser.

Negotiation. We view negotiation as a process of arriving at a common understanding through mutual responsiveness, problem solving, or bargaining. Negotiation, in the context of Zero Base Pricing, is the process of preparing, planning for, and conducting discussions on all aspects of the proposed contract. The preparation phase, the most crucial to a successful negotiation, draws heavily on the analytical techniques developed in this book. Since buyers change and the human memory is frail, the buyer should document the negotiation as it occurs.

Purchasing Research. Purchasing research provides information which helps buyers who are preparing for negotiations, searching for new sources, using economic forecasts, and developing escalator clauses.

On-Line Data Bases. New services provide a way to get up-to-the-minute data on suppliers, materials, indexes, the economy, and industry trends. Such services make the vast amount of information available via a computer or daily facsimiles.

Purchasing/Quality Teamwork. The buyer has many responsibilities to perform to ensure that the desired level of quality of incoming material is achieved. The purchasing/quality team plays a major role in reducing the quality portion of all-in-cost.

Proactive Procurement. With this approach, the purchasing department is involved in the requirements process where it provides information on the commercial implications of alternate materials, equipment, and services. Purchasing takes the initiative to make savings happen throughout the procurement system. With proactive procurement, all members of the procurement system—whether forecasters in marketing, designers and cost estimators in engineering, production planners and inventory managers, quality assurance personnel, the purchasing staff, or others—recognize their role in the procurement system. They cooperate in making the organization more profitable through more effective procurement. The procurement system is portrayed in Figure 1.7.

Procurement System Review. A review of an organization's procurement system facilitates the development of proactive procurement and of productive internal partnerships. Teamwork allows us to maximize value internally and reduce all-in-cost.

Documenting Cost Reductions and Quality Improvements. One of the keys to developing and maintaining a successful Zero Base Pricing system is to systematically document and publicize the resulting benefits.

PLAN OF THE BOOK

This chapter has described Zero Base Pricing and its benefits. The chapter has introduced the concept of all-in-cost and has established the need for buyers to work with both internal customers and suppliers to minimize this cost.

Chapter 2, "Maximizing Value Internally," investigates the development of requirements for production materials. A major portion of the savings and quality improvements resulting from Zero Base Pricing occurs during the new product design and development process. We also look at the important role of the purchase description in controlling all-in-cost.

Chapter 3, "Value Engineering and Value Analysis," discusses another key tool in an effort to obtain the right all-in-cost.

Chapter 4, "The Buyer's Role in Capital Expenditures," describes two of the most complex procurements confronting the professional buyer. These procurements have profound impacts on the responsiveness (cycle time), capacity, profitability, and productivity of the organization. These procurements require considerable planning, coordination, and cooperation on the part of all involved per-

Figure 1.7   The Procurement System

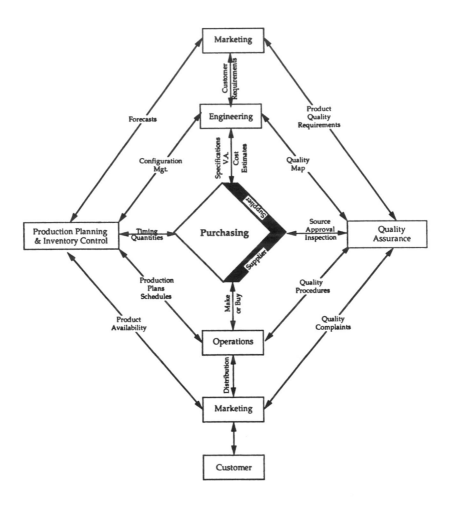

sonnel. The professional buyer has key roles to play in the procurement of equipment and plant.

Chapter 5, "Services," describes the procurement of services and the key role to be played by the buyer. Many managers who buy services, especially professional services, don't appreciate the dollars that purchasing can contribute to the bottom line. Early purchasing involvement in the development of services requirements results in significant dollar savings and a higher level of customer satisfaction.

Chapter 6, "Pricing Theory and Competitive Pricing," introduces the economic principles which are the foundation of modern pricing. The chapter provides an understanding of what a price represents and discusses how prices tend to vary under differing economic conditions.

Chapter 7, "Price Analysis," discusses the relationship between price and cost analysis and establishes the need for some form of analysis on every purchase. The chapter then describes four approaches to conducting price analysis.

Chapter 8, "Cost Analysis and Cost Models," describes three methods of obtaining cost data: through partnership relations, from suppliers in response to requests for proposal requirements, and through the development and use of cost models. The chapter then addresses the buyer's role in analyzing the available cost data.

Chapter 9, "Cost-Volume-Profit Analysis," analyzes how a supplier's profit is affected by contract cost elements and by changes in volume. When preparing for negotiations, the buyer needs to know how changes in volume will affect the supplier's total and unit costs.

Chapter 10, "Analysis of Direct Costs," discusses the dual importance of direct costs: frequently they represent 35-60 percent of a supplier's costs, *and* they usually are the basis for allocating most indirect (overhead) costs. The chapter pays particular attention to ways of controlling direct labor costs.

Chapter 11, "Analysis of Indirect Costs," addresses three crucial issues: the equitableness of the supplier's indirect costs, the role of the supplier's forecast in allocating indirect costs, and the supplier's basis of recovering allowable indirect costs.

Chapter 12, "Profit Analysis," introduces an objective approach to establishing the supplier's profit goal. The approach helps the buyer evaluate the profit component in relation to the supplier's requirements.

Chapter 13, "Contract Compensation Arrangements," introduces a wide selection of compensation arrangements, thereby providing the buyer with the flexibility needed for the procurement of a large variety of supplies and services. These arrangements reflect a range of both cost (risk) responsibility assumed and profit potential.

Chapter 14, "Negotiation," shows how to apply the various price and cost techniques during negotiations. The chapter also describes the documentation required in anticipation of subsequent questions and possible changes.

Chapter 15, "Zero Base Pricing's Effect on Product Quality," takes a system's point of view in eliminating incoming defects. Supplier quality problems arise from many sources: sudden schedule changes; insufficient teamwork in new product development; designs which cannot be produced economically by suppliers; poor source selection; faulty pricing; insufficient attention to supplier management; reliance on inspecting quality (in lieu of designing and building-in quality); and a widespread belief that suppliers are our adversaries, not our partners.

Chapter 16, "How to Implement Zero Base Pricing," describes two approaches to gaining the benefits of ZBP. Zero Base Pricing can start in the purchasing department. Purchasing then can build on its successes to increase the recognition of what purchasing can contribute to the firm's profitability. Or, top management may sponsor or direct the required changes. The Procurement System Review provides a proven approach to identifying needed changes in the procurement system and implementing the required changes.

RECOMMENDED READING

Richard Schonberger, *World Class Manufacturing,* (New York: The Free Press, 1986).

Chapter 2

Maximizing Value Internally

In Chapter 1 we established that the process of obtaining the lowest all-in-cost begins during the determination of what to buy and how to describe this requirement. To do this, the buyer must work with the internal customer. The professional buyer does *not* wait until a requisition lands in his or her in-basket or shows up on the computer screen. Rather, such a buyer is involved early in the process of deciding what will be purchased. Many experienced buyers estimate that the savings potential of an effective requirements process is equal to or greater than that of effective buying. In this chapter, we look at how the professional buyer maximizes value inside the company for production materials requirements. Chapter 4 describes this process for capital equipment and buildings and Chapter 5 describes the process when purchasing services.

THE DESIGN AND DEVELOPMENT PROCESS: PRODUCTION MATERIALS

Purchasing is moving to earlier and earlier involvement in the new product development process because it can make large contributions to quality, cost, and market availability. Many companies find that scientists and engineers trained in purchasing are a necessary part of the design team. Other companies have had success assigning purchasing professionals to their design teams. Such early purchasing involvement almost always coincides with early involvement of one or more prospective suppliers.

Early Supplier Involvement

The move to early supplier involvement is a result of the following five trends:

- Quality and reliability demands are increasing
- Faster product development has become a major competitive weapon
- Materials and component technologies are changing rapidly and supplier innovations need to be incorporated at the design stage
- Product life cycles are becoming shorter
- Purchases by manufacturing companies are increasing as a percent of the cost of sales

Improving quality and reliability generally requires additional development time. Thus, the first two trends are in conflict! The most cost-effective way of dealing with this conflict is to involve suppliers early in the design process. Early purchasing involvement (EPI) generally results in improved quality and reliability for the new product and substantial savings in development time and material cost, since the supplier is allowed to contribute its technical expertise and information on its manufacturing and quality capabilities.

Suppliers have long interacted with design engineering in an effort to have their products "spec'd in," usually on a sole source basis. In many cases, such action was to the benefit of both the supplier and the manufacturer. Unfortunately, many problems arose in other situations. Frequently, there was no competition, so the "best" item and the "right" price were not obtained. The majority of engineers focus on technology, performance, and reliability. They pay relatively little attention to supplier capacity, manufacturing and quality systems, financial strength, and related nontechnological issues. Their involvement in price often creates false expectations.

Early supplier involvement (ESI) is a component of the early purchasing involvement program. With ESI, suppliers are carefully prequalified to ensure that they possess both the desired technology and the right business/manufacturing capability. In the vast majority of cases, early supplier involvement under EPI involves only one, two, or three prequalified potential suppliers. Thus, we gain the technological benefits of early supplier involvement with due attention paid to the commercial aspects of the relationship. At last, we are able to enjoy the best of two worlds.

Requirements for production items originate during the design (and possibly, redesign) of the firm's products. Design is the progression of an abstract notion to something concrete that has function and a fixed form. This form is then described so that it can be produced at a designated quality. A 1984 survey by *Machine Design* indicates that the average development time for new products is 14 months from the start of development, through design and manufacturing, to readiness for sale.[1] The design stage is frequently the only point at which a majority of the cost of making an item can be reduced or controlled. If costs are not controlled here they may be built in permanently, resulting in an expensive, noncompetitive product. Later cost reductions are a poor substitute for having the lower cost design from the beginning.

Quality and Reliability

The desired levels of quality and reliability must be engineered into the item at the design stage. We now recognize that higher product quality will lead to increased market share. Internally, improved quality leads to less test, less rework, and less scrap, resulting in improved productivity and job satisfaction. In turn, lower costs and higher profits result.[2] Purchased materials which are virtually free of defects are a prerequisite to the successful implementation of just-in-

---

1. Raymond E. Herzog, "How Design Engineering Activity Affects Suppliers," *Business Marketing*, November 1985: 136-143.

2. David Garvin of Harvard University writes that "in the room air conditioning industry U.S. companies with the highest quality were five times as productive, when measured by units produced per man-hour of assembly line direct labor, as companies with the poorest quality." "What Does Product Quality Really Mean," *Sloan Management Review*, Fall 1984: 25–43.

time (JIT) manufacturing. With JIT, we no longer have inventories of materials available to draw on if a defect is encountered. Some of the benefits of improved quality are shown in Figure 2.1.

Design Teams

Progressive companies view the design process as one to be conducted by a team representing many functional areas. Product planning, design engineering, reliability engineering, purchasing, manufacturing engineering, quality engineering, finance, and field support all are represented, as appropriate. The turnaround of many now successful manufacturers during the 1980's resulted from replacing departmental walls with teamwork among those who should be part of the design process.

Companies that do not have cooperative teamwork among functions often have a design function that operates in an information vacuum. The result is designs which

- are not responsive to customers' demands for style, quality, and easy maintenance,
- are not optimized for quality,
- fail to consider manufacturing's capabilities,
- fail to consider supplier capabilities, are not designed for low-cost, high-quality service support, or
- are not designed for simplicity and maximum use of standardized, proven high-quality, readily available purchased parts.

Inadequate teamwork among divisions frequently is accompanied by major scheduling problems which delay development and production times and impede early recognition of problem areas. Results often include extensive redesign, rework, and retrofit operations.

The traditional approach to new product development is portrayed in Figure 2.2.

Figure 2.1 Benefits of Improved Quality

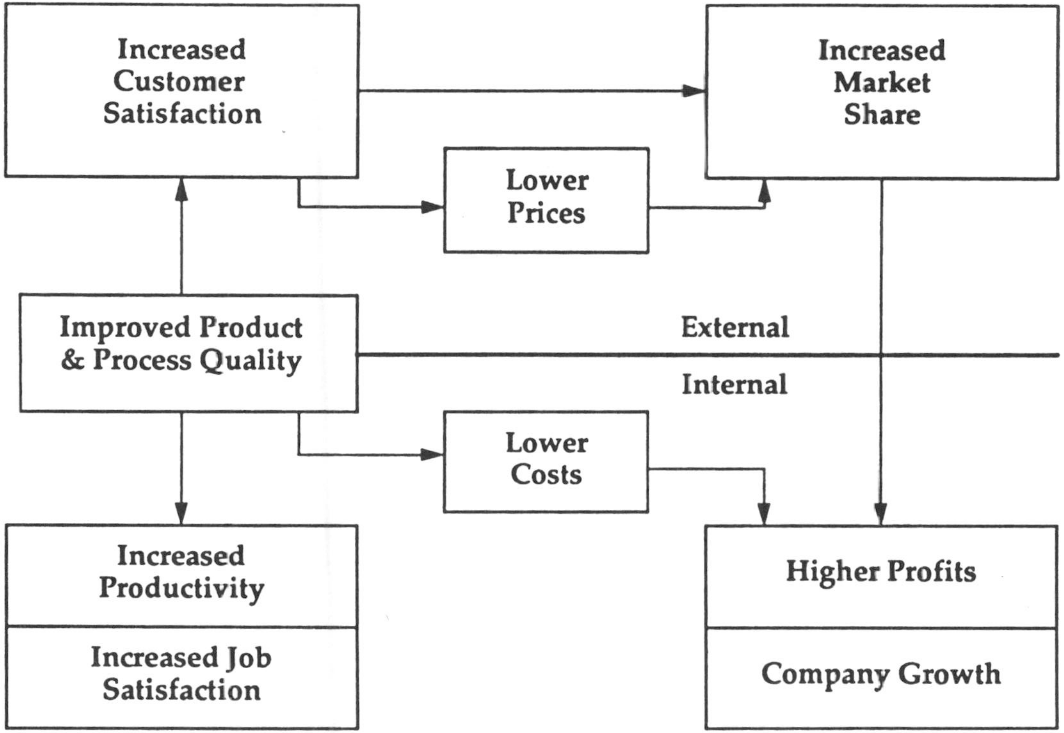

Figure 2.2   The Traditional Approach to New Product Development

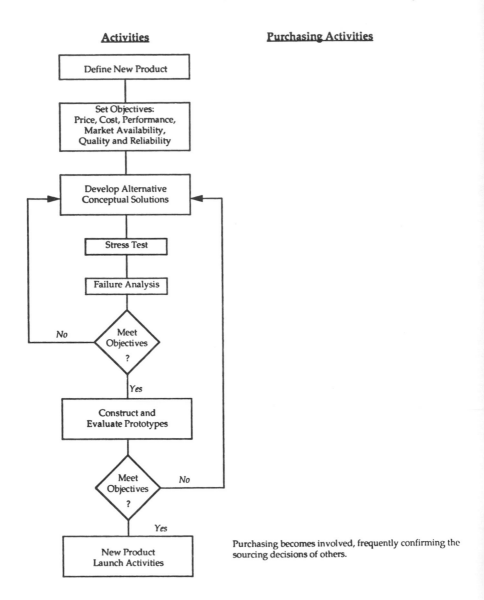

THE MODERN DESIGN AND DEVELOPMENT PROCESS

Leading firms such as Polaroid, Xerox, Ford, and General Electric have learned that early involvement of their potential suppliers results in significant cost reductions. When Jim Walz was Material Manager at G. E.'s Evendale plant, he contrasted the traditional approach to design and supplier selection with G. E.'s "new" early supplier involvement program. Under the traditional approach, engineering would design a component based on textbook principles or on what could be manufactured within G. E. A specification would be developed and forwarded to purchasing, which would attempt to secure competitive quotes from potential suppliers. Once a supplier had been selected, the fun began. The supplier's manufacturing equipment and/or processes would have to be altered to allow production of the specified material. Delays and quality problems were the norm. As would be expected, this approach to procurement was expensive. When G. E. began planning the development of its new commercial jet engine, sixteen design teams were established. Each team contained three members of the procurement department. These procurement personnel participated in the selection of suppliers who were invited to participate in the design and development of components which they could supply—usually without having to make expensive equipment or process changes. The savings to G. E. were in the hundreds of millions of dollars.

Xerox reports that a combination of early supplier involvement as well as the volume leverage that results from a reduction in its supplier base netted cost reductions of close to 10 percent *a year* for the period 1980-1984.[3]

Today, much more planning, coordination, and reviewing takes place during the design and development process than previously was the case. Paper reviews, prototype analysis, failure analyses, stress analyses, and value engineering all are conducted in an effort to develop *producible,* defect-free products. The modern design and development process and the part purchasing should play are shown in Figures 2.3 (a), (b), and (c).

---

3. Somerby Dowst, "Skill in Managing Suppliers Makes Xerox Our '85 Medalist," *Purchasing,* June 27, 1985: 58-76.

Figure 2.3 (a)   The Modern Design and Development Process (Investigation Phase)

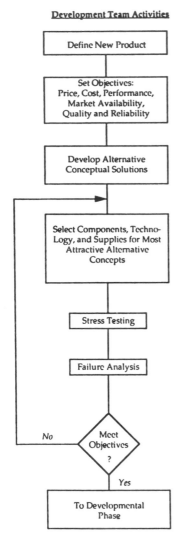

<u>Development Team Activities</u>

Define New Product

Set Objectives:
Price, Cost, Performance,
Market Availability,
Quality and Reliability

**Develop Alternative
Conceptual Solutions**

**Select Components, Techno-
Logy, and Supplies for Most
Attractive Alternative
Concepts**

Stress Testing

Failure Analysis

No — Meet Objectives ?

Yes

To Developmental Phase

<u>Purchasing Activities</u>

Purchasing provides a window to new components which suppliers have developed. This information may cause marketing and engineering to identify new product possibilities.

Purchasing provides information on the cost, performance, market availability, quality, and reliability of components which may be used. Purchasing works with other team members to identify and qualify potential supply partners. Such partners will be invited to participate at this or the conceptual solution phase.

Purchasing provides input on the economy and availability of materials required with each approach.

Purchasing develops preliminary supply plans.

Copyright © 1990, Burt, Norquist, and Anklesaria.

Figure 2.3 (b)   The Modern Design and Development Process (Development Phase)

Development Team Activities
From Investigative Phase

Purchasing Activities

Purchasing solicits and screens supplier value analysis suggestions which may result in an established product being returned to the development phase in an effort to reduce costs, increase quality, or both.

Purchasing provides input on the impact of specifications on cost and availability. Purchasing monitors impact of design on company's standardization program.

- Design and Build Prototype
- Design Review
- Meet Obligations ? — No
- Yes
- Qualification Testing
- Failure Analysis
- Meet Technological Objectives? — No
- Yes
- Value Engineer

Purchasing provides input on cost and availability of alternative materials.

- Design Changes? — Yes
- No
- To Production Phase

The authors gratefully acknowledge the assistance of Richard Y. Moss II, Reliability Engineering Manager, Hewlett Packard Corporation, in the development of Figures 2.3 (a), (b), and (c). Additional, more detailed information on the reliability aspects of the design process may be found in Chapter 9, "Engineering In Reliability" by Mr. Moss, contained in the *Reliability Handbook*, edited by W. Grant Ireson, McGraw-Hill Publishing Company, 1988.

Figure 2.3 (c)   The Modern Design and Development Process
(Production Phase)

Development Team Activities   Purchasing Activities
From Developmental Phase

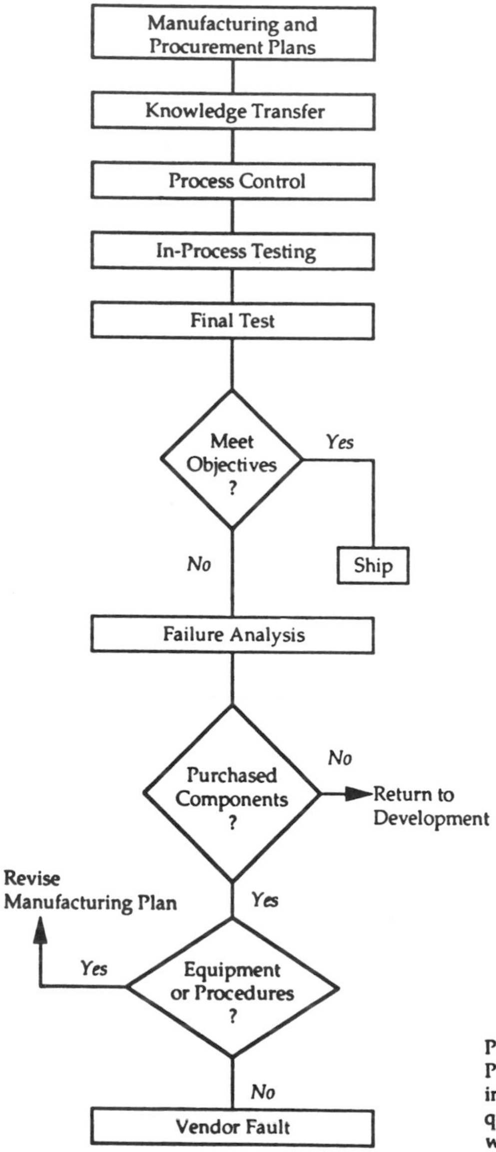

Purchasing formalizes sourcing decisions.

Purchasing notifies sister divisions of problem.
Purchasing directs supplier to develop and
implement corrective action plan. Purchasing,
quality and manufacturing, as appropriate, work
with supplier to correct problem.

Copyright © 1990, Burt, Norquist, and Anklesaria.

The Investigation Phase. The modern design and development process begins with the investigation phase. First, the new product is defined. This function normally is performed by marketing.

Next the needs, desires, and objectives for the product are established. These needs are based on marketing's perception or knowledge of what customers want, balanced against the company's objectives and resources. Needs that are potentially compatible with the firm's objectives (profit potential, sales volume, payback period, etc.) and resources (personnel, machines, and management) are considered for development. Product objectives, including performance, price, quality, and market availability, are then established and become the criteria that guide subsequent design, planning, and decision making.

Alternative ways of satisfying these needs, desires, and objectives should be developed and then evaluated against the criteria. Often, an engineer has a need that must be filled: a gear ratio, a structural component, a capacitance, a memory requirement. This need could be met in more than one way, yet many times the engineer may not be aware of the options available. Here the buyer can supply suggestions. A gear, for example, might be machined of bronze or steel, die cast in aluminum or zinc, molded from plastic, or formed by powder metallurgy. All of these options may meet engineering's constraints while offering a wide range of cost, availability, and reliability choices.[4] Purchasing and potential suppliers provide information on the availability of the materials and sub-assemblies to be purchased under each approach.

The early involvement of quality engineers allows advanced quality planning to commence in a timely manner. quality standards are developed to ensure that what is being designed can be produced at the quality specified. Specifications for test equipment and procedures are developed. Required test equipment is carefully selected and purchased. The firm's and its potential suppliers' quality management systems are reviewed to ensure that once production begins, defect-free materials result.

---

4. Jim Esterby, "Design Stage Is the Best Time to Prevent Quality Problems," *Purchasing,* December 8, 1983: 78 A1.

The selection of components is facilitated by the availability of an internal current catalog of items and sources which have been prequalified.[5] The use of such a catalog simplifies the design engineers' job while simultaneously supporting the efforts of materials management to standardize the items used.

There are many hidden costs associated with an unnecessary variety of production items or purchased components:

- Excess paperwork
- Short, needlessly expensive production runs
- Higher inventory costs
- Higher unit costs of small quantities of purchased materials
- Additional order processing costs
- Higher inspection and materials handling costs
- Additional quality problems
- An increased probability of stock outages
- Field support problems

The use of standard materials, production processes, and methods shortens the design time and lowers the cost of designing and producing an item.

The selection of technologies is a complex issue due to inherent cost/benefits trade-offs and functional orientations. Engineers are eager to incorporate the latest technology. The marketplace often richly rewards those who are first with improved performance; therefore, there is a strong case for incorporating new technology or processes before they are perfected.

But the cost of such a decision can be high. Not only does such an approach result in a proliferation of components to be purchased and stocked, but it frequently results in the use of items whose production processes have not stabilized. quality problems, production disruptions, and delays frequently result. Engineering, quality, pur-

---

5. This catalog is developed by the joint efforts of engineering, reliability engineering, purchasing, and manufacturing engineering. It is a result of a team effort which considers the technical and commercial implications of the items included. The internal catalog is in contrast to a supplier's catalog which, while simplifying the engineers' efforts to describe an item, places the firm in a sole source posture.

chasing, and manufacturing personnel *must* ensure that both the costs and benefits of such advanced developments are properly considered. The design team should design new products to the requirements of the customer, not necessarily to the state-of-the-art.

When a component or subsystem is to be developed by an outside supplier, one, two, or three carefully prequalified potential suppliers may be asked to design and develop the required item. Potential suppliers are given performance, cost, weight, and reliability objectives and are provided information on how and where the item will fit (interface) in the larger system. These potential suppliers must develop quality plans during the design of the item to ensure that the item will be producible in the quality specified. Selection of the "winning" supplier is a team effort with purchasing, design engineering, reliability engineering, product planning, quality, manufacturing, finance, and field support participating. Performance, quality, reliability, and price are all considered.

Development Phase. In this phase, breadboard and hardware prototypes are developed so that the design team may conduct tests on the integrated system to eliminate performance and quality problems. Approaches are reviewed in detail for feasibility and likely risk. Efforts are taken to reduce risk to acceptable levels by developing and testing prototypes for high-risk items.

The first complete prototypes of the new product are designed, built, and tested. Documentation such as material lists, drawings, and test procedures is created. It is not unusual to repeat this phase more than once, perhaps building the first prototype in the laboratory to test the design and the second generation in manufacturing as a test of the documentation. The design should not leave this phase until a prototype has met all the design goals, although it may not be possible to demonstrate the reliability goal because of the small number of prototypes available to test.

The design review is the point at which the new design can be measured, compared to previously established objectives, and improved. Purchasing participates in the design review and provides information on the effect of specifications and the availability of items. The buyer must ensure that the specification or other purchase description is complete, unambiguous, and provides necessary information on how items furnished under it are to be checked or tested. The buyer should be satisfied that the purchase description is written in terms relevant to and understandable by potential suppliers.

The value engineering (VE) techniques described in Chapter 3 are applied to improve quality and reduce cost. Purchasing works with potential suppliers to obtain VE suggestions for consideration.

The Production Phase. In the production phase, the manufacturing plan and the procurement plan (frequently in the form of a bill of materials) are finalized. As a result of its early involvement in the design process, purchasing has developed its procurement plans. Purchasing has worked with design engineering to select the appropriate type of purchase description (specification). The appropriate plans are now formalized and implemented.

Engineering Change Management

Engineering change management controls the changes to a product's design; specifically, its form, fit, and function. Any changes in components or the product itself may have profound effects on its cost, performance, appearance, and acceptability in the marketplace. Changes, especially at the component or subassembly level, can have a major effect on manufacturing and purchasing. There is often pressure to make problem-driven (i.e., poor performance, early failures, and safety hazards) design changes quickly. These problems are often the result of inadequate prototype tests. Design changes made as a result of such pressure often create unforeseen problems. Unless changes to the configuration of an item and its components are controlled, your company will encounter one or more of the following:

- Uncontrolled changes where quality and reliability requirements have been compromised without appropriate testing
- Inventories of materials that require needlessly expensive rework to be adapted to the new configuration
- Useless inventories of unusable raw materials
- Subassemblies that are no longer required

Adherence to this or a similar design process is key to the firm's success. Product quality, cost, and availability all must receive proper attention. And, as seen previously, engineering, manufacturing, marketing, quality assurance, and purchasing all have vital roles to play in the design process.

FIVE WAYS TO DESCRIBE PRODUCTION MATERIAL REQUIREMENTS

The purchase description is the heart of any procurement. Whether or not a purchase will satisfy the organization's needs satisfactorily is determined at the time the purchase description is selected or written. In no other form of communication is there a need for greater clarity and precision. The extent of this precision has a major bearing on the successful completion of the procurement.

Purchase descriptions serve a number of purposes:

- To tell the buyer in the purchasing department what to buy
- To tell prospective suppliers what is required
- To serve as the heart of the purchase order
- To establish the standard against which inspections, tests, and quality checks are made

The purchase description can influence the amount of competition. The amount or "breadth" of competition has a major effect on the purchase price.[6] The purchase description also may affect the

---

6. Two studies conducted by one of the authors emphasize the importance of competition in achieving purchasing's economic objectives. The first study, "Effect of the Number of Competitors on Costs," was published in the November 1971 issue of the *Journal of Purchasing*. The article indicated that over the range of one to five competitors, prices tended to decrease by 4 percent each time one additional qualified supplier submitted a price. Thus, an item costing $100 when only one bid had been obtained would tend to cost $92 if three bids were available. The second study, "Reduction in Selling Price After Introduction of Competition," was published in the May 1979 issue of the *Journal of Marketing Research*. This study found that an average savings of 12.5 percent resulted when material that previously had been purchased on a sole source basis was purchased under competitive conditions.

"depth" of competition, thereby having an even more pronounced effect on the purchase price. For example, an explicit performance specification which describes the intended use of an item allows potential suppliers to bid on alternate approaches. Such performance specifications can result in a "competition of concepts" or a depth of competition with great savings enjoyed by the purchaser. The five common approaches to describing production requirements are listed in Table 2.1.

Brand or Trade Name. The simplest way to describe what to purchase is to specify a brand or trade name. When buying by brand name, the purchaser has every right to expect that additional purchases will have the same quality as the original.

The expression "or equal" should be used immediately following a brand name to allow competition. Then the salient physical, functional, or other characteristics of the referenced products that are essential to the purchaser's needs should be listed. The term "or equal" means that any proposed item should be able to perform the function to the same level of satisfaction as does the specified brand.

Specification by brand name is the approach that is the farthest from the ZBP method and its objectives. The use of brand names, while simplifying procurement, tends to be expensive. Brand name products generally cost more than unbranded products of similar quality. Even when competition is introduced by the "or equal" provision, prices are usually higher than when alternate approaches to describing the item are employed.

Samples. The need to develop a purchase description sometimes is avoided through the use of samples. Prospective suppliers are invited to match or duplicate the buyer's sample. This approach may be appropriate with special, nonrepetitive items such as clothing, briefcases, handcrafts, and printing. In order to avoid incurring any undue obligation or commitment, a leading computer manufacturer pays for all samples.

Standard Specifications. The need for a consistent level of quality has led industry and government to develop commercial standards, federal specifications, and international specifications. These documents describe the quality of materials and the quality of

Table 2.1 Advantages and Disadvantages of Five Approaches to Describing What to Purchase

Approach	Advantages	Disadvantages
Brand or Trade Name	Easily described Easily purchased Readily available Facilitate obtaining special workmanship Promotional pull of incorporated brand name Easy inspection Avoid testing Assurance of quality	Limited competition Higher prices Miss competitors' improvements
Samples	Easy communication of requirements	May require detailed test/inspection No definite standards
Standard Specification	Facilitate communication Avoid cost of developing design specification Wide competition Facilitates standardization program Readily available materials	Specifications may be dated May require expensive manufacturing processes High test costs Purchaser has responsibility for suitability of purchased item Standardized material may conflict with marketing's desires for unique products
Design Specification	Avoid sole source Avoid premium prices Facilitates standardization program	Expensive to prepare Purchaser responsible for adequacy of specification Miss latest technology Higher cost than standard item Less readily available More expediting problems Late deliveries Larger inventories
Performance Specification	Easily prepared Gain latest technology Obtain specified level of performance Increase depth of competition Matches design to supplier's own process, which should result in low cost	Possible loopholes in specifications Decrease breadth of competition

workmanship to be used in manufacturing the item. Testing procedures are included to ensure that those quality standards are met.

Design Specifications. Design specifications and engineering drawings spell out

- the materials to be used
- their sizes, shapes, and tolerances
- exact physical and chemical characteristics, and
- how the item is to be fabricated.

Design specifications provide a completely defined item capable of manufacture by a competent manufacturer. They also describe test procedures to be used to verify that all stated requirements have been met. The specification must meet the needs of many departments in the firm:

- Engineering's concern with technical adequacy
- Marketing's concern with customer acceptance
- Manufacturing's concern for ease of production
- Purchasing's concern for availability and economy

Since design specifications frequently are the basis of competitive bidding procedures, it is essential that they communicate what is needed without need for further clarification. Thus, critical dimensions must be spelled out in detail (including realistic tolerances), and all necessary quality requirements must be fully described. At the same time, the specification must avoid imposing unnecessary conditions. It is important to convey a complete and accurate understanding of what is required. The same word or expression is subject to varying interpretations by different people. Suppliers will interpret specifications to their advantage.

Unfortunately, written descriptions can be costly. Actual products can be used as standards. If one were buying and reselling briefcases, two identical briefcases agreed upon could serve as the specification. These models of the quality desired and promised would spell out many requirements with greater accuracy and lower cost for the visual quality requirements than any written description.

If the design specification is ambiguous, the ambiguity will be construed against the drafter (i.e., the firm using the specification to purchase the item). When design specifications control performance, there is a presumption that the specifications are adequate for the purposes intended and that, if followed, the desired result will be obtained. There is an implied warranty that the specifications are adequate. Thus, the supplier who produces under the customer's specification is not responsible for the suitability or acceptability of the resulting product.

As might be expected, design specifications must be reviewed periodically and updated. Several years ago, an attempt was made to buy bread with the "current" federal specifications. The wheat called for had not been grown for 20 years!

Performance Specifications. Performance specifications describe a product by its capacity, function, or operation instead of by its physical, chemical, or quality characteristics. The supplier need only demonstrate performance (within required parameters) to achieve acceptance of its product.

A performance specification provides a description of the intended use of an item (whether component, plant, or equipment) and frequently includes a statement of the qualitative nature of the item required. When necessary, it may set forth those minimum essential characteristics and standards to which such an item must conform if it is to satisfy its intended use.

Although a performance specification is shorter and easier to develop than a design specification, caution must be exercised in its development. Once again, the requirements of engineering, marketing, manufacturing, and purchasing must be considered.

The following general principles apply to the development of performance specifications:

- The performance specification must not be so narrow that it stifles creativity.
- The performance specification must be sufficiently specific to obtain desired objectives. If it is written too broadly, potential suppliers may not respond because of the risk involved, their inability to relate work requirements to their talents and capabilities, or difficulties in estimating costs.

- The performance specification is the nucleus of the purchase order or contract. How well the item performs is a direct function of the quality, clarity, and completeness of the specification.
- The risk to the supplier inherent in producing under the performance specification should affect the type of pricing on the resulting purchase order (e.g., firm fixed price, fixed price incentive, etc.). We will examine the relationship between the degree of risk and uncertainty and selection of the right contract compensation arrangement in Chapter 13.

The performance in terms of speed, rpms, light output, etc., should be specified and controlled in terms of average performance as well as the maximum and minimum acceptable. Generally the average performance determines the cost of manufacture. One does not want a supplier to cut cost and compromise quality by reducing the variation and then using the bottom of the specification's performance range.

While the use of a performance specification may appear to be very attractive, its use is constrained by the ability of the purchasing department to select capable and honest suppliers. The supplier assumes the entire responsibility for providing a product that meets the purchaser's need.

HOW TO SELECT THE RIGHT APPROACH TO DESCRIBING REQUIREMENTS

While the decision on what type of purchase description to use may appear to be simple, there are many factors that complicate the issue. For administrative procurements such as office supplies, brand names or samples frequently describe requirements best. Their use is appropriate

- to obtain the desired level of quality or skill when these are not described easily,
- to gain the benefits of wide advertising of the brand named purchased material. For example, DuPont's name on carpet and clothing aids in promotion of the end product, and

- to accommodate users who have a preference for a particular brand.

When brand names or samples are inappropriate methods of describing our requirements, some type of specification will be employed. When selecting or developing the specification, consideration must be given to the importance of competition and the desirability of avoiding unnecessarily restrictive criteria. Quite obviously, this is one of the buyer's many responsibilities.

Once a need has been identified and functionally described, and when the size of the contemplated purchase warrants, purchasing research and analysis should be conducted to investigate the availability of commercial products capable of meeting the company's need. Normally, these commercial products will be described by one of the standard specifications. This research and analysis also should provide information to aid in developing a procurement strategy appropriate to the situation. At this stage of the procurement process, purchasing research and analysis involves obtaining the following information as appropriate:

- The availability of products suitable to meet the need (with or without modification)
- The terms, conditions, and prices under which such products are sold
- Any applicable trade provisions or restrictions or controlling laws
- The performance characteristics and quality of available products, including quality control and test procedures followed by the manufacturers
- Information on the satisfaction of other users having similar needs
- Any costs or problems associated with integration of the item with those currently used
- Industry production practices, such as continuous, periodic, or batch production
- The distribution and support capabilities of potential suppliers

When ordering a nonstandard item, a determination should be made on whether to use a design or a performance specification.

EARLY PURCHASING INVOLVEMENT IN THE CHEMICAL INDUSTRY*

The preceding section deals with the design of mechanical and electronic items. But, what about buyers in other industries? We can best answer this question by examining Polaroid's experience in purchasing over 500 different inorganic and organic chemicals. The chemical industry has a unique technology and a unique culture. Buying chemicals involves significant differences from buying plastic moldings, capital equipment, or packaging materials.

Traditional Purchasing of Chemicals

Until a few years ago, Polaroid chemical purchasing personnel located chemicals, negotiated prices, specified packaging, worried about deliveries, and occasionally tried to play matchmaker between supplier and customer. Six forces sparked a change from this traditional approach to the procurement of chemicals to a proactive one:

- The need to reduce the all-in-cost of purchased chemicals
- The need to consolidate the requirements of decentralized Polaroid manufacturing groups in order to benefit from volume price breaks
- The need to have advance notice about chemicals coming from Polaroid Research that would need sourcing
- The need to know what influences choices of materials
- The need to develop optimum specifications
- The need to manage Polaroid chemical inventories better

---

*This section is abstracted from an article by Earl J. Forman. It is reprinted with permission from "Buy with Care" by Earl J. Forman from CHEMTECH, 1987, 17: 728-731. Copyright © 1987 American Chemical Society.

A Proactive Approach

In reaction to the above forces, the Chemical Purchasing and Materials Management group at Polaroid was set up as an entity within the general purchasing and materials management division. Chemical purchasing now focuses on developing and using professional skills and talents in the chemical world.

The chemical group consists of an organic chemist, an analytical chemist, and a planner. This group makes a powerful contribution to Polaroid's success. The group's corporate overview compliments the parochial needs and interests of the decentralized manufacturing organizations. The chemists coordinate research and development efforts at specification and analytical method development with plant lab efforts so that the right resources are working on the right projects at the right time. Working closely with purchasing, they also provide sound technical and strategic input useful in the development of negotiation strategies. They can assess supplier technical capabilities. The planner sees and quantifies the big-picture inventory trends and the small-picture volume effects of any proposed change in sales forecast, product mix, or production schedules. The result is a powerful support team. Polaroid's experience is that this team yields a significant return on investment.

Early Involvement. Research organizations that synthesize chemicals generate far more compounds than ever survive the gauntlet to actual use in products. For every surviving compound, the buyer must locate raw materials, negotiate prices, characterize properties, develop quality and safety specifications, heed government regulations, and attend to a myriad of other details. Purchasing clearly is responsible for directly accomplishing some of these tasks and is a logical choice to make sure that other tasks are not ignored.

If the buyer waits for the Darwinian process which results in selection of the surviving new chemicals to be completed before addressing the issues, it is too late to provide all desired assistance. If the buyer is to play the major coordinating role, the sooner he or she knows where research is going, the more effective the preparation for smooth progression into the manufacturing world. Hence, early intelligence is a preliminary requirement. What is research doing?

How is the work progressing? What is surviving? What are the needs?

Purchasing not only gains the early warning desired, but also influences the direction of research by having these issues monitored by a respected organic chemist assigned to the materials organization. The issue of the cost and availability of proposed raw materials is raised before the synthetic route is frozen. Alternative synthesis routes that might be more cost-effective or produce less deleterious side products can be suggested. Preliminary make and buy discussions can be initiated, and potential outside suppliers can be identified. These benefits result from the teamwork between research, manufacturing, and purchasing.

At Polaroid, an organic chemist from purchasing attends R&D review meetings. By combining a commercial point of view with technical competence, the chemist gives purchasing a major head start in preparing to introduce a new chemical to Polaroid's product line.

Is there really only one molecule that will perform a given function? On a number of occasions, Polaroid's scientists have quickly found alternatives when told by purchasing's organic chemist that their initial chemical choice would be very expensive or that the choice contained photographically active impurities as a result of its synthesis route. One chemical buyer found an off-the-shelf and workable analogue of the custom molecule she was requested to locate, at less than 1% of the price of the originally desired material. Bringing price considerations into focus early in the product invention and development process has been an enlightening as well as an economically attractive exercise. Research chemists at Polaroid now have more understanding of product costs and quality and the way their choices can influence these issues.

Developing Optimal Specifications. The chemistries of photographic processes are often sensitive to small changes in amounts or kinds of impurities, or variations in morphology or molecular weight, or any of several other variables, all of which are common in manufactured chemicals. Finding out what tolerances are needed often is a time-consuming and costly process. On the other hand, attempts to avoid this issue by specifying that everything be super purified can be even more costly. Chemical costs typically go up exponentially with purity demands. In many instances, the need for Herculean purification efforts puts great strain on suppliers' resources.

Universal purification can be a flawed strategy for another reason. There are instances where specific trace impurities enhance the functional utility of the chemical. Discovering such situations and ensuring inclusion of the specific trace impurity in the raw material specification gives analytical chemists both challenges and satisfaction. There is a cost-benefit optimum to the quality of raw material to be purchased. In a high value-added product, it pays to find that optimum point through preproduction experimentation and analysis rather than through the postmortem process of determining what ruined the last production run.

Polaroid operates on the premise that whenever possible, testing to specifications should be analytical rather than functional. Frequently suppliers cannot perform functional testing, making it difficult to be sure that they are producing salable material. When purchasing a custom chemical, the customer pays one way or another, i.e., either ending with a processing charge under a toll conversion contract when the off-grade material is accepted, or the supplier's risk is built into the price when off-grade material can be returned. Functional specifications normally result in larger inventories based on the need for a greater safety stock.

All of these forces have lead to the conclusion that an analytical chemist, armed with the early warning intelligence provided by purchasing's organic chemist, who has access to all of the company's analytical chemistry resources, is a valuable catalyst for development of technically and commercially sound specifications. Purchasing's chemical buyers provide technical guidance to develop tests that ensure the quality of raw materials needed to produce high-quality products while simultaneously providing a counterpressure to those espousing the old "nothing is too good for us" philosophy.

Control of Chemical Inventories

The third leg of Polaroid's purchasing and materials support group is a professional planner. Much of Polaroid's production is serial, creating long pipelines and long-term inventories. Some photographic components are aged before they are assembled and sold. A raw material coming into a warehouse may be in the pipeline in one form or another for over two years before it leaves as a finished product. This time span does not even include the custom chemical supplier's pipelines, raw material commitments, and inventories. The inventory carrying costs, warehouse space needs, and the possibility of being stuck with obsolete, expensive custom chemicals all speak of the need for good planning. Has the sales forecast changed? Are there plans to change the product mix? Will new products change our requirements for specific chemical raw materials? The ability to understand the effect of any of these factors on purchasing requirements and inventory strategy is of enormous value.

CONCLUDING REMARKS

The professional buyer has much to contribute during the requirements process. It is estimated that half of the savings resulting from a proactive approach to procurement occur during the determination of what should be purchased and how the requirement should be described. Thus, early involvement by the buyer in the requirements process is absolutely essential. In our next chapter, we look at the role of value engineering and value analysis in refining the requirements to be purchased.

RECOMMENDED READING

John A. Carlisle and Robert C. Parker, Beyond Negotiation, (Chichester, UK: John Wiley & Sons). An interesting discussion of the role of the supplier in the development of new products.

Edward G. Krubaski, "Customize Your Product Development," *Harvard Business Review,* Nov-Dec, 1988.

James W. Dean, Jr., "Organizing for Manufacturable Design," *Harvard Business Review,* Jan-Feb, 1989.

Richard Y. Moss II, "Engineering in Reliability," in *Handbook of Reliability Engineering and Management,* edited by W. Grant Ireson and Clyde F. Coombs (NY: McGraw-Hill Book Company, 1988).

Chapter 3

Value Engineering and Value Analysis

Before a new product reaches production, value engineering should be performed. Value Engineering (VE) systematically examines every element of cost in a part, material, or service to make certain that it fulfills the required function at the lowest possible cost. VE identifies the functions the user wants from a product or service and establishes the appropriate cost for each function. Then the product's designers use knowledge, creativity, and intuition to provide the required function at the desired cost. Although VE focuses on the relationship between function and cost, it should *never* sacrifice *required* function for lower cost.

VE plays an important role in reducing total costs. Savings resulting from VE are difficult to estimate, however, since they result in cost avoidance. Dr. William H. Copperman, a former Corporate Manager of Value Engineering at the Hughes Aircraft Company, is now President of CAVE, Inc., a California firm specializing in value management. He estimates that a minimum of ten dollars are saved for every dollar invested in value engineering. (The resulting design cost avoidances are generally understated.) The professional buyer has a key role to play in VE, being a source of both necessary information and suggestions for value studies.

Despite its obvious benefits, VE is often skipped in new product development. The most common explanation offered is that there simply is not enough time. Recognizing the presence of time pressure when VE studies are conducted, the professional buyer and the entire purchasing organization must be highly responsive to value engineers' requests for information on cost, market availability, capacity, and so on. Purchasing research groups should be major contributors to buyers' requirements to assure timely and accurate data.

Value Analysis (VA) is similar to VE but is performed *after the fact* when the buyer's firm has already entered into a contractual relation with the supplier. Value analysis frequently is based on suppliers' suggestions. Several studies published in *Purchasing* indicate that VA returns $25 or more of cost reductions for every dollar invested since the items are already in production.

Value engineering and value analysis are merging as purchasing groups are becoming involved early in new product development. In the absence of established value engineering or analysis programs, purchasing is the logical department to initiate, promote, and sponsor such activities for many reasons:

- Since every requirement and specification for material passes through purchasing, this department can be the logical organization to review and identify products for value studies
- Buyers have the responsibility of obtaining maximum value for all materials to be purchased. They also have the responsibility of challenging any requirement that appears to be questionable
- Buyers have many of the skills and perform many of the tasks required in formal value programs
- Through daily exposure to sales representatives' product offerings and literature for new products, buyers are in an excellent position to identify suitable substitutes.

Dr. Copperman has developed the following "job plan" (Figure 3.1) which depicts value programs from the beginning to the selling of the resulting proposal.

Figure 3.1 The Job Plan

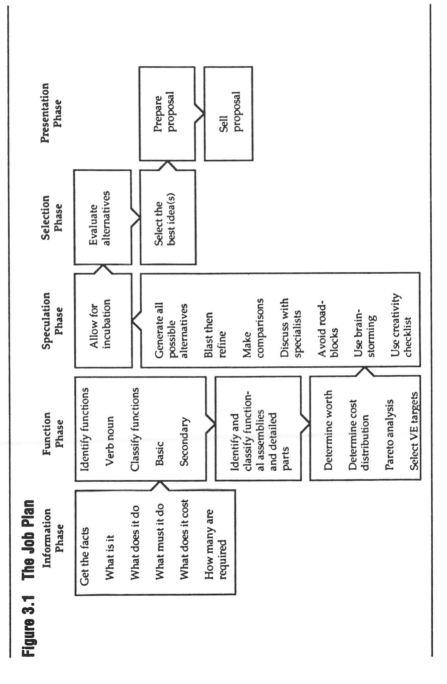

Information Phase	Function Phase	Speculation Phase	Selection Phase	Presentation Phase
Get the facts	Identify functions	Allow for incubation	Evaluate alternatives	Prepare proposal
What is it	Verb noun			
What does it do	Classify functions	Generate all possible alternatives	Select the best idea(s)	Sell proposal
What must it do	Basic	Blast then refine		
What does it cost	Secondary	Make comparisons		
How many are required		Discuss with specialists		
	Identify and classify functional assemblies and detailed parts	Avoid road-blocks		
		Use brain-storming		
	Determine worth	Use creativity checklist		
	Determine cost distribution			
	Pareto analysis			
	Select VE targets			

VALUE TECHNIQUES

There are five basic phases to a successful value program.

Information Phase: Getting All the Facts

This phase governs the selection of the product or component to be analyzed and selection of members of the value team. Concentration should be on items which have the highest cost reduction potential. These are high price items, large quantity items, and those with high total cost in relation to the function performed. This phase answers the following questions:

- What is the item?
- What must it do?
- What *does* it do?
- How much does it cost?
- What are its component costs?
- Are there key tolerances?
- What do they cost?
- What production quantities have been forecast?
- Does the product life justify investigation of cost reduction?

Function Phase: Analyze the Facts

In this phase, the analyst identifies the function in its simplest terms. What does it do? The answer should be phraseable in two words, a verb and an object: "conducts current," "supports weight," "saws wood," or "makes toast." Being forced to simplify the function's description prevents inadvertent combining of functions.

Speculation Phase: Suggest Alternative Methods to Provide the Same Function

This phase entails the study of the product with cost savings ideas. It considers the following:

- What is the most critical (basic) function?
- What are the secondary functions?
- How important are they to total performance?
- Do similar functions have equal cost and performance?

- Can the functions be modified, magnified, minified, reversed, rearranged, substituted, simplified, combined, or eliminated?

Questions like the following should be asked during this phase to stimulate the creativity of product designers and evaluators:

General

- Can the design be changed to eliminate the part?
- Can the present design be purchased at lower cost?
- Can a standard part be used?
- Would an altered standard part be more economical?
- If the part is to be improved in appearance, is this justified?
- Does a less costly part exist that will perform the same function?
- Can the design be changed to simplify the part?
- Will the design permit standard inspection equipment to be used?
- Can a part designed for other equipment be used?
- Can a less expensive material be used?
- Can the number of different materials be reduced?
- Are there newly developed materials that can be used?
- Can we produce all or a portion of a purchased part in our own plant with less expense?
- Should we buy parts currently produced by the shop?
- Would investment in new equipment result in reduced costs?

Machining and Assembly

- Are all machined surfaces necessary?
- Will a coarser finish be adequate?
- Does design permit the use of standard cutting tools?
- Are tolerances closer than necessary?
- Can another material be used that would be easier to machine?
- Can a fastener be used to eliminate tapping?
- Can weld nuts be used instead of a tapped hole?
- Can two or more parts be combined into one?
- Can parts be made symmetrical?
- Is there a newly developed fastener to speed assembly?
- Are a minimum number of hardware sizes used?

- Are stock components called for where possible?
- Can roll pins be used to eliminate reaming?

Specifications and Standards

- Is there a standard part that can replace a manufactured item?
- Can an altered standard part be used instead of a special part?
- Is standard hardware used?
- Can any specification be changed to effect a cost reduction?
- Are all threads standard?
- Can standard cutting tools be used?
- Can standard gauges be used?
- Is material available with tolerance and finish that will eliminate machining?
- Are SAE and other national standards used where possible?
- Could standards that are established by a supplier be used?
- Could wider tolerances be used to
  - eliminate finishing operations
  - reduce scrap or rework
  - reduce machining time on an operation
  - permit use of more economical processes or methods
  - reduce inspection, or
  - eliminate chronic material review or salvage problems?

Detailed checklists for substitution, elimination, standardization, combination, and simplification of parts are in Appendix B.

Next, a list of possible alternative solutions to the need should be generated. What else would do the job? This is perhaps the most difficult phase of the analysis. The comprehensiveness of the answer determines, to a large degree, the success of the entire value program. Obviously, the professional buyer will be a prime source of suggestions. No matter how thorough the search, there remain alternatives.

While alternatives can be obtained by various means, many people advocate the use of "brainstorming" sessions. In any event, the search for alternatives must be an exhaustive one.

Selection Phase: Analyze the Alternatives

If the speculation phase has been conducted properly, the evaluation and selection of the best idea(s) is relatively straightforward. If the effort has been an internal one, acceptance and implementation of the recommended changes is simple since design engineering has been an active participant in the process.

If, on the other hand, a supplier has conducted the analysis and is recommending the change, the buyer should strive to get the proposed change evaluated without delay. Delays in evaluating supplier cost reduction suggestions weaken the buyer's resolve to hold down prices and weakens the buyer's future negotiating position. Such delays project a lack of interest in cost reduction by other functions and weaken the seller's commitment to the program. Further, the seller will use a lack of responsiveness on value proposals to prove the buyer's company is not cost conscious and therefore, the seller's problems justify relief in the form of higher prices.

Presentation Phase: Sell the Idea

The buyer should develop a concise summary of findings (with particular emphasis on cost avoidance or cost reduction). He or she then submits the proposal to the firm's value committee or to design engineering.

Value engineering is receiving increased attention as American firms battle to regain or maintain their competitiveness in the global marketplace. VE requires team members from different disciplines to determine the essential functions of products, to develop creative lower cost (without sacrificing quality) or higher quality solutions, and to plan steps necessary to implement the required changes. These teams include representatives of design engineering, purchasing, manufacturing engineering, and industrial engineering. Progressive firms include potential suppliers and shop foremen on their VE teams.

The principal benefits of VE are in the following areas:

- Improved reliability (quality)
- Improved producibility
- Reduced cost

Example

Recently, a manufacturer of gas turbine engines applied value engineering during the development of an auxiliary power unit (APU) for large commercial aircraft. The APU required a new engine based on the firm's proven design, but with twice the horsepower of previous engines.

As the program developed, estimated production costs grew to more than twice the team's design-to-cost objective. As a result, an effort was undertaken to reduce costs. The VE program has reduced estimated production costs from $150,000 to $60,000 per APU.

Cost savings on the main air bleed control valve are typical of the results from the VE program. The control valve which had been designed into the new APU was technologically advanced. Its unit cost (from engineering's recommended source) was $1,085. The purchasing representative on the VE team contacted other qualified potential valve suppliers. One such supplier proposed an off-the-shelf valve which required minor design modifications (including a weight increase of four ounces and a simple revision to the electrical harness). The price for this valve was $724. Since the proposed valve was of a standard, proven design, the VE team felt that less technological risk would result from its use when compared with the valve specified by engineering.

The VE team decided that the cost savings and risk reduction were sufficiently attractive to call for use of the lower cost valve. Engineering was directed to reduce the weight of the housing to offset the four ounce weight addition. When the VE effort on the valve was completed, the engine's cost had been reduced by $361.

VALUE ANALYSIS

Value analysis may be conducted either as an in-house activity or as a program under the responsibility of purchasing with supplier participation. As might be expected, the greatest benefits result when the two activities are pursued simultaneously.

In-House Activity

Many savings result through the identification of items that are promising candidates for value analysis. The selection of candidate items should be based on maximizing returns on VA investment. Generally, potential savings are greatest on those components representing the largest annual outlay. Complexity also provides a clue. Usually the more complex an item, the greater the potential for improved value. An item that was developed in an accelerated time frame frequently will be overdesigned and may be a good candidate for VA study. Nonstandard industrial items have more potential for savings than do standard ones. Items with high scrap or rework costs and those requiring many operations also are good candidates for the VA program. Once a candidate has been identified, the VA procedures described for value engineering should be applied with the objective of improving marketability or reducing cost, or both.

Three approaches to in-house VA programs are common: (1) dedicated value analysts assigned to the purchasing office, (2) the committee approach, and (3) the integrated approach. The employment of dedicated value analysts is common in large manufacturing firms. The ideal value analyst has a background in design engineering, industrial engineering, and purchasing. He or she possesses knowledge of basic physics, strength of materials, and manufacturing processes and is familiar with the firm's product lines, suppliers, and principal customers. Of even greater importance, a good value analyst possesses an open, inquisitive mind and develops close relations with top management. Thus, a good value analyst has considerable informal authority and is able to overcome resistance to his or her proposals. The most obvious disadvantage of this approach is its cost. Such experienced personnel are not inexpensive. But savings of five to twenty times their salary expenses result.

The committee approach calls for the assignment of experienced personnel from engineering, production, purchasing, quality assurance, industrial engineering, and marketing. Each operating participant develops a better awareness of the techniques and potential contribution of value analysis. Ideally, this carries over to the individual's day-to-day activities. The VA committee reviews proposals submitted by employees under a VA or cost reduction program. Promising proposals are reviewed by a working subcommittee that asks the questions listed earlier in the chapter. The committee coordinates implementation of recommendations based upon its studies. The committee approach employs teamwork to overcome resistance to change. However, it has the two inherent weaknesses of most committees: an inability to gain support and cooperation and conflicting demands on committee members' time.

The integrated approach requires the exposure of operating engineering, purchasing, and other selected personnel to VA training *on a repetitive basis.* The objectives of this training program are to develop an awareness of the importance of value analysis, an understanding of how to conduct a VA study, and a dedication to the use of value analysis. This approach serves to reduce the resistance to changes in product design and specifications that frequently is encountered. The training program does, however, require time and money.

Supply Program

Suppliers are a gold mine of ideas for the VA program. Usually a supplier knows more about products and their capabilities than does the customer. Once an item has gone into production, it is possible that suppliers will be able to make suggestions that lead to significant savings. Frequently, they will be aware of suitable lower cost substitute items than those being purchased. A supplier's assistance may be obtained in two ways: informally and contractually.

With the informal approach, the purchasing firm may include a supplier checklist with request for quotations and/or with purchase orders. Figure 3.2 contains such a checklist. The firm may conduct value analysis clinics or post VA project candidates in an effort to obtain VA suggestions. A supplier who submits a suggestion that is implemented should be rewarded with a share of the savings.

A formal VA program calls for the inclusion of a VA provision in the purchase order or subcontract. In this VA provision, the purchasing firm agrees to share in the savings resulting from an implemented proposal. One major purchaser includes such a clause in all purchase orders of over $100,000. This purchaser agrees to share net savings resulting from implemented proposals on a 50/50 basis. This

---

Figure 3.2 Supplier Checklist for Value Analysis Study

Part name and number _____

Estimated annual usage _____

Buyer _____

Questions	*Yes*	*No*	*Recommendations*

Do you understand the part function?

Could costs be reduced by relaxing any
of the following requirements?
- Tolerances
- Finishes
- Testing
- By how much

Could costs be reduced through changes
in any of the following?
- Material
- Ordering quantities
- The use of castings, stampings, etc.
- By how much

Could you suggest other changes that
would achieve any of the following?
- Reduce weight
- Simplify the part
- Reduce overall costs

Do you feel that any of the
specifications are too stringent?

How can we help alleviate your greatest
element of cost in supplying this part?

Do you have a standard item that could
be substituted for this part?

Other suggestions?

Supplier _____ Date _____

Address _____

Signature _____ Title _____

Please add additional comments

---

purchaser also agrees to share savings on future buys for a period not to exceed beyond three years, but at a reduced rate. Many firms have had good success with informal programs, but more positive motivation in the form of a sharing of the savings results in wider and more active participation by suppliers and even greater savings.

Example
A California developer of tract homes recently applied value analysis techniques in dealings with its suppliers. A framing subcontractor suggested substituting waferboard for roof sheathing. Waferboard, created by the lumber industry as an alternative to plywood, is made of layers of cross-aligned wood strands that are blended with a tough phenolic resin (glue) under intense heat and pressure. The framer's cost for plywood was $250.00 per 1,000 board feet. The cost for waferboard was $188.00 per 1,000 board feet. The use of waferboard would save $6,095.70 for the 32 homes under contract.

Quality was a great concern of the developer. According to the framer, waferboard is as good as plywood, if not better. Waferboard is consistent, where plywood may have core voids, knotholes and such. Due to this, the waferboard lies flatter and stiffer, which makes it easier to work with. Waferboard is more water-resistant than plywood because of the resin which holds the particles together.

The developer reviewed the proposal with its architect and concluded that as long as the waferboard were not exposed, it could be used. As a result, the developer saved $6,095.00. The supplier's payoff was enhanced customer relations and the prospect of additional business.

IMPLEMENTING VALUE PROGRAMS

The key prerequisite to successful VE/VA programs is a cooperative attitude on the part of all involved departments and their personnel, especially those in design engineering. It is essential that those responsible for developing, implementing, and managing the programs recognize people's inherent tendency to identify with what they create or initiate. Care must be taken to ensure that designers realize that they are not being second-guessed. Those participating in the value programs should have the benefit of different points of view, experience, and knowledge. The initial design serves as an essential first step. Its subsequent review and possible revision must be seen as a necessary and normal process of product development.

VE/VA programs will be easier to develop and implement and will be more successful if purchasing and design engineering work as a team. The managers of these two activities have the same end objectives—the survival and profitability of the organization.

Assuming that a cooperative atmosphere exists, several approaches to initiating the program are possible.

- The purchasing manager and the chief engineer together attend a value seminar.

- The purchasing manager provides the chief engineer relevant and succinct literature on the subject.

- A buyer who has especially good relations with a design engineer plants the seed so that the idea for a value program emerges in engineering.

- The purchasing manager discusses several recent friendly examples of informal value engineering or value analysis (involving purchasing and engineering) and suggests that the program be formalized.

When relations with engineering are somewhat more formal, purchasing has two logical allies in its efforts to develop and implement a value program: finance and marketing. The chief financial officer should be concerned with anything that will make the firm more profitable. The manager of marketing is equally concerned with anything that will result in goods of a higher quality at the same cost or goods of the same quality at lower cost. If resistance on the part of design engineering occurs, purchasing should obtain the cooperation and support of these two departments in an effort to enlist engineering's cooperation.

A value program can be implemented as a result of a directive from top management. But such an approach frequently encounters informal resistance from some of those involved. This resistance severely limits the success and profit contribution of the program.

Frequently, spectacular success will be experienced during the first year or two of the program's life. But after these initial successes, enthusiasm may begin to wane. Since significant savings still are possible and likely, it is important that action be taken to foster a positive attitude toward value engineering and value analysis. Possible actions include the following:

- If dedicated value analysts are employed, management should avoid the temptation to assign non-VE/VA work to VE/VA personnel.
- If the committee approach is employed, the committee should meet on a periodic basis and ensure that a sufficient number of projects are undertaken. (Value analysts, by their nature, will take action.)
- The company newspaper, bulletin boards, and other media should be utilized to report on successful projects.
- Lobby displays and contractual VA clauses should be utilized to encourage supplier participation.
- VE/VA workshops should be conducted to bring design engineers, purchasing personnel, and suppliers together.

CONCLUDING REMARKS

It is the authors' observation that VE and VA receive much lip service, but relatively little management attention. As the Director of Purchasing of a Fortune 100 company recently told one of us: "Guess what? We just discovered value engineering." When prodded, he continued: "Yep, we discover it every six or seven years, go full speed ahead, and then forget it for four or five years!" The savings and quality potential of VE/VA are too great to ignore.

We now shift our focus to the buyer's role in capital expenditures.

RECOMMENDED READING

Lawrence D. Miles, *Techniques of Value Analysis and Engineering,* 2nd. ed., (N.Y: McGraw-Hill Book Company, 1982). The father of value management speaks.

Carlos Fallon, *Value Analysis,* (Irving, TX: Triangle Press, 1980).

Thomas J. Snodgrass and Multhiah Kasi, *Function Analysis: The Stepping Stones to Good Value,* (Madison, WI: University of Wisconsin, 1986). Mr. Snodgrass is considered by many to be the nation's leading academic in the field of VE/VA. The University of Wisconsin Engineering Program offers several excellent programs and related services for the serious value student.

William H. Copperman, CVS, *A Guide to the Contractual Aspects of Value Engineering,* (Raleigh, NC: North Carolina State University, 1986). Dr. Copperman is considered one of the nation's leading practitioners in the contractual aspects of value engineering.

Additional information on VE and VA may be obtained from the
Society of American Value Engineering
60 Revere Drive
Northbrook, IL 60062

Chapter 4

The Buyer's Role in Capital Expenditures

The procurement of equipment and buildings has a profound impact on the time required to launch new products, responsiveness (cycle time), capacity, profitability, and the productivity of the organization. Such procurements are complex. They require considerable planning, coordination, and cooperation on the part of all personnel. These procurements have a significant impact on fixed overhead costs and break-even levels.

PURCHASING CAPITAL EQUIPMENT

The Equipment Procurement Process

The purchase of capital equipment should involve personnel from many areas of the firm. Technical experts put emphasis on the areas they know, but frequently fail to consider the commercial aspects necessary to assure performance and a meeting of minds. When purchasing is left out of the process or is brought in to ratify the technical expert's commitment, the following generally have not been considered at all (or only superficially):

- Alternative suppliers
- Payment Terms: The technical expert frequently is agreeable to too much too soon

- Warranties: Performance requirements are not in writing
- Remedies: Agreement on penalty for noncompliance is missing
- Proper sourcing for accessories: Accessories frequently are bought by the supplier and marked up 100 percent and more when sold to the buying firm
- A reasonable cancellation clause that establishes commitment costs at each milestone
- Installation cost
- Equipment compatibility (computers, mobile equipment, etc.)
- Training—initial and follow-on
- Maintenance—responsiveness, who pays, and so on
- Repair parts and kits
- Ownership and liability during shipment

When the purchase of capital equipment is conducted properly, plant engineering, manufacturing, design engineering, finance, and purchasing are involved early in the requirements process. (See Table 4.1.) The general flow of an equipment procurement is described in Figure 4.1.

Standard Equipment. Normally, an adequate level of competition can be obtained by specifying an item that is standard to an industry and that is produced by three or more potential suppliers. This competition results in the right quality of equipment and service at attractive delivery and price terms.

Customized Equipment. Frequently standard equipment must be customized to meet the purchaser's unique needs or match other equipment in a line. When this happens, the required unique feature must be clearly defined so that it can be completely understood by all potential suppliers. The potential suppliers should be required to indicate in their bids exactly what each additional feature will consist of, how it will affect the machine's operation, and what it will cost.

Unique Equipment. Two approaches commonly are employed to meet unique equipment requirements: performance or detailed specifications. The use of a performance specification is appropriate when the procuring organization is concerned with what the machine

Table 4.1   Responsibilities of the Capital Equipment Procurement Team

Organization	Responsibilities and Concern
Plant Engineering	Physical size and mounting dimensions Detailed specifications for interface to other or matching equipment Power and maintenance requirements Safety features—OSHA requirements Pollution—EPA requirements Capital budget prioritization Spare parts inventories
Manufacturing	Capacity Ease of use Setup times Run time Product yields Uniqueness Capital budgeting requests
Design Engineering	Ability to produce items meeting design standards Ability to meet likely future requirements
Finance	Initial cost Payback period Credit terms Possible leasing Supplier financial review Coordinate capital requests
Purchasing	Coordinate above functional areas in dealings with suppliers Obtain and consolidate required information Maintain competition Captain source selection team Price (total cost of ownership) Terms and conditions Spares and services Warranty by OEM's (original equipment manufacturer) on purchased equipment Warranty by supplier Management of resulting contract Ownership of design or intellectual properties (if special design)
Maintenance	Supplier responsibilities, responsiveness, etc. Availability of spares and parts kits and confidentiality agreements

Figure 4.1   The Procurement of Capital Equipment

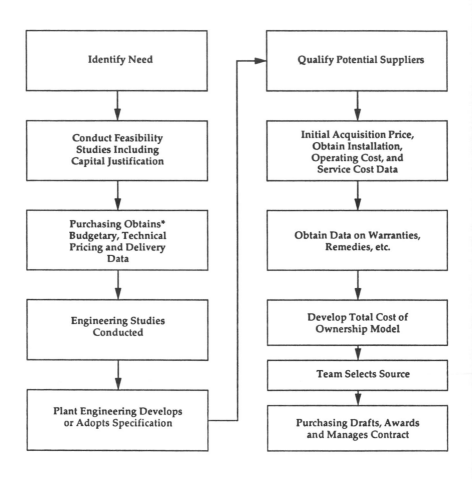

*If at this point a potential supplier deals directly with the engineer, it can result in a single source procurement incompatible with the lowest all-in-cost.

Copyright © 1990, Burt, Norquist, and Anklesaria.

will do and some freedom exists in how the machine will accomplish the task. The previously developed statement of what the item is to do and the identified technical characteristics will serve as the basis of such a specification. Competition can and should be solicited. Source selection utilizing the principle of the total cost of ownership (as shown in Figure 4.2) is relatively simple and straightforward.

The detailed specification approach may be through the firm's own engineering staff or through a professional services contract. Either alternative allows the firm to solicit competition for the fabrication of the required unique equipment. A less-preferred third alternative is to invite two or three carefully prequalified engineering firms to submit proposals for the development of the required specifications under a cost plus fixed fee basis. The firms invited to submit proposals should indicate their planned technical approach, rates, overhead, fee structure, and ceiling price for the work. The procuring organization should specify that it retains the right to award the follow-on fabrication work to the selected engineering firm or such other supplier as it may choose. Material, labor, overhead rates, fee structure, and ceiling price should be obtained for fabrication.

Other Terms and Conditions. Many standard and several nonstandard issues must be addressed in the terms and conditions in the request for proposal and resulting contract. These include the following:

- Payment terms
- Performance standards
- Inspection procedures
- Warranties against defects
- A performance warranty
- Supplier responsibility for postsale services
- Indemnity for patent infringement
- Operator training responsibility
- Installation responsibility
- The extent of liability for employee accident
- Maintenance program
- Patents or new designs from nonstandard items—does the customer share in the success of the new design?

- Provision if the new design *does not* work
- Compliance with state and OSHA safety requirements
- The supplier's responsibility for maintaining an inventory of spare parts at a stated price for a specified period
- Most favored price clause if supplier later markets the equipment and the customer had contributed to the design

The professional buyer should include a provision in development contracts restricting the supplier from producing similar items for other customers. An alternative is to include a royalty agreement. The request for proposal should request prices for periodic and emergency maintenance and repairs. The time to get such prices is when competition exists.

In many situations, the needs of purchasing's customers are best satisfied *at the lowest total cost* through the use of performance specifications. Thus, the professional buyer should advance the use of such a purchase description when it appears to be applicable.

Total Cost of Ownership

The use of performance specifications frequently will result in the receipt of bids or proposals for two or more items which will satisfy the company's needs. These items will have different prices and other characteristics such as operator requirements, fuel consumption, expected life, maintenance, and likely salvage values. The total cost of ownership approach to pricing allows the purchaser to determine the most likely cost of owning and operating an item over its anticipated productive life. This is the only rational approach to determining a true basis for comparing the costs of owning and operating equipment. Further, by considering all the significant costs over the life of the item instead of merely the initial acquisition cost, the firm may gain from increased competition. Firms whose products have higher initial prices but lower subsequent ownership costs may be able to compete.

The cost of ownership includes

- the initial cost of the item together with installation and start-up costs

- the likely cost of operating it (fuel or power consumption, salaries for operators required, etc.)
- finance costs
- training costs
- maintenance costs (a function of the reliability and the maintainability of the equipment)
- insurance costs
- tax considerations
- upgrades and/or overhauls expected during the useful life, and
- the likely salvage value of the item.

The present value of the expected stream of expenditures less the expected salvage value should be employed to accommodate the time utility of money. This concept is expressed in Figure 4.2 for a simplified example wherein initial (acquisition) cost, training costs, operating costs, maintenance costs, and salvage value are the only variables under consideration.

When comparing two or more pieces of capital equipment, the buyer must use the item's total cost of ownership, *not* the initial acquisition price.

Figure 4.2 Total Cost of Ownership

$$TCO = A + P.V. \sum_{i=1}^{n} \left(T_i + O_i + M_i - S_n \right)$$

where

TCO = total cost of ownership
A   = acquisition cost
P.V. = present value at the company's cost of money[1]
Σ = the sum of the terms in ( ) from years i to n
T_i = training costs in year i
O_i = operating costs in year i
M_i = maintenance costs in year i

---

1. This allows for different occurrences of these expenditures or salvage and for the time value of money.

Financing and Leasing

Once a decision has been made on which item to purchase, one other issue must be addressed. Many equipment suppliers now provide excellent financing packages. The cost of such financing should be compared with the cost of alternate sources of funds. If supplier financing appears to be of interest, the buyer must recognize that the rates and duration may be as negotiable as are price and delivery terms.

LEASING

PRO	CON
• Can defer income tax if leased	• Total cost generally higher
• Payments exceed latest depreciation allowances but can't be a tax dodge	• Lease interest generally higher than loan interest
• Avoid capital outlay	• May be restrictions on operating or changing equipment
• Maintenance provided by lessor (a convenience)	• Can often buy maintenance for less than maintenance cost component in lease
• Sometimes reduces risk of obsolescence	

PROCURING BUILDING CONSTRUCTION

Major construction work is not only one of the largest purchases most companies ever make but is also a commitment for the future. In 1988, the cost of a typical 130,000 square foot light manufacturing plant was about $8 million. Of equal importance, the availability of new plant facilities has a major impact on the firm's ability to introduce new products or to enter new markets in a timely manner. It affects the firm's cycle time. The productivity of the entire organization is affected by the physical layout of the building.

The professional buyer has much to contribute to the team responsible for the procurement of building construction. Application of sound procurement principles and practices, *including selection of the most appropriate method of procurement,* frequently results in

- cost reductions of 20-40 percent and
- reductions of 25 percent and more in the time required to obtain the required building.

In order for the buyer to make a full contribution to the procurement, he or she must be familiar with the five most commonly employed methods of purchasing building construction and of the cost and timeliness implications of each. Once the procurement team has selected the most appropriate method, the buyer has several responsibilities. Buyer responsibilities, under the two most commonly employed methods of purchasing building construction, are described near the end of the chapter.

Five Methods of Procuring Building Construction

Normally, the expression "methods of procurement" calls to mind methods of compensating the supplier for its goods or services. Firm agreed price, cost plus a fixed fee, cost plus incentive fee, and other methods of reimbursement come to mind. However, the phrase "methods of procurement," as used in this chapter, concerns the accountability of the designer and the builder to one another and to the owner. The following diagram (Figure 4.3) is introduced to assist in visualizing the relations among the various parties on a construction project and the sequence of the steps involved with each procurement method.

The Conventional Method. Under the conventional method, the firm selects a designer (generally referred to as the architect, the engineer, the architect-engineer, or simply A-E) to plan and design a structure to satisfy the organization's requirements. The buyer (with the assistance of plant engineering and/or the A-E) prepares the bid and contract documents, selects potential bidders, assists in bid review and award, and oversees the actual construction. A firm fixed price is the most common basis for payment under the conventional method. Various cost reimbursement procedures occasionally are employed.

Figure 4.3 Sequence of Steps Involved with Alternative Methods

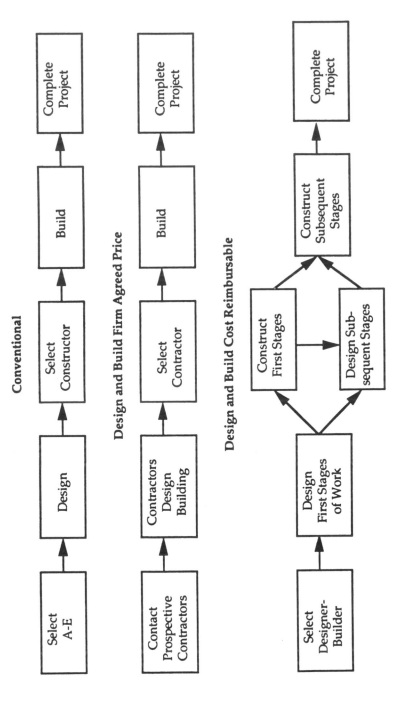

Conventional

Select A-E → Design → Select Constructor → Build → Complete Project

Design and Build Firm Agreed Price

Contact Prospective Contractors → Contractors Design Building → Select Contractor → Build → Complete Project

Design and Build Cost Reimbursable

Select Designer-Builder → Design First Stages of Work → Construct First Stages / Design Subsequent Stages → Construct Subsequent Stages → Complete Project

Building Team

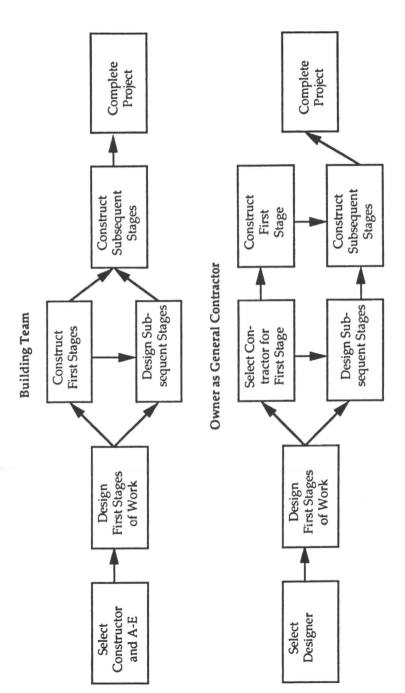

Select Constructor and A-E → Design First Stages of Work → Construct First Stages → Design Subsequent Stages → Construct Subsequent Stages → Complete Project

Owner as General Contractor

Select Designer → Design First Stages of Work → Select Contractor for First Stage → Construct First Stage → Design Subsequent Stages → Construct Subsequent Stages → Complete Project

The following are distinguishing characteristics of the conventional method.

- The design phase is performed by designers (architects and/or engineers) without the involvement of the builder.
- The design phase is completed before any construction begins.
- Two separate organizations are responsible for two separate phases of the work.
- Normally, the specified construction is performed for a firm agreed price.

The Design-and-Build Methods. Under the design-and-build methods, normally only one contract is awarded by the owner to a builder for both the design and the construction of the required structure. The design-and-build method is frequently referred to as the "turnkey" approach. After negotiating the contract with the builder, the owner may sit back until ready to turn the key of the finished building. Two compensation approaches to the design and build method are to design and build with firm agreed price and to design-and-build with cost reimbursement.

Under the design-and-build firm agreed price method, all or the majority of the design is provided by the prospective general contractor and its prospective subcontractors. Prospective subcontractors develop technical and cost proposals for their specialty areas. On receipt of these proposals, the prospective general contractor (builder) selects the most favorable one for each work element that will not be performed with its own forces.

The following are distinguishing characteristics of the design-and-build firm agreed price method.

- The builder has ample opportunity to influence the design of the required facility.
- Basic design is completed prior to award of the construction contract.
- One organization is responsible for both the design and the construction phases of the project.
- A firm price is agreed to for both design and construction.

Under the design-and-build cost reimbursable method, design normally does not commence until award of a contract. Design is accomplished by architects and engineers employed by, or retained by, the general contractor.

A construction project may be visualized as a group of work elements (structural, mechanical, plumbing, etc.) which, when properly integrated and completed, result in a building. With the design-and-build cost reimbursable method, the contractor may undertake a work element when its design has been completed. This is in contrast to the conventional approach, wherein the design of all elements must be completed before construction starts.

The following are distinguishing characteristics of the design-and-build cost reimbursable method.

- The builder has ample opportunity to influence the design of the required facility.
- Construction proceeds prior to completion of the total design of the project.
- One organization is responsible for both the design and construction phases of the project.
- The owner agrees to reimburse the contractor for its allowable costs. (Normally, a ceiling price or a guaranteed maximum price is incorporated in the contract.)

The Building Team Method. As with the conventional method, the owner retains both an A-E and a builder. But the builder is retained during the design phase and is expected to contribute information on costs, procedures, and time requirements not ordinarily available to the A-E.

Building team contracts are customarily awarded on a cost reimbursable basis. The builder, in return for its fee, attends to all matters pertaining to purchasing, expediting, letting of subcontracts, hiring of labor, and supervision of the construction. Frequently, all of the actual construction is subcontracted, although the builder may choose to perform certain work with its own forces.

As the A-E completes the plans and specifications for a logical work element (excavation, steel erection, mechanical, etc.), the builder either accomplishes the work with its own forces or obtains prices from several qualified specialists in the work (subcontractors) and awards the work to the qualified subcontractor making the best offer (price, quality, and time considered). As with the other methods, the builder oversees and integrates the efforts of the subcontractors.

The following are distinguishing characteristics of the building team method.

- The builder has ample opportunity to influence the design of the required facility.
- Construction proceeds prior to completion of the total design of the project.
- Two separate organizations are retained, each with responsibility for the area in which it has expertise. However, these two organizations work together as a team during both the design and the construction phases.
- The owner agrees to reimburse the builder for its allowable costs. (Normally, a ceiling price or a guaranteed maximum price is incorporated in the contract.)

The Owner As General Contractor. With this method, the owner contracts directly for accomplishment of the various work elements. The owner performs the integrating and controlling functions normally accomplished by a general contractor. Since contracts are awarded on a work element basis, it is possible for construction to proceed prior to completion of the total design phase. Frequently, a significant portion of the design work is accomplished by the owner's full-time employees.

The following are distinguishing characteristics of this method.

- Several contracts are awarded. Contracts may include such work elements as design, excavation, structure, mechanical work, etc.
- Construction may proceed prior to completion of the total design of the project.
- With the exception of the design work, the contracts generally are awarded on a fixed price basis.

Cost and Timely Availability

Cost and timely availability are two variables of key importance to the buyer of a new plant. In 1970, research was conducted on the cost and timeliness (i.e., how long does it take to gain beneficial occupancy of the building) implications of the above five approaches to procuring light manufacturing plants. One hundred and twelve buildings were in the study. The typical building consisted of approximately 130,000 square feet and cost $7,981,353 (in 1988 dollars). Without going into burdensome statistics, it is possible to project the cost and time implications of each of the five methods of procuring new plant construction to 1988 dollars.[2] Total cost includes the A-E fee, if applicable. Total time includes design and construction time. All data shown in Table 4.2 are for an identical 130,000 square foot building.

Table 4.2   Effect of Contract Method on Total Cost and Total Time Required

(for standard 130,000 sq. ft. building)

	Cost	Time in Months
Conventional	$7,981,353	16.16
Design-and-Build, FAP	5,553,091	11.54
Design-and-Build, CR	7,532,570	12.16
Building Team Method	7,747,289	12.18
Owner/General	7,538,925	15.41

---

2. The authors recognize the dangers of drawing conclusions from 20-year-old data and would much prefer to base the findings on current data. Unfortunately, no more current study is known. The findings of the 1970 study are of such potential value to the professional buyer that the authors have chosen to present them with appropriate caveats.

Selection of the Right Method of Procuring Construction

As might be expected, no one method is appropriate *under all conditions*. When aesthetics are of major consideration or when risk dictates, the conventional or the builder team methods frequently are appropriate.[3] With both of these methods, the A-E is in a lead role. In other cases, a particular method may appear to be the most appropriate, but suitable suppliers who operate with the method may be unavailable.

But, for the majority of standard building procurements, the design-and-build firm agreed price method results in significantly lower cost and earlier availability than with the other methods. Several years ago, Peter J. Cassimatis offered insight into some of the disadvantages of the separation of design and construction (as results with the conventional method):

> One great difference between the manufacturing industries and the construction industry is the role the designer plays on production costs. In manufacturing, product design is an integral part of production management, i.e., the product is designed in such a way as to achieve two objectives simultaneously: (1) to fulfill its aesthetic and functional requirements; and (2) to minimize production costs.

> It is apparent that the separation of the architect (or engineer) and the general contractor has enormous effects on the cost of construction projects. The designer cannot possibly foresee who the general contractor of the project is likely to be. Consequently, the designer is not aware of the type of labor, equipment, and construction methods the general contractor will utilize. This lack of information on the input factors of production forces the architect or engineer (1) to ignore these factors, or (2) to design the project in such a way that it can be constructed by any one of the several general contractors in the area, or (3) to assume

---

3. For additional insight into the issue of risk, see John D. Macomber, "You Can Manage Construction Risk," *Harvard Business Review*, Mar-Apr 1989: 155-165.

what is euphemistically known in the trade as the 'prevailing construction practices.' The obvious consequences of these practices are that the designer is reluctant to introduce new construction materials, fearing the contractors will either refrain from bidding or bid high prices.

Another consequence of the dichotomy of design and production is that this practice fails to promote cooperation between the architect and the builder. New ideas in design can be introduced with new methods of construction, but this implies that the general contractor will exchange information with the designer with regard to the cost of new materials and cost of installation. Since the contractor does not know whether he will obtain the job, he is not likely to provide the architect (or engineer) with any cost-reducing information that might jeopardize his competitive position. The designer, for his part, cannot offer any assurances to a contractor without violating his impartial role in the bidding.[4]

It is the authors' observation that there are three additional reasons for buildings constructed under the conventional method to be overdesigned and needlessly costly.

- The architect frequently dreams along with the owner without paying adequate attention to the budget.
- In many cases, the A-E fee is related to the cost of the completed project. When the A-E fee is based on a percentage of the final cost of construction, the architect's financial interest is inconsistent with the obligation to serve the best interest of the client.
- Frequently, the wrong A-E is retained. The design of industrial plants is a specialty, as is the design of churches and schools. Many owners are guilty of selecting a design firm which does not have sufficient experience with industrial facilities but has a

---

4. Peter J. Cassimatis, *Economics of the Construction Industry*, (New York, NY: The National Industrial Conference Board, Inc., 1969) 117–119.

well-known name. The owner, not the A-E, is at fault. And it is the owner who pays for this failure.

Buildings purchased under the design and build firm agreed price method tend to be functional structures. Following are two reasons for this tendency.

- The design work is being performed by firms and individuals who have had experience with the construction of similar structures.
- The design work is performed under competitive conditions. The firms which develop the design and cost proposals know that they are operating in a competitive environment. Award is based on how well the various design plans meet the owner's requirements and at what cost.

Thus, there frequently are many benefits flowing to the future plant owner who selects a method of procurement which involves the constructor in the design process. (In many ways, this is very similar to the idea of early supplier involvement discussed in Chapter 2.)

Specific Buyer Responsibilities

Figures 4.4 and 4.5 identify the buyer's responsibilities when procuring building construction with the conventional method and the design-and-build firm agreed price method. As previously indicated, the buying team must ensure that suitable qualified suppliers which operate under the specific method are available before selecting the specific method of procurement.

Figure 4.4   Buying Construction: Conventional Method

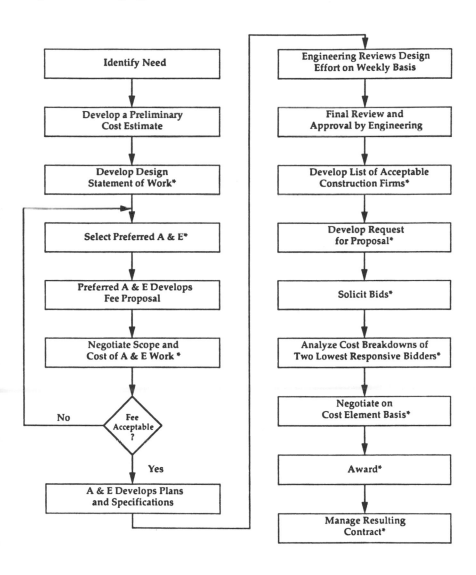

*Buyer has primary or secondary responsibilities for these items.

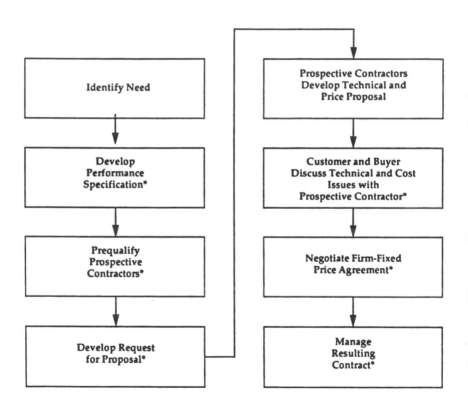

Figure 4.5   Buying Construction: Design-and-Build Firm Agreed Price Method

*Buyer has primary or secondary responsibility.

Copyright © 1990, Burt, Norquist, and Anklesaria.

CONCLUDING REMARKS

The professional buyer has many key responsibilities when the firm initiates a procurement of equipment or building construction. The buyer must be involved "up-front" if the lowest all-in-cost is to result.

We now focus our attention on the buyer's role in the procurement of services.

RECOMMENDED READING

Joseph Auer and Charles Edison Harris, *Major Equipment Procurement,* (New York: Van Nostrand Reinhold Company, 1983).

Chapter 5

Services

The procurement of services is an important activity. Commercial firms, not-for-profit organizations, and government buy more outside services each year. Requirements ranging from architectural-engineering, promotion, and advertising to software development are of critical importance to the operation of the organization. More mundane purchases, such as cafeteria and janitorial operations, affect the morale of employees.

THE BUYER'S ROLE IN PURCHASING SERVICES

The purchasing department can contribute its skill to buying services but unfortunately frequently is bypassed. Many managers who buy services, especially professional services, don't appreciate the dollars purchasing could save. Suppliers of specialties and services not only assess their cost but also their customers when establishing prices. If the customer is not knowledgeable about the product or service and has little price negotiating experience, the price will be significantly higher than need be. As one sales training expert put it, "Raise the price (with extras) until the customer flinches."

Evaluating the price for services on the basis of whether it is within the amount budgeted for the project is not cost-effective. However, this frequently is the criterion used by department and division managers.

On the other hand, if instead of encountering an "amateur" the potential supplier deals with a purchasing professional who is knowledgeable, experienced, and prepared, and the supplier knows the purchaser has the support of his or her company, the final price will represent value.

Listed below are service areas where purchasing often is not involved. Large savings have been obtained when purchasing has become involved. But purchasing must invest energy in learning about an area before it offers to provide professional buying. A background in the field is a big help.

- Print ad production
- General consultants
- Computer consultants
- Television ad production
- Outplacement agencies
- Training consultants
- Network TV time
- Market research

- Financial auditors
- Training courses
- Per diem help
- Placement agencies
- Technical consultants
- Spot TV & radio time
- Annual reports

Many of these areas are sacred cows. Yet Polaroid purchasing, for example, has become part of the team engaging these services at documented savings of approximately 25 percent with no sacrifice in quality or service.

Buying Services versus Products

Buying services, such as those listed, is very different from buying products. In dealing with product suppliers, the professional buyer generally

- knows the material costs
- has had a continuing dialogue on cost
- has both domestic and overseas competitors
- knows the specifications and quality desired, unless the product is a new item
- buys to a fixed price per unit
- documents all change requests, and
- writes the contract.

Buying professional services is very challenging. The value received often is intangible, costs are mainly for labor, frequently domestic competition is limited by customer preferences, and there hardly ever is offshore competition.

Without purchasing involvement

- the amateur buyer settles for vague agreement on output
- statements on overall price frequently are only the minimum or starting point
- verbal requests and changes, when documented at all, are documented by the contractor, and
- the customer usually has let the contractor propose the contract terms.

Purchasing professionals who want to bring their expertise to the professional service area should recognize that service contractors frequently work very hard to keep purchasing out. The service contractors' trade magazines say "avoid purchasing." By avoiding purchasing, contractors avoid

- written specifications
- any detailed analysis of costs
- breaking down billing charges and requirements for receipts, and
- negotiating—"just accept our professional rate!"

There's a Sucker Born Every Minute

Managers who buy without purchasing assistance often are seen as easy marks by sellers. The seller of professional services such as consulting, auditing, or advertising knows that the top manager or officer in that function may be at a disadvantage concerning price. The manager will be too busy to

- get details
- know the current market
- negotiate patiently, or
- check the bill in detail.

The seller of professional services is trained to convey the message through subtle pressure that price haggling should be beneath such managers. If subtle pressure isn't enough, the seller will imply that any lower price would mean lower quality, missed critical dates, and a spoiled "relationship."

Selling Your Services

The following list shows how to promote purchasing's contribution in the procurement of services.

- Study the area; learn from others before offering to purchase services in a new area.
- Sell purchasing as a service that can help get what your internal customer wants.
- Sell purchasing as a function that can help by separating the professional relationship from the pricing and billing relationship. This will be well received by many managers, as they really don't feel comfortable discussing price and would prefer to delegate the responsibility.
- Question managers as to how comfortable they are questioning and analyzing price before they buy.
- Show management that one-stop shopping can be costly. For example, the decorator who recommends and then buys furniture may have had a reasonable hourly rate as an advisor. But the effective hourly rate will prove to be staggering when it is determined how much less the furniture would cost without the decorator's markup or commission.
- If the manager is worried by the salesperson's scare tactics, contrast the purchase with other difficult ones where such tactics are regularly surmounted.

THE STATEMENT OF WORK

Before writing the statement of work (SOW) for the service, the customer and the buyer should develop a procurement strategy. Three critical issues should be addressed:

- Competition or directed single source

- Qualifications of sources: this information allows purchasing to begin developing a "long" list of potential contractors
- The need for early supplier involvement: in many instances, it is advisable to invite two or three prequalified potential contractors to help develop the statement of work. Early suggestions from a potential supplier can help formulate the SOW and enhance the customer's ultimate satisfaction

Whenever practical, competition should be employed when purchasing services. Competitive bidding is *not* appropriate for the sourcing of professional services, since price normally is not the only variable. When purchasing technical and operating services with a good SOW, competitive bidding may be practical.

The customer may want to use a particular contractor. In such a situation, the customer should be asked for a detailed justification showing why this supplier should be considered as the only source. Experience has shown that purchasing should challenge sole source justifications that are not realistic or in the best interest of the total firm.

The most critical ingredient for a successful complex services procurement is the development of the statement of work. The SOW identifies what the contractor is to accomplish. The clarity, accuracy, and completeness of the SOW determines, to a large degree, whether the objectives of the contract will be achieved. The following general principles apply:

- The SOW must identify the primary objective clearly and then identify subordinate objectives so that both the buyer and seller know where to place their emphasis. For example, is timeliness, creativity, or artistic excellence the primary objective?
- The SOW must not be so narrow that it stifles the contractor's creative effort.
- If a SOW is written too broadly, firms may not respond because of the risk and uncertainty involved, because they cannot relate work requirements to their talents and capabilities, or because of pricing difficulties.

- A contractor, taking its ultimate direction from the SOW alone, should be able to perform the required work without further guidance.
- The SOW affects the administration of the contract. The manner in which the scope is defined will govern the amount of direction that the buyer can give during the contract's life.
- The SOW must be written clearly so that more than one interpretation is virtually impossible. On a large contract the SOW may be read, interpreted, and acted upon by contractors and buyers, engineers, functional experts, price analysts, negotiators, lawyers, and contract administrators, all of whom have different backgrounds, orientations, and biases.

Planning the Statement of Work

Certain basic questions must be answered and understood before developing the SOW:

- What are the objectives of the project?
- Where did the objectives come from, who originated them, and why were they originated?
- What is the current status (resource and schedule constraints), of the effort?
- Based on the current status, what is the risk involved in meeting the objectives?
- What are the resource, schedule, and compensation constraints for the project?
- What buyer and contractor participation is needed for the project? Specifically state all buyer support (i.e., buyer furnished equipment, materials, facilities, approvals, etc.) to be furnished.
- Challenge the tasks identified as to their sequencing and interrelationships.
- Identify contractor delivery requirements. Include details about the schedule, type, and quantity of any deliverables.
- Specifically identify any technical data requirements (e.g., plans, specifications, reports, etc.). A periodic written report by

the contractor can improve the quality of work and help focus on what is being delivered. The outcome can be used immediately and, at the same time, is recorded for future review. Many resources are wasted restudying questions because the current management does not have access to previous studies.

- As with all other requirements, the SOW requirements should be challenged prior to completing the document. Many of the value engineering questions of Chapter 3 apply:
  - ➤ Why is the task needed in the project?
  - ➤ Does it contribute tangible benefits?
  - ➤ How much does the task cost in terms of the technical effort to be performed?
  - ➤ Is the value of the task to the project worth the cost associated with its accomplishment?
  - ➤ Is there another way to accomplish the task? Has it been considered?
  - ➤ What is the effect on the project if the task were deleted?

A Few Special Issues

The following issues deserve special attention. Required provisions may be in either the SOW or terms and conditions included by the buyer:

- A performance plan. Require the contractor to develop a non-subjective, quantifiable blueprint for providing the services. After developing the blueprint, all required processes should be identified by the contractor. Next, the contractor should be required to establish fail-safe measures to minimize quality problems.
- Personnel plan. Require the contractor to develop and maintain recruiting and training programs acceptable to the buyer.
- Environmental factors. Identify any such factors which may affect the work.
- Administrative factors. The following and similar administrative factors should be described:

- ➤ Contract award procedures
- ➤ Time required for proposal evaluation and award
- ➤ Liability insurance
- ➤ Bonding requirements

- Termination. A two-way, no-cause termination provision allowing either party to end the agreement with 30, 60, or 90 days of notice is a common practice. A "for-cause" termination clause will allow the buyer to terminate immediately under certain specified conditions.

- A Program Organization Chart. The contractor should designate his program manager and show the key members of the organization by name and function. The program manager's functional authority should be clearly defined.

- Milestone Plan. This plan should identify all major milestones on a time basis.

- Funds Commitment Plan (cost reimbursement contracts only). This should show estimated commitments on a dollar-versus-month basis and on a cumulative dollar-versus-month basis.

- Labor Commitment Plan. This should show estimated labor loading on a labor-hour basis.

- Monthly Progress Information. This report should be submitted 10 days after the close of each month. The report normally should contain:

A narrative summary of work accomplished during the reporting period, including a technical progress update, a summary of work planned for the next reporting period, problems encountered or anticipated, corrective action taken or to be taken, and a summary of buyer-seller discussions.

A list of all action items, if any, required of the buyer.

An update of the milestone plan showing actual progress against planned progress.

An update of the funds commitment plan showing actual funds committed against the planned funds by time (incentive and cost contracts only).

A report on any significant changes in the contractor's program personnel or in the financial or general management structure, or any other factors that might affect the contractor's performance.

Missed milestone notification and recovery plan—The contractor should notify the buyer by phone within 24 hours after discovery of a missed major milestone or the discovery of an anticipated major milestone slip. The contractor should provide the buyer with a missed milestone recovery plan within seven working days after notification.

Such information can be costly and should be requested only when its cost and the cost of using it will result in savings.

SELECTING SERVICE CONTRACTORS

Selecting the "right" source is much more of an art when purchasing services than when purchasing materials. Based on the complexity of many service procurements and the unexpected problems which tend to arise, it usually is desirable to choose established, reputable suppliers. Unless one supplier has a unique reputation or a special skill, selection of the supplier should be based on a careful review of the competing firms.

When a large number of potential contractors is available, the buyer and the customer should reduce the list to three to five firms. The purchasing/customer team should interview prospective contractors' management, talk with previous customers, and check out employees through random interviews.

During source selection, emphasis should be placed on the *total* cost and *total* benefits to the buying organization. Assume, for example, that two architect-engineering (A-E) firms are under consideration for the development of plans and specifications for a new building estimated to cost $10 million. Firm X has a reputation for designing functional buildings whose costs are relatively low. Firm Y has a reputation for designing more elaborate, aesthetically more attractive buildings whose costs tend to run 10 percent more than X's. X's fees tend to run 10 percent more than Y's. These assumptions are used in Figure 5.1.

Figure 5.1   Total Costs for Construction Project

	Firm X	*Firm Y*
	Firm X	*Firm Y*
Design Fee	$726,000	$660,000
Construction Cost	$10,000,000	$11,000,000
Total Cost	$10,726,000	$11,660,000

Unless the customer determines that the aesthetic features likely to result from Firm Y's work are worth $934,000 more than X's design ($11,660,000-$10,726,000), selection of X (at the higher fee) results in a lower all-in-cost!

Consulting Services

The procurement of consulting is especially challenging. When the scope of work is definable, use of a lump sum price is recommended. A lump sum is far easier to administer and it avoids the tendency of some consultants to prolong a job unnecessarily. If considerable uncertainty is present or if your management wants to purchase a level of effort or temporary manpower, a daily or monthly rate is more appropriate and often insisted on by the consultant. Except in unusual cases, the consultant should be required to provide a written report before payment is made. Figure 5.2 is a checklist for purchasing consulting services.

In addition to the traditional concerns with a prospective contractor's financial strength, management, experience, and reputation, the area of technical capabilities requires special analysis.

Technical Contractors

A recent article in *Purchasing World* identifies the following issues to be addressed when selecting a contractor for computer maintenance. The list is introduced as an example of the depth of analysis required when selecting a contractor for a critical service. Based on past history, does the prospective contractor

- maintain *all* of the equipment in a computer installation
- *quickly* correct problems

Figure 5.2   A Checklist For Consulting Contracts

1. Break the statement of work into milestones, with a product at each milestone.

2. If feasible, request pricing on a lump sum basis.

3. Establish budgeted man-hours for each milestone, if compensation is based on daily or monthly rates.

4. Agree on the people to be assigned.
   - Numbers
   - Levels
   - Specific names
   - Qualifications

5. Establish lump sum prices with payment milestones or billing rates at a daily or monthly rate by individual consultant. Tie payment to completion of specific milestones.

6. Agree on the amount of the customer's involvement.

7. Agree on the manner in which the consultant will work:
   - Total independence?
   - Under direction of the customer's representative?
   - Frequency of reporting? To whom?

8. *Expense Control*

   A. Which consultants are local, which not, and what travel costs will be reimbursed?

   B. What over expenses will be reimbursed? Receipts required?

9. *Advanced Agreement in Writing*

   No work to commence until the buyer has agreed in writing to the proposal.

10. *Billing Detail*

    Invoices to be documented by specific time period covered.
    - Payment milestone (if lump sum)
    - Man-hours used
    - Billing rates on a monthly basis
    - Expenses
    Expenses documented by receipts.

11. *Project Escalation*

    No increase in scope will be allowed without advance agreement in writing as outlined above.

12. Completion of Nondisclosure Agreement if appropriate.

13. Ownership of product or output.

14. Will your company allow the use of its name in the consultant's promotional activities?

- have a field engineering office close to your facilities
- specialize in your type of equipment
- have a prescribed schedule of service calls
- have troubleshooting escalation procedures, skilled field engineers, and readily available spare parts
- have proven successful experience moving computers
- offer equipment brokerage
- have the technical ability to make low-cost modifications to your equipment (if so, can the firm support the resulting system)
- service refurbished equipment
- have high hiring standards, require appropriate training, and equip field service personnel with appropriate tools and equipment
- supply maintenance documentation
- develop custom products for special needs, and
- show flexibility in meeting specific requirements?[1]

Repairs

Anticipation is the best way to cope with emergency repairs. Vehicles, office machines, and plant equipment do break down. Sewer lines do get clogged. In many cases, it is possible to establish the source and a better price for such repair services before the emergency occurs.

Transportation

When buying transportation services, consistent on-time pickup and delivery, equipment availability and service to particular locations normally are more important than price.[2]

---

1. "How to Choose a Computer Maintenance Service," *Purchasing World*, August 1987: 73.

2. James R. Stock and Paul H. Finszer, "The Industrial Purchase Division for Professional Services," *Journal of Business Research*, February 1987: 3.

Recurring Services

Competitive prices should be solicited every two or three years for recurring services. Such action avoids complacency and helps to maintain realistic pricing. More frequent changes in contractors cause too many service disruptions.

PRICING SERVICE CONTRACTS

Procurement authority Louis DeRose writes that "the competitive process is not truly efficient in services markets. It is constrained by (three) forces and factors of supply":

- One of the strongest factors influencing competition and prices—a continuing or cumulative supply—is absent.
- Interchangeable services generally are not available due to the personal effort and involvement of the supplier.
- The supply of services is more easily restricted or restrained than it is for commodities or products.

It is for these reasons, DeRose writes, "that buyers must negotiate service agreements."[3]

Certainly there are situations where competitive bidding is an effective method of determining both source and price. An example of this situation would be a janitorial services contract for which there is intense competition. But in the majority of instances, we agree with Mr. DeRose that negotiation will result in better pricing.

Frequently, the pricing of service contracts is not tailored to motivate the supplier to satisfy the organization's *principal* objective. Once the primary requirement (artistic excellence, timeliness, low cost, etc.) is identified, the buyer must ensure that the resulting contract motivates the supplier to meet this need. When conditions require, the contract should reward good and penalize poor service.

---

3. Louis J. DeRose,"Not by Bids Alone," *Purchasing World*, November 1985: 46.

PROCURING THREE TYPES OF SERVICES

Professional Services

Architect-engineering (A-E) firms, lawyers, consultants, and education authorities are representative of the individuals and firms that provide professional services. The buyer must consider the relationship between the price mechanism (e.g., firm fixed price, cost plus incentive fee) and the contractor's motivation on critical professional services contracts. For example, fixed price contracts reward suppliers for their cost control. For every dollar in reduction of supplier's costs is a dollar of additional profit. Consider the procurement of A-E services. A fixed price contract places the supplier in a most awkward position. If costs are carefully controlled, the A-E's profits increase. But such cost control may result in designing a building whose construction cost is excessive. A cost plus award fee contract (where the fee includes a guaranteed minimum, plus a bonus for effectively controlling the building's construction cost) normally will result in lower *total* costs.

Cost type contracts should be considered when

- there is considerable uncertainty concerning the amount of effort which will be required
- there is insufficient time to develop a realistic SOW, and
- the dollar amount involved warrants the administrative cost and effort involved.

For lower dollar amounts, a time and materials or labor hour contract should be considered to avoid contingency pricing. Such contracts require close monitoring to ensure that the specified skill of labor is furnished and that the hours being billed are, in fact, required.

Administratively, it may be impractical to use other than a fixed price contract or an hourly rate price for relatively small contracts. Even on larger dollar amounts, the suppliers' reputation may allow the use of a fixed price contract. But buyers should be aware of the potential effect of the pricing mechanism on the contractor's performance.

Technical Services

Such services include research and development (R&D); software development; repair service; printing; promotion; insurance; the development of technical manuals; transportation; radio and TV production and spot advertising; per diem help; heating, ventilating, air conditioning, and elevator maintenance; window washing; pest control; parking services; energy management; accounting; bookkeeping; payroll; mailroom; copyroom; and messenger service.

R&D services normally are purchased through one of two methods of compensation: a fixed price for a level of effort (e.g., 50 days) or a cost plus fixed or award fee. Software development lends itself to cost plus award fee contracts (as described in Chapter 13). This approach rewards excellent performance and punishes poor performance while ensuring the supplier that its costs will be reimbursed and at least a minimum fee received.

Once a good SOW is available for services such as printing, promotional services, and the development of technical manuals, competition should be employed to select the source and determine the (fixed) price.

Operating Services

Janitorial, security, landscaping, and cafeteria operations are typical of operating services. Experience has shown that performance of such services can be very challenging to administer. Accordingly, the compensation scheme should reward the supplier for good service and penalize it for poor service. Such an approach to pricing aids in the administration of the contract and results in a higher level of customer satisfaction.

Insurance, plant and equipment maintenance, and anticipated emergency services should be sourced and priced through the use of competition among carefully prequalified suppliers. Unanticipated emergency repairs normally will be purchased on a not-to-exceed time and materials basis (as described in Chapter 13).

MANAGING PERFORMANCE

Prework Conference

When the dollar magnitude, complexity, or critical nature of the service or uncertain working conditions dictate, a prework meeting should be held with the prospective contractor before awarding the contract. The customer, inspector, key site personnel, and purchasing should be represented at this meeting. The following related items, as appropriate, should be reviewed:

- Invoicing and payment provisions
- Terms and conditions
- Schedule
- Staffing and supervision
- Site conditions, work rules, and safety
- Invoicing procedures and documentation (for incentive and cost contracts)
- Material purchase procedures (for incentive, cost, and time and material contracts)
- Background checks and security clearances
- Insurance certificates and permits
- Possible conflicts with other work
- Submission of time sheets (for cost contracts and time and material contracts)
- Buyer responsibilities. Buyer supplied items such as tools, equipment, facilities, etc. must be identified. Timeliness of buyer reviews and approvals for studies, reports, plans and specifications, etc. must be established and accepted by both parties.

In many instances, the buyer needs to know who the supplier's key personnel are for the project. When purchasing the development and production of a technical manual, the project leader and one or two creative artists may spell the difference between a successful and a marginal project. The site supervisor for a janitorial or a food service contract frequently makes the difference between a smoothly running operation and a troublesome one. Ideally, these issues should be addressed during the development of the SOW, and provisions made to obtain the information and reports required.

Monitoring Progress

When evaluating a contractor's progress, the purchaser is interested in actual progress toward completing the work. Progress data may be obtained from many sources: ongoing information from the contractor's process control system, progress conferences, visits to the field, and periodic progress reports from the contractor.

When appropriate, the contractor may be required by the terms of the purchase order or subcontract to submit a phased schedule. Such a requirement should be made a part of the invitation to bid or request for proposal and the resulting contract. A phased production schedule shows the time required for the operating cycle: planning, design, purchasing, hiring, training, performance, monitoring the quality of performance, and so on.

The purchaser may include a requirement for progress reports in the invitation to bid or request for proposal. Desired reports should be specified in the resulting purchase order or subcontract. Such reports show the supplier's actual and forecasted progress compared with the contract schedule, delay factors if any, etc. The report also should contain narrative sections in which the contractor explains any difficulties. Progress reports do not eliminate field visits on crucial contracts. On major critical subcontracts, it may be desirable to establish a resident monitor at the supplier's facility.

Controlling Changes

The buyer should be present when the project manager discusses possible changes in the original SOW with the contractor. When such changes are necessary, the new price should be negotiated by the buyer and agreed to prior to an agreement to implement the necessary changes. The buyer negotiates from a position of weakness if changes are agreed to before agreement is reached on the change in price.

Controlling Buyer's Representatives

Monitoring supplier progress frequently calls for the assignment of one or more individuals from the customer's department to act as inspectors. These individuals should be carefully selected. They should be briefed by the buyer on their responsibilities, authority, and the legal implications of their dealings with the supplier and the supplier's personnel. Normally, such inspectors derive their authority from the buyer. They are the buyer's representatives. Experience has shown that the buyer must periodically make field visits to monitor progress and to minimize the possibility of inspectors abusing their authority.

CONCLUDING REMARKS

The procurement of services is a little-understood, but increasingly important, activity. The professional buyer must be as effective at obtaining services as in obtaining materials, equipment, and supplies. The keys to successful service procurement are the buyer's knowledge of the service, a sound statement of work, selection of the "right" source, a fair and reasonable price, and aggressive management of the contract.

Having developed the "right" requirement, our focus now is directed at obtaining the "right" price.

Chapter 6

Pricing Theory and Competitive Pricing

The objective of procurement is to obtain necessary materials, equipment, and services of the desired quality, in a timely manner, and at fair and reasonable prices. Within this framework, the objective of contract pricing is to establish and administer a pricing arrangement that results in payment of a fair and reasonable price. A fair and reasonable price is defined as one that is fair to both parties of the transaction, considering the quality and timeliness of contract performance. From the supplier's point of view, such a price generates a reasonable return on its investment.[1] From the buyer's point of view, this price is a function of need and market conditions. This chapter provides an understanding of what a price represents and discusses how it tends to vary under differing economic conditions.

PRICE

Price is the monetary amount a buyer pays a seller for the delivery of a product or the performance of a service. There are at least three different views of what constitutes a fair and reasonable price.

---

1. Under temporary conditions, a seller may be willing to forego immediate profit in order to meet long-term objectives.

To a seller, a reasonable price is the full cost to produce plus his or her idea of a reasonable profit.[2] What is a reasonable profit is affected by the market-place, which varies with

- the number of buyers
- the number of sellers
- the degree of risk in cost estimates
- the degree of risk in achieving product or service performance
- the cost to produce
- the intensity of demand
- the availability of alternatives capable of satisfying this demand
- the time it takes to add capacity, and
- the time it takes to develop substitutes.

To a buyer, a reasonable price generally is the lowest price required to get the desired product. How much a buyer is willing to pay is influenced by

- the intensity of the need (frequently affected by the lead time available)
- the ability to obtain delivery, and
- the alternatives that are available.

Utility is hard to measure. If a particular product is required to perform a vital function, that product will have a high utility. On the other hand, if substitutes are available, or if the function is not really vital, the product may have low utility. The buyer's immediate need is to satisfy the funded purchase request. The need for, and utility of, a particular product is decided by someone else. As a result, the buyer generally believes that his or her job is merely to buy at the lowest price to which a seller will agree. If that price is higher than the funds authorized by the purchase request, the buyer must go back to the person who originated the request. Need and utility may be re-evaluated as a consequence of that action and appropriate

---

2. The very serious reader is encouraged to read Donald N. McClouskey, *The Applied Theory of Price* (New York: Macmillan Publishing Company, Inc., 1982).

changes may be made in the requisition. Even when the money provided covers the price agreed to, the buyer should revalidate the requirement before awarding a contract. While these steps are sound and necessary, they are of little comfort to the buyer who must make a determination that the price is reasonable.

From an economist's point of view, the market price is the best approximation of a fair and reasonable price. Competitive forces determine what quantities will be bought and sold and the prices charged under specific market conditions at any time. This viewpoint is based on the presence of competition among suppliers and competition among buyers. Even with these assumptions, market prices will vary due to length of the contract, size of the order, the buyer's negotiating skill, and similar factors.

The Theory of Price

Adam Smith promulgated the theory that every individual, in pursuing his or her own selfish good, would be led to achieve the best good for all. Smith reasoned that prices and price levels are regulators that tend to bring supply and demand into equilibrium and to cause, in the long run, the most efficient allocation of scarce resources. He postulated that demand in excess of available supplies will lead to higher prices in the short run, and if strong demand continues or appears likely to continue for an appreciable period of time, the higher prices will attract new suppliers. Conversely, supply in excess of demand will lead to lower prices in the short run as sellers attempt to move their products. If demand and prices remain or appear likely to remain weak, this will cause some sellers to quit the market.

In order to increase the supply in any one product market, additional production resources, called the factors of production, must be committed. Land, labor, and capital—factors of additional resources—come to one market from other markets. They come from markets where they are used less efficiently, as measured by the lower prices, profits, and returns on investments they command. It is this migration of resources which supports the role of price as the regulator that controls the allocation of scarce resources for their most efficient use.

Perfect competition is defined as a market in which there are many fully informed sellers and buyers of a homogeneous and perfectly interchangeable product, all free to enter or leave the particular market at will. Under perfect competition, the price is determined in the marketplace solely by supply and demand. Neither the seller nor the buyer can control the price level.

Degrees of Competition

Modern price theory classifies markets by degrees of competition—a relative concept—and develops theories about the relationship of demand, supply, and price levels under different competitive conditions. A company may sell similar products in different markets with different degrees of competition at different prices. For instance, a tire company will make tires with different tread designs, tread thicknesses, and mileage guarantees, while incurring similar production costs for the different tires. The tires will be marketed under a brand name to the original equipment market and the replacement market. Other tires with modified treads and markings will be sold to oil companies and chain stores for resale. The prices at which the manufacturer sells to these markets vary.

The principal classifications are shown in Figure 6.1.

Under the **perfect** and **effective** classes of **competition**, the buyer and seller have no control over price. The closer the seller is to being the only one offering the particular product, the more control he has, as long as there are many buyers. The closer the buyer is to being the only customer, the more control she has, as long as there are many sellers.

Effective competition is similar to perfect competition, except that the number of sellers is limited. However, there must be enough sellers so that no one seller dominates the market. All sellers are independent and active rivals, and new firms can enter the market easily.

Monopolistic competition is similar to perfect competition except that there is product differentiation; that is, the sellers are able to establish real or illusory differences among the products they offer for sale. The seller is able to control price to some degree if

Figure 6.1 Market Advantage

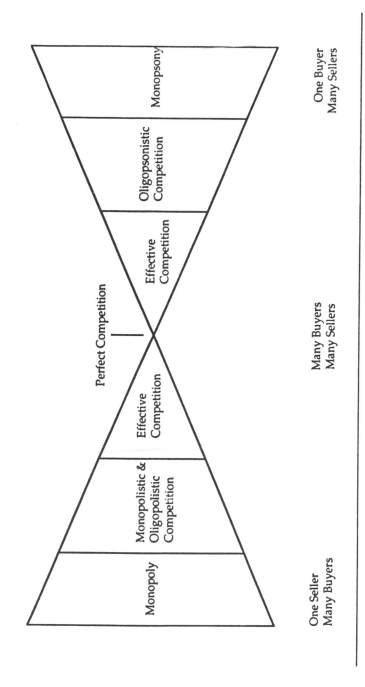

High Seller Power

High Buyer Power

Monopoly

Monopolistic & Oligopolistic Competition

Effective Competition

Perfect Competition

Effective Competition

Oligopsonistic Competition

Monopsony

One Seller
Many Buyers

Many Buyers
Many Sellers

One Buyer
Many Sellers

she can convince buyers that the product is different from those of other sellers. Most retail trade falls in this category.

Oligopolistic competition exists when there are few sellers and many buyers of products that have degrees of difference. The seller, through advertising and quality differentiation, is able to control price to some extent. This kind of competition exists with steel and aluminum, for example, where there may be little real difference in product, and with automobiles, major appliances, and machinery through product differentiation.

Oligopsonistic competition is like oligopolistic competition except that there are many sellers and only a few buyers.

Monopoly exists when there is one seller and many buyers of a product that has no close substitutes. The seller has considerable control over price. The prices of some sellers, such as utilities, are regulated to protect, to some extent, the public. The seller's control over price varies according to circumstances that determine his bargaining strength.

Monopsony exists when there are several sellers and one buyer of interchangeable products. In this case, sellers tend to have little control over price.

Cost Based Pricing

The reader may be thinking that all of this business about monopolies, oligopolies, and monopsonies is interesting, but what has it got to do with pricing? As previously stated, the seller probably considers a reasonable selling price to be the full cost of production plus a reasonable profit. Therefore, a supplier facing little or no competition will tend to charge what the market will bear. Wholesale outlets and retail outlets add a markup which includes their costs plus a profit to their purchase prices. The cost-plus approach is used widely in the defense industry where other price competition is not particularly intense, the product is highly differentiated, and the seller has some advantage. On the other hand, a defense contractor has one customer—the federal government—and is often legally required to disclose its costs.

The cost-plus approach will vary, depending upon the user and what portion of costs are to be recovered. Both the manufacturer and the middleman use it to figure sales prices. Studies show that most manufacturers use the cost-plus method of pricing. Their costs cover the value of the resources required to produce the product. The resource costs include both direct and indirect costs. Direct costs are the costs of material and labor directly associated with certain items or services provided. Indirect costs are costs of operation not directly associated with the production of a certain item or service, such as plant maintenance, warehousing, and general company management. The expenditure of resources is measured in terms of dollar value.

There are several techniques that suppliers use to establish their pricing range including straight mark-up pricing, rate-of-return pricing, and incremental or marginal cost pricing.

Straight Mark-up Pricing. Under straight mark-up pricing, the firm establishes its prices based on total cost plus a percentage markup for profit. There may be one standard markup for each product line or individual markups for individual products or product lines. Under this procedure, the individual establishing prices will do the following:

- Estimate the product's cost
- Determine the mark-up rate to be used
- Apply the mark-up rate to the product cost to establish the price

Suppose the costs of an item totaled $80 and a markup of 20 percent on cost is determined reasonable for that product. The price would be $96.

Rate-of-return Pricing. Rate-of-return pricing is similar to straight mark-up pricing in that profit dollars are added to estimated costs. However, instead of being based on estimated costs, profit dollars are based on the desired return on investment. The basic steps of this form of pricing are listed below:

- Determine the desired rate of return on investment
- Estimate the required investment
- Estimate the sales level
- Estimate the unit cost at the forecasted sales level
- Calculate the desired dollar return and add this amount to the dollar cost

Suppose the product discussed above required a $600,000 investment at the desired level of sales, 5,000 units. The unit cost is still $80, and the manufacturer desires a 15 percent return on investment.

Unit profit dollars are determined by dividing the desired return by the estimated sales in units.

$$\frac{.15 \times \$600,000}{5,000} = \$18 \text{ profit per unit}$$

Estimated cost + Desired profit = Unit selling price

$80 + $18 = $98 unit selling price

Variable or Incremental Pricing. Under certain circumstances, a supplier may quote a price which does not cover its total costs. Instead, it may cover only variable costs. This approach is used most widely when business is depressed, the firm is selling outside of its normal market, or the firm has considerable unused capacity. For example, a supplier may quote below the full costs in order to get a job that would cover variable costs if needed to keep the business going or to prevent terminating part of the labor force. The concept of incremental pricing is discussed further in Chapter 9.

COMPETITIVE PRICING

As a general rule, a supplier will quote a price that will be low enough to place it in an area for consideration and, at the same time, high enough to return a satisfactory profit in case it receives the award. Therefore, prices quoted are based on a combination of what it costs to produce an item and what the supplier thinks other suppliers will bid.

The process of arriving at an agreement on a price (assuming well-prepared negotiators) is depicted in Figure 6.2.

For a sale to occur, the maximum price the buyer is willing to pay must be at or above the absolute minimum the seller will take.

Figure 6.2   Establishing a Price

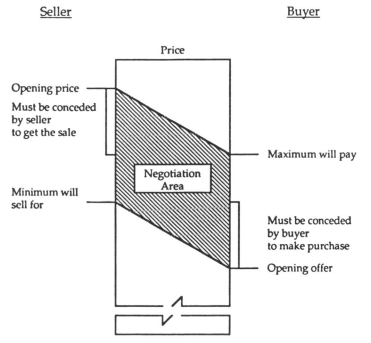

Copyright © 1990, Burt, Norquist, and Anklesaria.

The difference between these two points is the only area of negotiation in which an agreement can take place.

In preparing for negotiation, the professional buyer analyzes the seller's situation and estimates the seller's opening price, and also the minimum price the seller might accept. The buyer will adjust his or her approach when the seller's offer is known.

The seller's offer will take into account one or more of the following considerations:

Seller—opening price
- Fully loaded costs and a profit
- Competition (what will the market bear?)
- Allowances for foreseeable future cost changes

- An assumption that the customer is desperate
- Anticipation that the customer is a potential source of more business
- Alternatives attractive to a buyer

The minimum a seller will consider might be based on a variety of goals:

Seller—minimum will sell for
- Sale will increase total profits
- Makes a contribution to fixed costs
- Based on making cost reductions in the future
- Chance for future business with the buyer
- Needed to maintain market share
- Needed to avoid layoffs or to use excessive capacity

The buyer's opening offer can be considerably below the seller's request, but it must be either reasonable or backed up with reasons the salesperson will be willing to counter in hopes of raising the buyer's offer. Otherwise there is a high probability that the salesperson will terminate discussions. The buyer will consider one or more of the following when developing his/her initial offer:

Buyer—opening offer
- Very low but can justify its consideration
- Plans on supplier yield increases
- Suspects supplier may need business now
- Uses an optimum cost model as a base
- Alternate sources available if supplier says "No"
- More than covers supplier's variable costs

The buyer also must determine a "maximum" in order to avoid paying more (during the heat of negotiation) than required for the other available alternatives. Of course, time constraints are a factor in this analysis:

Buyer—maximum will pay
- Has good alternate suppliers at this price
- Project cannot be justified above this point
- Analysis indicates more than a fair profit to the supplier, and alternatives are present

- Special features justify this price
- Will manufacture before going any higher

In many situations the buyer already will have obtained agreement to the "minimum" and "maximum" from his or her management before embarking on the negotiation. In most cases the "absolute maximum" is held back and comes into play only after further discussion and reconsideration by upper management. These issues will be more fully discussed in Chapter 14.

If the business is important enough, the supplier may forgo all profit and even a portion of the cost if the contract can be secured. In such an instance, the supplier will quote low in order to undercut all competition. This is called "buying-in" or "cost optimism." It is frowned on because, in many cases, this approach may result in either of three unsatisfactory situations for the buyer: (1) a default through the inability or unwillingness of the supplier to perform, (2) an inordinately high price quote on the follow-on business for the item, or (3) an immediate request for correction after award.

A supplier also may look to a follow-on advantage by paying for all tooling and setup expenses required to make the item on the initial contract. As a result, the supplier alone may have the production experience, know-how, and the use of fully amortized tooling to undercut all competition for follow-on business while making an exorbitant profit. Under another pricing strategy, the supplier may hope to recover costs through contract changes and amendments or orders for spares that are developed after securing the contract.

CONCLUDING REMARKS

The professional buyer recognizes the market conditions, the degree of competition present, and the pricing technique which the supplier has employed when developing its price proposal. Such insight allows the buyer to anticipate the need for cost analysis and to better prepare for negotiations. When preparing for negotiations, the professional buyer analyzes the seller's situation and estimates the seller's opening price and the minimum price the seller may accept. The professional buyer is sensitive to the supplier's realistic profit needs to allow for investment in research and development, plant, and equipment and to reward investors with a realistic return on investment.

Having established this theoretical foundation, we next turn our attention to price analysis.

Chapter 7

Price Analysis

The buyer's objective in performing price analysis is to ensure a fair and reasonable price for the timely delivery of the desired quality of an item or service. The conclusion that a price is fair and reasonable must be based on some form of analysis. There are two basic types of analysis:

- **Price analysis** is the evaluation and review of the total price of an item without regard to the individual elements of cost or profit. Price analysis focuses on the "bottom-line" price.
- **Cost analysis,** on the other hand, looks at more than just the "bottom line" price. Cost analysis looks at the necessity and reasonableness of every cost element, including profit.

The professional buyer must conduct some form of analysis on every purchase. The degree, extent, and method of analysis depends on the situation and the specifics of each proposal. In most instances, price analysis alone is adequate to determine the reasonableness of a proposed price. Price analysis is a relatively simple and inexpensive method of analysis. It involves no in-depth fact-finding, no audit, no cost negotiations. Therefore, it is an efficient and cost-effective method.

In many cases, however, price analysis alone will not provide an adequate basis for the determination of price reasonableness. In these cases, cost analysis (the element-by-element evaluation) must be performed. The question arises, however, whether performing cost analysis eliminates the need for price analysis. In other words, if the buyer decides that cost analysis is needed, is there any reason to bother with price analysis? The answer to that question is "Yes." The following example demonstrates why.

Suppose you were asked to submit a proposal to build a car. Your proposal might look something like this:

Materials	$ 1,500
Labor	3,000
Overhead	2,500
Miscellaneous	1,000
Profit	500
Start-up costs	2,000,000
TOTAL	$2,008,500

Based upon cost analysis alone, the buyer would very likely determine that your proposal was indeed reasonable. Each element is necessary and reasonable, even the $2 million for start-up, assuming you've never built a car before. But obviously the total price is not reasonable since a car can be obtained elsewhere for much less. The conclusion that the price is not reasonable is gained through price analysis, not cost analysis. So while price analysis alone can be adequate to make a determination of reasonableness, cost analysis alone usually cannot. Normally, a sound conclusion on value cannot be made on the basis of cost analysis alone; price arrived at by cost analysis must be corroborated by price analysis.

One may conclude, therefore, that price analysis is always required. Sometimes it is performed alone, sometimes in conjunction with cost analysis, but it is always done.

How is price analysis performed? Since price analysis evaluates only the bottom-line price, the analysis must involve some form of comparison. There are four basic types of comparison that may be employed when conducting price analysis. These include a comparison of prices with the following:

- Competitive price quotations
- Regulated prices, published market prices, or catalog prices when there are price lists issued on a competitive basis or regulated prices

- Historic prior quotations and contract prices for the same or similar end items
- Independent estimates developed with the firm

COMPETITIVE PRICE QUOTATIONS

In Chapter 6, competition was discussed in some detail. With perfect or effective competition, the market price represents a price at which buyers are willing to buy and sellers are willing to sell. In other words, perfect or effective competition will normally result in a price fair and reasonable to both buyers and sellers, provided that the following prerequisites are satisfied:

- The specifications for the item or service to be purchased must be clear and adequate so that prospective suppliers may estimate their costs with a high degree of precision. If such a degree of accuracy is not present, suppliers may submit bids or quotations, but these bids will include contingencies to protect the suppliers from any uncertainties. Such situations frequently are present with high technology requirements, with items requiring a long time to develop and produce, and under conditions of economic uncertainty.
- There is sufficient time for qualified suppliers to develop realistic and accurate proposals.
- Price must be the only variable. If quality, service, schedule, or similar requirements are not firmly established and known by all competitors, then negotiation is the preferred method of establishing the terms (including price) of the resulting contract.
- The requirement is firm, with little likelihood of a change in specifications or other aspects of the contract. When suppliers anticipate changes, they may "buy in" with the expectation of reaping their normal profit plus "windfall" gains on the resulting changes.
- Special tooling and/or setup costs are *not* major factors in the procurement. The allocation of such costs and title to the special tooling are issues best resolved through negotiation.

It is a general principle that open competition is the one sure way to get a fair and reasonable price. The professional buyer reviews each potentially competitive procurement to determine if effective competition exists. Competition may be considered effective when each of the following conditions are met.

- There are at least two offers.
- Offerors must independently contend for the contract award.
- Offerors must be able to satisfy the buyer's requirements efficiently.
- Offerors must submit priced offers responsive to the requirements of the solicitation.

Once it is determined that effective price competition exists, the actual comparison of the prices will vary from easy, for directly comparable products like fuel oil, to more difficult, for items like standard motors, to very difficult when buying machinery with complex features and accessories. When these prerequisites are satisfied, the buyer can accept the lowest responsible and responsive quote meeting the requirements of the solicitation. In making the comparison, the buyer should consider such things as available prompt payment discounts and transportation costs from different FOB points. Additionally, the buyer should consider any price adjustment factors required by the solicitation.

A price can be based on adequate price competition even when there is no current direct competition between would-be sellers. The price may appear to be reasonable when compared with current or recent prices for the same or similar items bought in similar quantities when price competition or cost analysis has proven their reasonableness. An example is the exercise of an option in a contract awarded under adequate price competition. Another example is the procurement of an item normally purchased competitively when only one offer is received. If the price appears reasonable in comparison with recent purchases of comparable quantities for which there was adequate price competition, the price may be considered fair and reasonable based on price competition.

Meeting the conditions described above for effective competition does not always assure the buyer that competitive prices have been obtained. Problems which may change the competitive picture include:

- The low offeror has a "lock" on competition.
- The conditions of the solicitation (e.g, restrictive specifications) unreasonably deny one or more known and qualified sources the opportunity to compete.
- The prices do not appear to be reasonable.

Lock on Competition

A lock on competition simply means that the low offeror has a competitive advantage. For example, all costs of special tooling and plant rearrangement may have been written off to earlier sales. Such a situation would significantly reduce this supplier's costs for the procurement when compared with those of another offeror who was about to make the item for the first time. Another common example is the case of one offeror controlling a vital component. Although this does not eliminate the independence of the various offerors, it gives that offeror a significant competitive advantage to control price and sales of that one component. It must be remembered that even if there are two offers, one from a wholesaler or jobber and another from a manufacturer who is the source of supply for both offerors, there is only one *real* offeror. Therefore, effective price competition does not exist.

Obviously, if a company has a lock on competition, the buyer cannot use competition to determine if a price is fair and reasonable. However, the presence of such a "lock" alone does not make the price unreasonable. It simply forces the buyer to use some other means of determining if the price is fair and reasonable.

Unreasonable Solicitation Conditions

This involves a question that faces the buyer at every stage of the procurement process. Are offerors required to furnish *realistic, minimum* needs only?

Often, users like school boards, governmental agencies, plant engineers, and design engineers, in their efforts to furnish detailed specifications, unnecessarily restrict competition. In some instances, these efforts result in specifications so restrictive that no one can make a responsive offer at a reasonable price. For example, a school board may gather specifications from several manufacturers who could meet its needs. After research, the board might include the best features of all items in a specification that no one supplier could meet without expensive modification of its production process. More often, school boards develop specifications for items like desks and chairs that are tied to one product, thereby excluding other satisfactory products. It might be noted that the job of a school furniture salesperson is to convince the school board to specify quality and features that will limit the competition on an item that would otherwise go to a lower bidder. Quite obviously, industrial sales engineers have similar responsibilities to "assist" the customer's engineers in the development of production materials and equipment requirements.

Procurement personnel are not immune from requiring more than is necessary in a solicitation or contract. Restrictive "boilerplate" clauses are often included as a matter of course, when in reality, they are not required. Such action results in the payment of a higher price than required for the *real* equipment.

Although it is imperative that the buyer be on the lookout for such restrictive provisions throughout the procurement process, he or she must be especially careful during price analysis. The buyer must carefully review exceptions taken by offerors to the specifications, delivery schedule, and other terms of the solicitation. Additionally, he or she must actively promote the consideration of exceptions that offer benefits in price or quality. If potential offerors were unreasonably denied an opportunity to compete, effective competition may not exist.

Unreasonable Prices

Even with apparent competition, prices sometimes may appear to be unreasonable. For this reason, it is important that the buyer considers offers against previous prices paid and prices on similar items. If the current prices do not appear fair and reasonable, further analysis is required. While unreasonable, overspecified requirements are the most obvious condition causing an unreasonable price relative to the organization's needs, requirements that are too general also may result in unreasonable prices.

Performance Specifications

The existence of effective price competition may be difficult to determine if one is buying to a performance specification. Under such conditions, all respondents may propose products to meet the performance requirement, but no two of the products may be alike in anything other than claimed performance. To use an unsophisticated example, assume a procurement uses a performance specification that calls for an eight-ounce coffee container. One offeror proposes to furnish a paper cup. The other proposes to furnish a ceramic mug. Both meet the requirements, but each has different characteristics.

Does the fact that the price proposed for the paper cup is lower than the price for the mug mean that the price of the paper cup is reasonable? It might not be if other companies sell paper cups that meet the specification requirements at lower prices. Additionally, the price might not be reasonable if the ceramic mugs last 100 times longer than the paper cups. In other words, where the specifications can result in proposals to furnish unlike products, the buyer needs to do further analysis beyond a comparison of competing prices.

When requirements are defined only by performance specifications, good procurement practice may dictate proposal evaluation using technical competition. After selecting the source on technical and quality grounds, price becomes the issue. Cost analysis probably will be required if the procurement is for a significant dollar amount. Alternatively, life cycle costs or the *total* cost of ownership (see Chapter 4) may be used to identify the supplier whose product will result in the lowest total cost of ownership.

REGULATED, MARKET, AND CATALOG PRICES

Regulated Prices

From a pricing standpoint, it is assumed that regulated prices normally are set by forces beyond the direct control of an individual company. When the price is set by law or regulation, the pricing job should be relatively easy. The supplier must identify the regulating authority and specify what the regulated prices are. The regulating authority for utilities is usually a local or regional government. State or federal units are usually the authorities for telephone and electric rates, and protected commodities.

With regulated prices, the control is obvious. Some governmental body (federal, state, or local) has determined that prices of certain goods and services should be controlled directly. Firms wishing to change prices must formally request changes from an established regulatory authority. Normally, approval of price changes requires formal review, hearings, and an affirmative vote of the regulatory authority. No firm may charge more or less than the approved price. On the other hand a recently deregulated item, like transportation, should alert buyers to the high probability of substantial savings.

Market Prices

Commodity items are generally sold at market prices. With market prices, no firm is ordered to sell its product at a certain price. Firms sell at that price because it is the price at which they are willing to sell and buyers are willing to buy the product in the marketplace. A variety of factors determine the market price. Cost of production, product quality, availability of substitutes, the industry reputation of the firm, and demand all have an impact on the product's price.

The job of price analysis is more complex with market prices. To determine if a price is fair and reasonable, the buyer must first determine whether the price of the product meets three criteria:

- There must be an established market price
- The item or service must be sold to a number of customers
- The item or service must be sold by several suppliers

Use of market prices to determine that a price is fair and reasonable cannot be accomplished until we confirm that the item's price meets the three criteria listed above. To do this, the assistance of an offeror is required. Our objective should be to cooperate with the prospective supplier and to pick whichever method will keep paperwork to a minimum. It frequently is possible to obtain special discounts or extra services which reduce all-in-cost by offering a guaranteed volume or a long-term contract.

Catalog Prices

When purchasing a large number of related commodities such as motors, switches, lighting fixtures, etc.; distributors' catalog prices well may be only the starting point in the efforts to establish a fair and reasonable price. In such circumstances, the buyer can request distributors of the required commodity group(s) to propose discounts from their catalog prices. On receipt of the catalog and proposed discounts, the buyer could compare catalog prices, less the appropriate discount and award a term contract (i.e., 12 months) for the commodity class to the lowest bidder. This approach allows procurement professionals to gain a large savings for a wide variety of unknown future purchases with a minimum of effort.

If others in the company commit the firm without involving the buyer, they often will be charged the full catalog price. Purchasing management should be alert to these missed savings when selling purchasing's role to top management.

HISTORIC PRICES

The professional buyer can perform price analysis by comparing a proposed price with historic quotes or prices for the same or similar item. In these comparisons, it is vital to insure that the base price is fair and reasonable, a valid standard against which to measure the offered price.

It is not enough for the present bid to be lower than the last price paid or even lower than all prices previously paid. Consider the example of an item bought repeatedly from the same company:

Buy	Quantity	Unit Price
1st	180	$86
2nd	200	79
3rd	172	70
Present	212	58

A steady downward trend in price often is nice but is not proof of reasonableness. Unless the reasonableness of one of the previous prices has, at some point, been established by competition, detailed cost analysis, an independent cost estimate, or testing the market for the same or a similar item, the present offer may be unreasonably high. Further, the reductions in price for follow-on orders may not reflect all the reduced costs which the supplier is experiencing.

When performing price comparison, the professional buyer requires easy access to pricing data on a line item basis. At a minimum, parts history cards and computer printouts or data displayed on a CRT showing price, quantity, contract, date, supplier, and delivery should be available in each buying organization. Care must be exercised in using these prices. *The mere fact that past prices exist doesn't make them a valid basis for comparison.* Several issues must be considered:

- How did the procurement situation affect the price fairness and reasonableness at the time of purchase?
- How have the conditions changed? For instance, have delivery requirements changed?
- What is the effect on price of changes in the quantity of a material or service purchased?
- Was the procurement competitive or sole source? If the procurement went from one mode to the other, pricing might be affected.
- Historic prices might involve onetime engineering, tooling, and other start-up costs. If they need not be duplicated, the buyer should exclude them from the price analysis base.

Changes in Buying Power

The professional buyer must contend with the changing value of the dollar over time when using historic prices as a basis of price analysis. Price index numbers provide a tool to analyze the effect of the changing value of the dollar on price. Price index numbers usually depict historical price changes with respect to time. They also can be used to analyze, compare, and predict prices for a specific product or service in a different time frame.

There are several reasons for using index numbers instead of the adjusted prices themselves to provide for comparison:

- To reduce the comparison to terms of a percentage increase or decrease, thus rendering price changes for high-priced items comparable to price changes for low-priced items
- To provide for comparing price changes of aggregates of different items, such as aggregative price changes for plywood or paper from one year to another
- To provide a vehicle for collecting samples of price changes for different items and using the collected samples to represent price changes for an entire population of items such as plumbing supplies, electric motors, etc.

The buyer can use price index numbers for three general purposes: (1) to deflate or inflate prices for comparison analysis, (2) to determine price or cost escalation or de-escalation in contractual documents, and (3) to inflate and deflate costs to facilitate trend analysis.

Price Index Numbers

Price index numbers are used in cost or price analysis to compare the proposed cost of an item with the cost of the same or similar item purchased in past years. Here, the index numbers are used to adjust prices for inflation so the comparison can be made in constant year dollars. Contract price escalation clauses (discussed in Chapter 13) usually call for some kind of after-the-fact pricing action to adjust the price paid to reflect actual price levels at the time of contract performance. These clauses usually use index numbers to measure changes in price levels. Index numbers also are used to facilitate trend or time series analysis of individual cost elements by eliminating or reducing the effects of inflation so that the analysis can be made in constant dollars.

Index numbers are defined as ratios, usually expressed in percentages, indicating changes in values, quantities, or prices. Typically, the changes are measured over time, each period price being compared with the corresponding figure from some selected base period. Simple index numbers deal with single commodities, such as plywood, steel, or grain. More commonly though, index numbers are aggregates of a number of different commodities, products, or services. For such index numbers, each item in the aggregation is weighted to represent a commodity, product, or service in proportion to its amount in a particular end item, industry, or geographical area.

Types of Indexes

Price index numbers represent changes in the prices of items, commodities, or industries over a period of time. *The Producer Prices and Price Indexes* (Bureau of Labor Statistics) give changes in the average wholesale price of commodities and products sold in the United States over a given period of time. Unfortunately, complex items such as cameras, computers, and stereo systems are extraordinarily difficult to index due to the rapid changes in features for these items. For example, cameras with many automatic features and very sophisticated electronic components now cost about the same as mechanical cameras did twenty years ago.

Quantity index numbers represent the change in the amount of a commodity or product output over a period of time. The Federal Reserve Board compiles a quantity index called the *Index of Industrial Production*. This index measures physical volume of factory production in the United States from one year to the next.

A value index combines changes in both price and quantity over time. Value indexes are the product of a price index and a quantity index. A commonly used value index is the Index of Retail Sales (published in the *Federal Reserve Bulletin*). This index reflects the changes in both prices and quantities of items sold by retail sales outlets across the United States.

As historical indicators, index numbers become more accurate if they are constructed using actual prices paid for a particular commodity, product, or service rather than using the more general aggregative index published by agencies such as the Bureau of Labor Statistics (BLS). The development and use of price indexes are described in Appendix C and price adjustment clauses in Appendix F.

Polaroid calculates the price change on the many items bought from a distributor by entering the BLS index numbers for each category into a personal computer. The change for the item and the weighted average of all items is quickly calculated. This approach avoids the reliance on a stack of price increase notices that the distributor often brings to negotiation.

Forecasting Index Numbers

Forecasting index numbers may be either a short-range problem or long-range problem. To this point, the discussions have focused on using index numbers as a measure of historic cost changes. The business of pricing is concerned with predicting or forecasting prices in the future. Accordingly, the buyer needs to be able to forecast index numbers as well as construct them from the appropriate literature.

There are at least two ways of forecasting in the short term. It may make good sense in short-range forecasting to put more weight on the most recent years of data. One method does this subjectively simply by ignoring the early years of data, graphically fitting a straight line through the most recent data, such as the last two years, and extending that straight line into future years for the forecast. On the other hand, the last two years may be atypical. In such a case, it might be more logical to use a trend line including other recent yearly data. The difference in projections can be seen by plotting the data in two different ways as shown in Figure 7.1.

The proper use of the straight line approach to forecasting depends on the forecaster's knowledge of current economic trends. Probably the most important single rule to remember about forecasting is that no one can predict an economic turning point. The analyst needs to get as much data as possible and look for trends and changes in trends. He or she should consider these changes in making projections. Some techniques, such as moving averages and exponential smoothing, may be of assistance in prediction but are beyond the scope of this text. Information on these techniques may be found in a basic forecasting text.

At Polaroid, the purchasing research group provides buyers with updated economic and supplier scenarios for both the domestic and overseas procurement climates. (Table 7.1 is a projection of the economy, and 7.2 is how suppliers would be affected.)

Figure 7.1 Index Forecasting

Year	Index
1981	105.0
1982	107.0
1983	110.0
1984	115.5
1985	119.0
1986	120.0

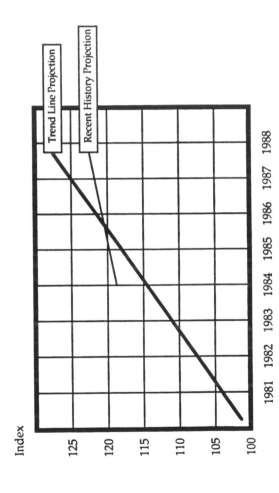

Table 7.1   1988 National *Economic* Scenario

Predictions (as of April '87) . . . . *Actual Outcome*

Predictions (as of April '87)	Actual Outcome
Inflation is Present	increasing
Unemployment in 6-7% Range	below 6%
Prime Rate Increases	2.5% from '87 low
Dollar Stabilizes	range 120-135 on yen
Corporate Profits Increase	up
Trade Deficit Still a Problem	over 100 billion
Higher Import Prices	up significantly
Supply More in Balance with Demand	more out of balance
Consolidation of Industries	airlines and others
Growing International Competitiveness	lower dollar helped us

Table 7.2   1988 National *Supplier* Scenario

Predictions (as of April '87) . . . . *Actual Outcome*

Predictions (as of April '87)	Actual Outcome
Selected Industries will be Strong	e.g., chemicals, paper
Generally, a Seller's Market	few exceptions
Labor Cost Pressure	just started
Capacity Utilization will Increase	new high
Increasing Lead Times	increased
Crude, Intermediate, and Finished Prices will Increase	increased, except oil
Interest Rates will Increase	up over 2%
More Overseas Export Opportunities	large increase
Suppliers will Try to Increase Margins	many succeeded

Polaroid buyers make use of economic scenarios to understand the probable viewpoint of salespersons. As a result, buyers are better prepared for negotiations. The increased understanding of the economy helps the buyer put what the seller has to say in a better perspective. The purchasing research group provides the buyer with detailed index data on specific products on request. Two examples of such reports are contained in Appendix D.

The Need for Judgment

Historical price comparison usually is a starting point that may reveal differences to be explained before a final price decision can be made. Sources include the experience and judgment of the buyer or the buyer's supervisor and that of representatives of other organizational elements. However, the proposed supplier may be the only source for some needed answers. The buyer needs to talk to the proposed supplier before making up his or her mind. However, when analyzing the differences, the buyer should not be misled into accepting a standard, but inaccurate, answer. For example, the supplier may contend that material and labor prices have gone up in the two years since the last purchase and that a higher price is justified for this part. But, a general increase in material and labor prices may not influence the unit cost of a particular part unless the cost of the actual material and labor used have gone up and no compensating production or overhead economies have been realized. The professional buyer is always on the lookout for such offsets!

INDEPENDENT COST ESTIMATES

When other techniques of price analysis cannot be utilized, the buyer may request a company cost engineer to develop an independent cost estimate. (In several firms, purchasing has one or more individuals with the skills to develop independent cost estimates.) This estimate can be used as the basis of price comparison in determining that the price is fair and reasonable.

Like other techniques of price analysis, this technique requires the buyer to determine that the price used for comparison is itself fair and reasonable. To do this, the buyer must determine the basis for the estimate and its reliability. Some questions for this evaluation of how the estimate was made include the following:

- What was the source of information?
- What information and techniques were used?
- How reliable were earlier estimates from this source?

The many different techniques of cost estimating may be grouped into three broad categories of estimating: round-table estimating, comparison estimating, and detailed estimating. Advantages and disadvantages of each of these categories are summarized in Table 7.3.

Round-table Estimating

In round-table estimating, experts in such functions as engineering, manufacturing, procurement, and finance are brought together to develop cost estimates based on experience, knowledge of the product or program, and knowledge of market conditions. The estimate developed by this approach is usually completed without benefit of detailed drawings or a bill of materials and with limited information on specifications.

Round-table estimating has the advantage of speed of application and is relatively inexpensive. An obvious disadvantage is the possibility that such a subjective evaluation will produce erroneous results.

Comparison Estimating

This broad grouping of estimating methods is a practical compromise between the expense of detailed cost-estimating analysis and the risk of error associated with round-table cost estimating. Comparison estimating requires the determination of the historic cost of the same or similar item as the one being estimated and adjusting or projecting the historic cost for future production. This comparison may be done at the cost element level, such as direct manufacturing labor, or at the total price level. One way to facilitate the task of estimating by comparison is to use mathematical or graphical models called cost-estimating relationships (CERs). CERs usually relate

Table 7.3   Methods of Estimating Contract Costs

Method	Advantages	Disadvantages
Round-table estimating	Estimate developed rapidly	Least accurate
	May be developed from limited information and specifications	No quantitative basis for determining realism
	Economical	Of limited use for follow-on contracts
Comparison estimating	Establishes a baseline of data for future uses	Need for adjustments for comparability
		Projects past inefficiencies
	Saves time	May require use of complex statistical techniques
	Relatively economical	May be subject to changes in time and technology
Detailed estimating	Most accurate for estimating direct cost of production	Most expensive
	Provides excellent historical basis for future estimates	Most time-consuming
	Is based on firm industrial engineering principles	Requires in-depth multi-talented team effort
		Requires detailed specifications

some physical or performance characteristic of the item being manufactured, or program being developed, to the cost of the item or program. Then, by defining the physical or performance characteristic of the new item or program to be produced, the cost can be predicted for the model.

Cost-estimating relationships are derived from observations of historical costs and the parameters, such as weight, speed, square footage, and cubic feet that are associated with those costs. The sciences of probability and statistics and a tool called regression analysis are used to discover and evaluate different cost models.

The use of cost-estimating relationships offers a practical alternative to the detailed analysis approach. For existing products, CERs offer the analyst a reasonable and practical way to check elements of the prospective supplier's proposal without duplicating the laborious process of detailed analysis.

Detailed Analysis Estimating

The classic approach to estimating costs is by detailed analysis. Sometimes known as the "grass roots" or "bottom up" approach, detailed analysis is characterized by a thorough review of all components, processes, and assemblies. Estimates for labor, tooling, material, and additional capital items may be made using this type of estimating. The application of labor rates, material prices, and indirect rates to the calculated direct cost estimates translates the estimate into total dollars. The detailed analysis estimate has the added important characteristic of producing complete records that are available for future use. Detailed analysis is the most accurate of the three approaches for estimating the direct cost of production. It also is the most time-consuming and the most expensive.

Generally, detailed analysis yields a more accurate estimate of the direct labor hours needed for a production process than an estimate produced by the round-table or comparison method. By breaking the estimate into a large number of small parts, one can take advantage of two facts. The first is that small items can be estimated more precisely than large ones. The second is that errors in estimating individual elements tend to offset each other. An accurate detailed estimate requires considerable data:

- Product specifications
- Delivery quantities and rates
- A bill of materials
- Costs of delivered purchased parts and material
- Detailed drawings of parts to be manufactured
- Parts routings
- Manufacturing equipment requirements
- Testing and inspection requirements
- Packing and shipping requirements
- Time factors (labor standards)
- Overhead rates

Suppliers who manufacture end items in quantity make extensive use of the detailed analysis method of estimating costs. The records and standards produced are the source data used by suppliers in their contract proposals. Ideally, the data could be made available to the analyst for review.

In considering the use of an independent cost estimate, the buyer needs to examine the estimator's track record in price estimation. If, in the past, the estimates have been close to contract prices determined to be fair and reasonable by some other means, reliance may be placed on the estimate. If estimates have been significantly above or below contract prices, then less reliance may be placed on current estimates.

Knowledge concerning the reliability of past estimates does not free the buyer from the obligation to review the estimate and the estimating methodology for accuracy on each and every proposal. Knowledge of past accuracy of the estimator and estimating technique is only one step in determining the acceptability of the estimate. The buyer must be aware that the detailed analysis method perpetuates existing practices and inefficiencies. The professional buyer is on the lookout for this tendency and makes appropriate adjustments before determining that a price is "fair and reasonable."

An Example

The following actual example (Tables 7.4(a) and 7.4(b)) demonstrates how a buyer used engineered cost estimates when conducting price negotiations to arrive at a "fair and reasonable" price for the construction of a remotely located facility when time was not available for competitive bids.

Table 7.4(a) Cost Comparisons

	Contractor's Bid	Engineered Estimate	Negotiated Result
Plumbing	$ 10,000	$ 10,000	$ 10,000
Mechanical/A/C	35,000	20,000	23,000
Halon System	20,000	17,000	20,000
Electrical	30,000	30,000	30,000
Computer Floor	25,000	16,000	20,000
Sprinkler System	8,000	8,000	8,000
Construction/Supervision	76,000	50,000	51,000
(See Table 7.4(b))	$204,000	$151,000	$162,000
O.H. and Profit (20%)	41,000	30,000	32,000
	$245,000	$181,000	$194,000

Table 7.4(b) Construction/Supervision Breakout

	Contractor's Bid	Engineered Estimate	Negotiated Result
Ceiling	$ 6,000	$ 6,000	$ 6,000
Walls/Glass	20,000	11,000	11,000
Doors (12)	10,000	6,000	6,000
Carpet/Paint	3,000	3,000	3,000
Misc.	25,000	10,000	11,000
Supervision	12,000	14,000	14,000
	$76,000	$50,000	$51,000

CONCLUDING REMARKS

We have seen that price analysis is a process of comparing. This comparison may be with other competitively submitted prices; prices on published price lists issued on a competitive basis, published market prices, or regulated prices; historic prior quotations and contract prices; or independent estimates developed within the firm. We also have seen that price analysis must always be employed when making a determination that a price is fair and reasonable.

Next we turn our attention to the challenging area of cost analysis.

RECOMMENDED READING

Phillip F. Ostwald, *Cost Estimating for Engineering and Management,* 2nd. ed. (Englewood Cliffs, NJ: Prentice-Hall, 1984).

Chapter 8

Cost Analysis and Cost Models

When preparing for negotiations, the buyer is interested in the cost of the item. Cost is a word we hear every day. However, the meaning of the word "cost" can be anything from total price to direct cost, indirect costs, or several other interpretations. In general terms, cost is a measurement of the amount of resources used for some contract or project objective. Resources include material, labor, and other inputs to production.

Earlier, cost analysis was described as a technique for evaluating the fairness and reasonableness of a price by analyzing individual elements of cost such as labor, material, indirect costs, and profit. Cost and pricing data consist of all the facts that can reasonably be expected to contribute to making sound estimates of future costs as well as evaluating the costs already incurred. The buyer obtains or develops cost data to prevent disagreement on the facts and to insure that he or she and the supplier start from the same point in estimating the costs of contract performance.

There are three methods of obtaining cost data: through partnership relations, from suppliers in response to request for proposal requirements, and through the development and use of cost models.

OBTAINING COST DATA FROM PARTNERS

Purchasing literature is filled with articles advocating the establishment of long-term, mutually beneficial partnerships with our suppliers. One of the hidden benefits of such partnerships is that the buyer will have access to the supplier partner's cost data. As a senior automotive purchasing executive recently remarked, "We don't make a big issue about cost data until the benefits of the partnership are obvious to the supplier. But as the relationship progresses, we insist on total access to the supplier's cost-accounting system."

At Polaroid, buyers employ a staircase of cost knowledge (Figure 8.1) approach to identify a supplier's position relative to eight graduated steps. Buyers can see how far they have traveled toward a complete understanding of costs by checking their progress on the staircase. Experience with the existing supplier base demonstrates that progression up the stairway is generally an iterative process. Buyers are encouraged to move up the staircase a step or two at a time in a spirit of trust and collaboration. Sometimes a supplier has gained a better understanding of his or her own costs; and more than one supplier has redone his or her overhead allocation rules.

Polaroid is not alone in this approach. Others have been moving in this direction. Instead of just negotiating, buyers at other progressive firms are working with their sellers' staffs to assure that their companies are receiving maximum value for their money.

As Fred McClintock, former manager of materials management at Xerox, told *Purchasing* magazine in the June 27, 1985 issue:

> We used to stress negotiation, but now our emphasis is on teaching what makes up the supplier's cost on a part: raw material, labor, overhead, etc. We want buyers to be able to go through such cost analysis with vendors, and determine ways they can make a reasonable profit and still reduce costs.

Polaroid's purchasing professionals have found that in many instances they have been successful at starting new suppliers or current suppliers on new programs near the top of the cost knowledge stairway.

Assurance of value through more cost knowledge has made program managers willing to narrow the choice to one or two sup-

Figure 8.1 The Staircase of Cost Knowledge

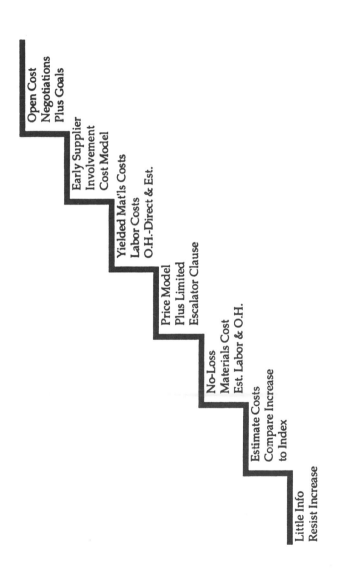

Little Info
Resist Increase

Estimate Costs
Compare Increase
to Index

No-Loss
Materials Cost
Est. Labor & O.H.

Price Model
Plus Limited
Escalator Clause

Yielded Mat'ls Costs
Labor Costs
O.H.-Direct & Est.

Early Supplier
Involvement
Cost Model

Open Cost
Negotiations
Plus Goals

pliers at the beginning of a program. Polaroid thereby gains the many benefits of early supplier involvement instead of waiting and bidding out the final design. Basically, Polaroid looks for suppliers that have outstanding management teams.

The national trend is to treat suppliers more as partners and extensions of one's own facilities. The extent of this trend depends on building up trust. Trust develops through shared data that allows both parties to receive fair treatment. In this partnership each is looking for these assurances:

Supplier	*Manufacturer, Customer*
• will be adequately compensated for suggestions and innovation	• supplier will keep current in technology of its field
• won't be left with losses on materials when production forecast is reduced	• supplier price will represent value even if there is no competition
• will be kept informed as forecasts change	• supplier won't take advantage of single source position

Increasing Role for Economic Price Adjustment (EPA) Clauses

Early design involvement, fewer suppliers, more single sources, and more long-term commitments mean that EPA clauses may play a larger role in purchasing strategy. In the past, EPA clauses frequently favored the seller. Cost analysis, cost modeling skills, and support from a purchasing research group now enable buyers to consider the use of EPA clauses which address possible changes in the cost of the supplier's inputs in an evenhanded manner. The development and use of EPA clauses is discussed in Chapter 13.

OBTAINING COST DATA AS A CONDITION OF BIDDING

A frequently asked question is "How do you obtain nonpartnership supplier cost data? Many suppliers resist sharing such data. They say it's proprietary and none of our business!"

The time to establish access to any and all of prospective supplier's data (including cost data) is when developing the Request for Quote or Request for Bids. Obviously, the professional buyer requests detailed cost data only when it will be essential in establishing a fair and reasonable price with the supplier or when there is a significant probability that changes from the original contract involving large amounts of money will occur.

If a supplier refuses to comply with such a condition in the RFP, there are several recourses available to the buyer:

- Threat of competition or perceived competition
- Work with the second lowest bidder, assuming that it has provided cost data
- Develop a cost model and renegotiate with the supplier
- Start developing a new source

Sometimes it may be necessary to discipline a supplier even when such action results in a higher price on the initial contract. When word gets out that a low bidder was found unresponsive in providing the required data, other prospective non-cooperative suppliers will tend to fall into line.

It is not enough for the offeror to set the cost or pricing data in front of the buyer with a "Here it is. Come and get it." announcement. The buyer should ask that the seller explain how the package was put together; how the supplier got from known, factual data to the estimate; and how the supplier tried to protect itself from the uncertainties of the future. In other words, the submission must include a narrative to go with the figures so that complete understanding is possible.

DEVELOPING COST DATA THROUGH MODELS

Sometimes a supplier may be reluctant or even refuse to supply requested cost data. The supplier's competitive position may be strong enough to allow such a refusal, or the supplier may not want the buyer to know how much or how little profit is included. Also, the supplier may want to avoid giving the buyer details that could be questioned.

A buyer can develop a cost model which will provide insight into the supplier's likely costs. Experience indicates that the buyer's possession of a realistic cost model frequently results in the supplier providing its cost data in rebuttal to the buyer's data. Two basic approaches to cost modeling, Zero Base Pricing and Should Cost models, are now described.

Zero Base Pricing Models

Developing a ZBP cost model is much like solving a jigsaw puzzle. The supplier's proposed price determines the overall size, but the objective also is to have the size of the material, labor, factory overhead, general and administrative overhead, and profit pieces. For instance, by weighing plastic moldings and knowing the resin cost, the no-loss material cost can be calculated. Yields at each stage of manufacturing will have to be estimated to get a total material cost.

With help from an industrial engineer, or through use of one of the techniques to be described shortly, the labor hours can be estimated. Labor costs will vary with the location of the manufacturing plant and can be estimated from published data. Estimates of space, energy, equipment, and supervision requirements can be used to develop factory overhead. Even if the initial estimates are incorrect, the discussion in future negotiations will help refine and improve the cost model. Requests for price increases should be tested against the model.

A Cost Model from the Process Industry

Figures 8.2(a) to 8.2(c) show how a cost model is constructed when only the current price and material costs are known or can be estimated. The buyer makes the assumptions shown at the top of Figure

8.2(a) before starting work on the model. A high-yield, low-labor assumption will force the buyer to evaluate overhead costs thoroughly. When only one model is developed, use of this assumption provides the buyer with the best starting position. Experience has shown that supplier overhead estimates are the hardest to negotiate down. Low yields and high labor can be changed with time to get lower prices.

The buyer works through Figure 8.2(a) to get a "high-yield" total material cost of $56.87. In Figure 8.2(b) the conversion costs of $5.57 per thousand linear feet are calculated using assumptions based on data the buyer has gathered.

Figure 8.2(c) shows the total material and conversion costs of $62.44. This is used together with an estimated profit of $8.23 to force an estimate of the supplier's overhead. In this example, the overhead allowance is calculated to be $19.83 per 1,000 feet of coated plastic.

The buyer next estimates (Figure 8.2(d)) overhead factors based on assumptions made at the start of the model (Figure 8.2(a)) and any additional estimates needed to get a possible range of overheads.

During negotiations with the supplier, the buyer would work to check out the assumptions on which the model is based. There are many possible scenarios for what the seller did to develop the price:

a. Low material yield and low overhead
b. High yield and high overhead
c. High yields but high labor and factory overhead and low nonfactory overhead
d. Combination of above

Maybe the supplier had used low yields in developing its price. In this case the buyer might accept the current price provided that the supplier establish a yield improvement program that will lower the total material costs and thereby the selling price over the coming year. The parties might agree that the buyer would supply technical help to the supplier.

If the supplier's overhead turns out to be from $10 to the $19.83 the buyer's model estimated, the supplier should be asked to explain the overheads used in setting the price. The buyer would use his or her estimated range of $9.20 to $14.30 (Figure 8.2(d)) to raise

Figure 8.2(a) Cost Model: Coated Plastic
Order Size: 200,000 Linear Feet (200 MLFT)
Material Costs

Purchasing's Assumptions:
    a. High yields
    b. No downtime except for setup time
    c. Low machine cost/hour because equipment is old
    d. Factory overhead of two to three times direct labor
    e. No engineering since product is mature
    f. Low selling cost since long-term customer

Raw Material Cost	*$ per MLFT*
Base plastic: $2.00/#; 30" width, no loss cost[g]	51.43
Coating solution, no loss cost (market price)	<u>2.97</u>
No Loss Cost	<u>54.40</u>

Adjustment to allow for scrap[h]:

Plastic: High Yields @ 96%: 51.43 ÷ 0.96 =	53.57
Coating: High Yields @ 90%: 2.97 ÷ 0.90 =	<u>3.30</u>
Total Material Costs	<u>$56.87</u>

Note:

(g) MLFT: 1,000 linear feet based on plastic weight and thickness calculated from cost per unit, assuming 14,000 sq. in. Thus, for a 30" width, there will be (14,000/30) 466.67 inches of plastic or 38.89 linear feet. Since the quote is per 1,000 linear feet (1 MLFT), $2 per 38.89 feet or (1,000 x 2) ÷ 38.89 = $51.43 per MLFT.

(h) Yields losses: edge trim, start-up, running losses.

Figure 8.2(b) Cost Model: Coated Plastic
Order Size: 200,000 Linear Feet (200 MLFT)
Conversion Costs

Manufacturing's Assumptions:
i. Machine speed: 525 ft/min or 525 x 60 = 31,500 ft/hr
j. Operators wages & benefits: $20/hour*
k. Two operators to run, two to set up @ 1.6 hours each

Running labor (@ 31.5 MLFT/hr): (assumption i)	$ 1.27
(2 x 20/31.5) (assumptions k and j)	
Setup labor for 200 MLFT:	.32
(1.6hr x 2 x $20)/200 (assumptions k and j)	
Direct Labor Total	1.59
Machine Cost: $100/hour/31.5 (assumption c)	3.17
Packaging: Buyer's estimate	.81
Total Conversion Costs	$5.57

*Source: Bureau of Labor Statistics.

Figure 8.2(c) Cost Model: Coated Plastic
Order Size: 200,000 Linear Feet (200 MLFT)
Calculation of Overhead and Profit

	$ per MLFT
Price quoted by supplier	90.50
Less: Materials costs (from Fig. 8.2(a)) 56.87	
Conversion costs (from Fig. 8.2(b)) 5.57	
	62.44
Overhead and Profit (difference)	28.06
Less: Profit (assumed @ 10% of cost or 10/110 of price)	
[90.50/11]	8.23
Overhead[1] (balancing figure)	19.83

Note:

(1)   Overhead: This is a 'forced' figure and represents one day's production of 200,000 linear feet. The buyer now estimates the overhead factors (see Fig. 8.2(d)) to challenge the $19.83 derived from the model.

Figure 8.2(d) Buyer's Estimate of Overhead Factors
[200 MLFT per shift]

| | *Buyer's Estimated Range* | |
| | *A* | *B* |
Factor	*$ per shift*	*$ per MLFT*
Engineering (see assumption e, Fig. 8.2(a))	0	0
Factory OH (assumption d, includes machine cost)	$636 to $954	3.18 to 4.77[m]
G&A (estimated by buyer)	1000 to 1500	5.00 to 7.50
Selling Expense (see assumption f, Fig. 8.2(a))	200 to 400	1.00 to 2.00
		9.18 14.27

Note:

(m)   Factory overhead is 2-3 times direct labor of $1.59 (see Fig. 8.2(b)) so the range/MFLT is (1.59 x 2) = 3.18 to (1.59 x 3) = 4.77.

questions. A reduction to the $10 to $14 range would appear to be a reasonable objective. With any reduction in overhead and total cost, the profit objective should be reduced a corresponding percentage. For example, if the buyer succeeds in negotiating a reduction of $8 on overhead, the savings would be $8.80, assuming a 10 percent profit margin.

Once the overhead issue is settled, the buyer can approach other issues like improved yields on long-term contracts, lower machine costs per hour, improved productivity, and so on. In the future, the supplier will view the buyer as a well-prepared professional and expect difficulty in pushing through unreasonable costs.

A Simplified Manufacturing Cost Model

The floppy disk cost models described on pages 156 to 161 involve many materials and operations. The model develops a material and labor cost for each operation using estimated yield losses and run times. To accurately account for the losses at each operation, in the final cost, the costs must be accumulated from operation to operation.

To those unfamiliar with this accounting method of developing product cost, a simplified direct-cost-only example is developed first. The model is based on two parts and a total of three operations. The two parts are a large square disk which costs $.10 and the label which costs $.04.

Figure 8.3(a) portrays the Simplified Manufacturing Cost Model. The rows and columns are numbered like a Lotus 1-2-3 spreadsheet. The formula and calculations for each position are shown in Figure 8.3(b).

The cost of the materials build to $0.159 and the labor to $0.144 because of yield losses and production run time of only 80 percent. The losses are compounded depending on the process. This compounding effect is why models that are more than approximations get very complex.

Figure 8.3(a) Simplified Manufacturing Cost Model

A	B	C	D	E
Item	*U/M*	*Material Cost*	*Price*	*No Loss Cost*
5 Steel Square	sq. ft.	1	.10	.10
6 Label	each	1	.04	.04

Operation	*Qt. Good per minute*	*Operations*	*Run Time*	*Mth. Yield*
19 Inspection	5/min	$10/hr	80%	95%
20 Cut	4.5/min	10/hr	80%	90%
21 Label & Stack	4.5/min	10/hr	80%	95%

Operation	*Mat'l. Cost*	*Lab. Cost*	*Cum. Mat'l.*	*Cum. Lab.*
31 Inspect	.1053	.0439	.1053	.0439
32 Cut	.0117	.0514	.1170	.0953
33 Label & Stack	.0420	.0487	**.1590**	**.1440**

Total Labor	.1440			
Total Material	.1590			
	.3030			

Figure 8.3(b) Cell Formulas & Calculations for Simplified Cost Model

E5	=	D5/C5	
E6	=	D6/C5	
B31	=	E5/E19	$.1/.95 = .1053$
C31	=	C19/(B19*60*E19*D19)	$10/(5*60*.8*.95)$
D31	=	B31	$.1053$
E31	=	C31	$.0439$
B32	=	(D31/E20) − D31	$(.1053/.9) − .1053 = .0117$
C32	=	C20/(B20*60*E20*D20)	$10/(4.5*60*.9*.8) = .0514$
D32	=	D31 + B32	$.1053 + .0117 = .1170$
E32	=	E31 + C32	$.0439 + .0514 = .0953$
B33	=	E6/E21	$.04/.95 = .042$
C33	=	C21/(B21*60*E21*D21)	$10/(4.5*60*.95*.8) = .0487$
D33	=	D32 + B33	$.117 + .042 = .159$
E33	=	E32 + C33	$.0953 + .0487 = .1440$
Total =		E33 + D33	$.1440 + .159 = .3030$

Third Model: A Complex Assembled Product

The third model is on a computer. It illustrates the buildup of manufacturing costs of a product, a 5¼" floppy disk. The manufacturing
process involves ten materials and nine operations. The modeling
method works as well on more complex products by accumulating
subassembly costs in individual models leading on to a final assembly model.

Figure 8.4(a) describes the process flow for the manufacture of
5¼" floppy disks. The process always needs to be understood before
an accurate detailed cost model can be developed.

Figure 8.4(b) shows a cost model for a floppy disk. The input
data is shown in boxes. All other data is derived with the logic
shown in Figure 8.4(c). Lines 5 to 14 develop the no-loss material
cost. Lines 19 to 28 give the estimated or known production rate,
labor rate, run time, and material yields. The packaging line requires
two people.

The cumulative costs of labor and material are developed on
lines 31 to 40. Where the operations are in sequence, the yields multiply. In this model (Figure 8.4(b)) the yield loss is high.

"What if" questions can be answered quickly by merely changing any input item. (Changes in manufacturing process however
would require modifying the logarithms.)

Calculation formulas can be found by relating to the coding of
the cell location, i.e., the calculation of the material cost at the lami-
nation operation is (E5 + E6)/E19 or (jacket cost + line cost)/lamina-
tion material yield and can be found at cell location B31. (Figure
8.4(c) shows the cell formulas.)

Figure 8.4(a) Manufacturing Process Flowchart: 5¼" Floppy Disks

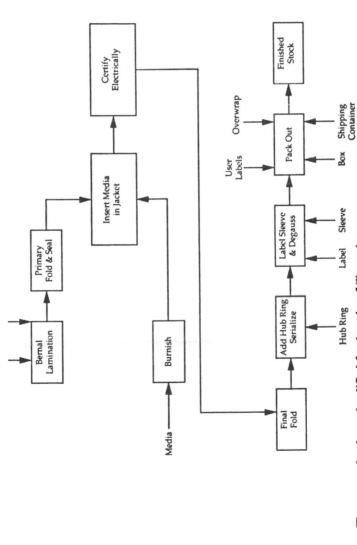

Note: The process has been simplified for the sake of illustration.
Copyright © 1990, Burt, Norquist, and Anklesaria.

Figure 8.4(b) Floppy Disk Cost Model

Columns	B	C	D	E
Item	U/M	Materials Conv Fctr	Price	No-Loss cost/disk
5 Jacket	1b	0.04	$1.5000	$0.0600
6 Liner	1f	0.04	$0.0500	$0.0020
7 Media	ea	1	$0.2000	$0.2000
8 Hub ring	1000	0.001	$15.0000	$0.0150
9 Label	ea	1	$0.0100	$0.0100
10 Sleeve	ea	1	$0.0400	$0.0400
11 User labels	ea	0.1	$0.1000	$0.0100
12 10 pack box	ea	0.1	$0.2000	$0.0200
13 Overwrap	ea	0.1	$0.0300	$0.0030
14 Crrgtd, etc.	ea	0.001	$1.3000	$0.0013
				$0.3613

Operation	Qt/min	Operations DL Rate	Run Time	Mt'l Yld
19 Laminate	100	$14.00	70.0%	95.0%
20 Primary Fold	35	$14.00	85.0%	99.0%
21 Burnish	100	$11.00	85.0%	99.6%
22 Insert	150	$11.00	50.0%	99.5%
23 Certif	45	$14.00	80.0%	65.0%
24 Fin Fold	40	$11.00	85.0%	99.2%
25 Hub Ring	50	$11.00	80.0%	99.6%
26 Label/Ser	50	$11.00	70.0%	99.9%
27 Box out	25	$11.00	85.0%	99.9%
28 Pack	500	$22.00	85.0%	99.9%

Operation	Mat'l Cost	Lab Cost	Cum Mat'l	Cum Lab
31 Laminate	$0.0653	$0.0035	$0.0653	$0.0035
32 Pri fold	$0.0007	$0.0079	$0.0659	$0.0114
33 Burnish	$0.2008	$0.0022	$0.2667	$0.0136
34 Insert	$0.0010	$0.0025	$0.2677	$0.0161
35 Certify	$0.1087	$0.0100	$0.3764	$0.0260
36 Fin Fold	$0.0030	$0.0054	$0.3794	$0.0315
37 Hub Ring	$0.0151	$0.0046	$0.3945	$0.0361
38 Lab/Ser	$0.0100	$0.0052	$0.4045	$0.0413
39 Box out	$0.0731	$0.0086	$0.4776	$0.0499
40 Pack	$0.0013	$0.0009	$0.4789	$0.0508

		Overhead		
42 Volume		1,000,000		

Item	Total	Unit Cost		
45 Indirect Lab.	$15,000	$0.0150		
46 Factory Ovh	$12,000	$0.0120	Grand Total	
47 Depreciation	$20,000	$0.0200		
48 Rent	$12,000	$0.0120	Tot mat'l	$0.4789
49 Utilities	$10,000	$0.0100	Tot lab	$0.0508
50 G&A	$15,000	$0.0150	Tot ovh	$0.0840
52 Total	$84,000	$0.0840	Grand Total	$0.6137

*Note: All information in bold is available to or estimated by the buyer.
Copyright ©1990, Burt, Norquist, and Anklesaria.

Figure 8.4(c) Cell Formulas

Material & Labor by Operation		*No-loss cost/disk*	
Location	*Formula*	*Location*	*Formula*
B31	(E5+E6) + E19	E5	D5*C5
C31	+ C19 + (B19*60*E19*D19)	E6	D6*C6
D31	+ B31	E7	D7*C7
E31	+ C31	E8	D8*C8
B32	+ D31 + E20 – D31	E9	D9*C9
C32	+ C20 + (B20*60*E20*D20)	E10	D10*C10
D32	+ D31 + B32	E11	D11*C11
E32	+ E31 + C32	E12	D12*C12
B33	+ E7 + E21	E13	D13*C13
C33	+ C21 + (B21*60*E21*D21)	E14	D14*C14
D33	+ D32 + B33		
E33	+ E32 + C33		
B34	+ B33 + E22-B33		
C34	+ C22 + (B22*60*E22*D22)		
D34	+ D33 + B34		
E34	+ E33 + C34		
B35	(B34 + B33) + E23 – (B34 + B33)		
C35	+ C23 + (B23*60*E23*D23)		
D35	+ D34 + B35		
E35	+ E34 + C35		
B36	+ D35 + E24-D35		
C36	+ C24 + (B24*60*E24*D24)		
D36	+ D35 + B36		
E36	+ E35 + C36		
B37	+ E8 + 25		
C37	+ C25 + (B25*60*E25*D25)		
D37	+ D36 + B37		
E37	+ E36 + C37	*Overhead Cost and Grand Total*	
B38	+ E9 + E26		
C38	+ C26 + (B26*60*E26*D26)	C45 =	B45 + C42
D38	+ D37 + B38	C46 =	B46 + C42
E38	+ E37 + C38	C47 =	B47 + C42
B39	(+E10 + E11 + E12 + E13) + E27)	C48 =	B48 + C42
C39	+ C27 + (B27*60*E27*D27)	C49 =	B49 + C42
D39	+ D38 + B39	C50 =	B50 + C42
E39	+ E38 + C39		
B40	+ E14 + E28	E52 =	D40+E40+C52
C40	+ C28 + (B28*60*E28*D28)		
D40	+ D39 + B40		
E40	+ E39 + C40		

Two Years Later. The model for the disk two years later (Figure 8.4(d)) shows the cost impact of several events which occurred during the two-year period. For the sake of illustration, only a few cost items are changed:

a. The price of the media has dropped.
b. Direct labor rates have risen.
c. Insertion run time has improved.
d. Certification yield has improved.
e. Packing line speed has doubled.
f. Depreciation is lower.

This model was developed by a purchasing manager and was used to track both actual and possible cost changes. It was used to negotiate price decreases based on these costs. If the supplier had not made the cost reductions, the manager asked, "Why not, and how soon can you, since these are the trends in the industry?"

Despite direct labor pay increases, the final cost is estimated to be down by more than one-third.

Figure 8.4(d) Floppy Disk Cost Model Two Years Later

	B	C Materials	D	E No-loss
Item	U/M	Conv Fctr	Price	cost/disk
5 Jacket	1b	0.04	$1.5000	$0.0600
6 Liner	1f	0.04	$0.0500	$0.0020
7 Media	ea	1	(a) $0.1000	$0.1000
8 Hub ring	1000	0.001	$15.0000	$0.0150
9 Label	ea	1	$0.0100	$0.0100
10 Sleeve	ea	1	$0.0400	$0.0400
11 User labels	ea	0.1	$0.1000	$0.0100
12 10 pack box	ea	0.1	$0.2000	$0.0200
13 Overwrap	ea	0.1	$0.0300	$0.0030
14 Crrgtd, etc.	ea	0.001	$1.3000	$0.0013
				$0.2613

Operation	Qt/min	Operations (b) DL Rate	Run Time	Mt'l Yld
19 Laminate	100	$15.00	70.0%	95.0%
20 Primary Fold	35	$15.00	85.0%	99.0%
21 Burnish	100	$12.00	85.0%	99.6%
22 Insert	150	$12.00	(c) 75.0%	99.5%
23 Certif	45	$15.00	80.0%	(d) 95.0%
24 Fin Fold	40	$12.00	85.0%	99.2%
25 Hub Ring	50	$12.00	80.0%	99.6%
26 Label/Ser	50	$12.00	70.0%	99.9%
27 Box out	25	$12.00	85.0%	99.9%
28 Pack	(e) 1000	$25.00	85.0%	99.9%

Operation	Mat'l Cost	Lab Cost	Cum Mat'l	Cum Lab
31 Laminate	$0.0653	$0.0038	$0.0653	$0.0038
32 Pri fold	$0.0007	$0.0085	$0.0659	$0.0122
33 Burnish	$0.1004	$0.0024	$0.1663	$0.0146
34 Insert	$0.0005	$0.0018	$0.1668	$0.0164
35 Certify	$0.0053	$0.0073	$0.1721	$0.0237
36 Fin Fold	$0.0014	$0.0059	$0.1735	$0.0296
37 Hub Ring	$0.0151	$0.0050	$0.1886	$0.0347
38 Lab/Ser	$0.0100	$0.0057	$0.1986	$0.0404
39 Box out	$0.0731	$0.0094	$0.2717	$0.0498
40 Pack	$0.0013	$0.0005	$0.2730	$0.0503

		Overhead		
42 Volume		1,000,000		

Item	Total	Unit Cost		
45 Indirect Lab.	$15,000	$0.0150		
46 Factory Ovh	$12,000	$0.0120	Grand Total	
47 Depreciation (f)	$15,000	$0.0150		
48 Rent	$12,000	$0.0120	Tot mat'l	$0.2730
49 Utilities	$10,000	$0.0100	Tot lab	$0.0503
50 G&A	$15,000	$0.0150	Tot ovh	$0.0790
52 Total	$79,000	$0.0790	Grand Total	$0.4023

Note: All information in bold is available to or estimated by the buyer.
Copyright ©1990, Burt, Norquist, and Anklesaria.

Should Cost*

This cost-modeling technique was developed by Mark Cohen of Pacific Bell. The objective of Should Cost is to provide Pacific Bell contract managers (buyers) with the same insight into a supplier's costs as the seller's representatives have. Should Cost consists of four phases: development of a generalized model, performing general geographic adjustments, performing further refinements to accommodate the potential supplier's labor rates, and making final refinements based on a plant visit.

Phase I. The buyer develops the model shown in Figure 8.5(a).

Phase II. Direct labor estimates are revised to adjust for applicable geographic wage rates (Figure 8.5(b)).

Phase III. In the previous phase, an adjustment was made for the general or average wage rate based on BLS data. In Phase III, an adjustment is made for the potential supplier's actual wage data (Figure 8.5(c)).

Phase IV. This is the most accurate phase of the study. The buyer gains additional information about the cost of the product (especially in the areas of direct labor and factory overhead) through a visit to the manufacturing location. The buyer observes the equipment used to manufacture the product and records the equipment brand and model number. The supplier is asked questions on productivity in units per hour, strikes per minute, setup times, etc. The buyer should observe the amount of direct labor supporting the machine. How many employees attend the equipment? The buyer should call the equipment manufacturer and learn what the productivity rates should be and what the cost of the installed machine was.

In Figure 8.5(a) observed direct labor is $1.00 rather than $2.56 (from Phase III) because the actual unit output per hour is determined to be 12 1/2 per average hour with only one employee attending the equipment, rather than 4-5 as originally estimated. A wage rate of $12.50 per hour applies. The other elements of cost, GS&A and profit should not be significantly different than in the previous

---

*Should Cost is copyrighted by Pacific Bell and is used with its express permission. No further reproduction of this material may be made without the express written permission of Pacific Bell.

Figure 8.5(a) Should Cost Model: Phase I
SIC Code 3444, Sheet Metal Work

Element		Information Source
Materials	$10.00	Bill of materials and inquiries to suppliers
Direct Labor	2.65	Direct Materials ÷ 3.77 (See Item 1,Table 8.1)
Factory Overhead	4.64	Direct Labor x 175% (See Item 2)
Factory Cost	$17.29	
GS&A (operating expenses)	4.41	Factory Cost x 25.5% (See Item 3)
Total Cost	$21.70	
Profit	1.26	Total Cost x 5.8% (See Item 4)
Estimate Price	$22.96	

Table 8.1 Should Cost Data Sources
All Data is for SIC Code 3444, Sheet Metal Work

Item

1. Direct Labor $= \dfrac{\text{Direct Materials}}{\text{Applicable Ratio}}$ Annual Survey of Manufacturers
   U.S. Dept. of Commerce, 1986

$$= \frac{\$10.00}{3.77}$$

$$= \$2.65$$

2. Factory Overhead: Pacific Bell study
   Semiautomated: 150–200%

3. GS&A (operating expenses):   Annual Statement Studies,
   $10MM-$50MM Assets: 25.5%   Robert Morris Associates, 1989

4. Profit: Annual Statement Studies,
   $10M-$50M Assets: 5.8%   Robert Morris Associates, 1989

Relevant data from the Annual Survey of Manufacturer, Pacific Bell studies and from the Annual Statement Studies is contained in Appendix E.

Figure 8.5(b)   Should Cost: Phase II
Direct Labor Estimates Revised to Adjust for Geographic Wage Rates

	Phase I	*Phase II*	*Source*
Materials	$10.00	$10.00	
Direct Labor	2.65	2.39	Bureau of Labor Statistics, U.S. Dept. of Labor
Factory Overhead	4.64	4.17	Direct Labor x 175% (Item 2, Table 8.1)
Factory Cost	$17.29	$16.56	
GS&A (operating expense)	4.41	4.22	Factory Cost x 25.5% (Item 3)
Total Cost	$21.70	$20.78	
Profit	1.26	1.21	Total Cost x 5.8% (Item 4)
Estimated Price	$22.96	$21.99	

Figure 8.5(c)   Should Cost: Phase III
Adjustment for Actual Wage Data

	Phase II	*Phase III*	*Source*
Materials	$10.00	$10.00	
Direct Labor	2.39	2.56	Wage rate from supplier or local Chamber of Commerce
Factory Overhead	4.17	4.48	Direct Labor x 175% (Item 2, Table 8.1)
Factory Cost	$16.56	$17.04	
GS&A (operating expense)	4.41	4.35	Factory Cost x 25.5% (Item 3)
Total Cost	$20.78	$21.39	
Profit	1.21	1.24	Total Cost x 5.8% (Item 4)
Estimated Price	$21.99	$22.63	

Figure 8.5(d)   Should Cost: Phase IV
Site Visit

	Phase III	Phase IV	Source
Materials	$10.00	$10.00	
Direct Labor	2.56	1.00	Site Visit
Factory Overhead	4.48	5.00	Site Visit (500% of Direct Labor)
Factory Cost	$17.04	$16.00	
GS&A (operating expense)	4.35	4.08	Factory Cost x 25.5% (Item 3, Table 8.1)
Total Cost	$21.39	$20.08	
Profit	1.24	1.16	Total Cost x 5.8% (Item 4)
Estimated Price	$22.63	$21.24	

phase studies. If there are substantial differences in these areas, they should be brought out in negotiations and evaluated accordingly.

With the information developed with the Should Cost model, the buyer is able to better evaluate proposals. Negotiations on price are less time-consuming and result in better pricing.

Consignment. It is possible to develop a Should Cost model when the purchasing firm furnishes all or most of the material. Assume that a buyer is requesting quotations from a supplier to connectorize cable to be furnished by the buyer's firm. This operation requires stripping 24 wire ends and clamping the stripped ends into a single 24-pair connector. Based on the description of this operation, the buyer can see that the labor performed has no logical relationship to the cost of the materials being modified.

The buyer's industrial engineer estimates the average time required to be five units per hour (allowing for some nonproductive setup time), with wages of $10.00 per hour. Accordingly, direct labor is estimated at $2.00 per unit.

In this method, SIC tables similar to those for the preceding product Should Cost analysis are employed. The operation is classified as "Assembly-Job Shop," Manual Hand Type Operations, SIC Code 3599. The buyer now develops the model shown in Figure 8.6.

Figure 8.6   Should Cost Model: Consignment

Element		*Information Source*
Direct Labor	$2.00	5 units/hour @ $10.00/hr. (Engineered est.)
Overhead	2.00	100% of Direct Labor (Item 1,Table 8.2)
Conversion Cost	$4.00	
GS&A (operating expense)	1.16	29.0% of Conversion Cost (Item 2)
Total Cost	$5.16	
Profit	.28	5.5% of Total Cost (Item 3)
Estimated Price	$5.44	

Table 8.2   All Data for SIC Code 3599, Assembly-Job Shop

Item
1. Overhead:
   Manual: 100%   Pacific Bell study
   Semiautomated: 100-200%   (See Appendix E)
   Full Automated: 225-400%

2. GS&A (operating expense):   Annual Statement Studies
   $10MM-$50MM Assets: 29.0%   Robert Morris Associates, 1989

3. Profit: Annual Statement Studies
   $10MM-$50MM Assets: 5.5%   Robert Morris Associates, 1989

ANALYZING AVAILABLE COST DATA

This section is written with the assumption that the buyer has the supplier's cost data and has access to additional supporting data. If cost data has been developed through the use of cost models, the buyer will have to temper the following guidance.

The buyer's detailed review and analysis starts with taking the supplier's summary apart, looking at the cost elements and their supporting data, one by one, and following the trail to other (referenced) data sources. After a detailed review and analysis have been completed, the elements are revised as necessary, put back together in summary form, and the results compared with the initial offer. Adequate evaluation of cost or pricing data submitted or identified may require examination of data beyond those used by the prospective supplier in preparing the offer. The buyer should request that the prospective supplier submit the additional pertinent data required for adequate evaluation.

The buyer should fight any temptation to insist on great masses of cost and pricing data. When competition is keen and the buyer requests data before narrowing the field, suppliers generally will provide cost summaries with the proposal and furnish most of the detailed supporting cost and pricing data by reference. Schedules and exhibits should be attached to the summary contract price proposal to identify the sources on which the numbers are based. To be complete, data identification must answer four questions:

- What data are being referenced?
- Where can the data be found if further analysis is necessary?
- What do the data represent? Are the data actual or estimated? (For actual costs, the buyer will want facts concerning their accumulation.)
- How are the data used in developing the cost estimate? (The buyer needs to know if the data were used directly or adjusted for use in the current proposal. If the data were adjusted, the factors used for adjustment also must be supported.)

In the absence of evidence to the contrary, the buyer ultimately must rely on the prospective supplier's representations that the most current data have been submitted or identified, that there are no errors in the data, and that all data relevant to the price decision have been submitted or identified. Despite this basic dependency, the buyer has the responsibility to determine that the data submitted and identified are adequate for pricing the contract. The buyer must seek out data from other sources when the prospective supplier's data do not satisfy his or her needs, or when the data do not appear truly representative.

The buyer could sit in judgment on the proposal and reject all data that are incomplete. He or she could wait until all data are in hand and then proceed with the analysis. The only trouble with such an approach is that the required delivery date has been moving inexorably closer while the buyer has had the purchase on hold. In addition, the buyer can't tell if the data as submitted really are complete until they are used in analysis.

Accounting Systems. The primary source of cost and pricing data is the prospective supplier's accounting system. An understanding of the principles, systems, and methods involved in accumulating this data is vital to understanding the basis of price development.

When negotiating prices with suppliers based on cost analysis, the buyer should be familiar with the supplier's cost-accounting system. This knowledge is necessary when determining that the component cost elements of the price are fair and reasonable. Systems for accumulating costs include actual or historical cost systems, standard cost systems, and combinations of the two systems.

Historical Cost System. Under a historical cost system, the supplier collects direct cost data as costs are incurred. Presentation of results is delayed until operations are completed. The cost center is then charged with the actual or historical cost of the operation. Overhead is charged to the cost center and is based on some factor of direct cost.

When this system of cost accumulation is used, management is required to make estimates of future costs using historic data. Estimates are based on past experience adjusted for anticipated changes. No claim is made concerning the perfection or scientific nature of these estimates. They are simply that—estimates. When actual costs are determined, variances between actual and estimated costs may be analyzed to determine causes of errors and to make more reasonable estimates of costs in the future.

Standard Cost Systems. A standard cost system uses standards of performance and price that are usually developed by a team of specialists based on a study of operations. *Standard costs* are based on a careful study and analysis of plant conditions and may involve experimentation, testing, and time and motion studies to establish reasonable standards for each operation. For each product, specialists determine the standard quantity of materials to be used, standard price of these materials, standard number of hours to be used, standard rate of pay for labor, and standard manufacturing overhead rate. The overhead rate is subject to the biggest variation from the actual rate because it is based on an assumed standard volume or operating level. Higher or lower volumes result in variances.

Whatever cost-accounting system the firm uses, there must be some method of tracing costs to the point where they were incurred. Two methods are routinely used: the job order cost method and the process cost method. These methods relate to the principal types of manufacturing organizations.

Job Shop. Under a job shop organization, the factory works on a series of individual jobs with individual specifications. The job is the control element. Thus, the job order cost method collects costs for each job as it moves through production across accounting periods. The job cost method accumulates costs by individual jobs.

- An individual job order is established for each job.
- Material and labor costs for the job are entered on the job order record.
- This job order record provides detailed information on the costs involved in both goods in process and finished goods.

A job order may cover the production of one unit or a number of identical units. If the contract is for just one unit, the entire actual cost of the unit is accumulated under the job order.

Because the physical units of producing under a job order cost system are identified with specific job orders and lots, the labor distribution and accumulation system used by the supplier will identify the direct factory labor cost associated with the units produced under such job orders and lots. When a job order or a lot thereunder is completed, an examination of supporting data will identify who worked on the items produced, how much time they expended, and the rate of pay.

Process Operations. The process cost method is appropriate when a single product or specific group of products is produced as a continuous flow of events. This method accumulates costs by process using the following steps:

- Costs of resources for the process are accumulated during the accounting period and charged to goods in process inventory.
- Cost elements, such as direct labor incurred throughout the period, are measured in terms of equivalent units of production. The cost for individual units is then found by dividing total cost by the equivalent units of production.
- Cost elements, such as direct material, are considered as having been incurred at the beginning of the manufacturing process. The unit cost for the period is determined by dividing material cost by the units started during the period.
- Costs of finished goods inventory and goods in process inventory are determined by the units completed during the period multiplied by the cost of these units. The cost of goods in process at the end of the period includes the material cost of these units, plus a share based on equivalent units of production and other costs incurred during the period.

The process cost method normally is used by suppliers who continuously manufacture a particular end item, like chemicals, for which there is a repetition of identical or highly similar processes. They are organized according to the process of activities that an item must pass through during the course of manufacture. The completed items result from a series of processes, each of which produces some change in the material. The number of processes involved will vary with the complexity of the items manufactured. Under a process cost system, direct costs are charged to a process even though end items (which may not be identical) for more than one contract are being run through the process at the same time. At the end of the cost-accounting period, the process costs incurred are charged to the units involved.

Under a process cost system, the buyer must be able to identify which factory employees charged their time to which processes, what their rate of pay was, and the total cost charged to the process.

During production, an item may go through more than one process. When an item comes out of one process and enters another, the cost of the process just completed will be charged to the next process, usually as direct material. This continues until the completed end item emerges from its final process. This charging hampers identification of the actual labor cost for specific end items that have completed all processes because cost elements lose their identity when they are charged to the next process as direct material.

Cost Principles. The total cost of a contract is the sum of the allowable direct and indirect costs allocable to the contract, incurred or to be incurred, less any allocable credits. In ascertaining what constitutes cost, any generally accepted method of determining or estimating costs that is equitable under the circumstances may be used, including standard costs properly adjusted for applicable variance.

Factors which the buyer should consider in determining the allowability of individual items of cost include (a) reasonableness, (b) allocability, (c) generally accepted accounting principles and practices appropriate to the particular circumstance, and (d) any limitations set forth in the contract. In addition, the following questions should be considered.

- Would the cost generally be considered necessary for the conduct of the supplier's business or the contract?
- Do federal and state laws and regulations or contract terms affect allowability?
- Would a prudent businessperson allow the cost considering his or her responsibilities to the owners, employees, customers, and the public at large?
- Are there significant deviations from the established practices of the supplier that are not justified?

- How would this cost look if headlined in the newspaper or brought to the attention of the buyer's top management?

A cost is allocable to the buyer's specific contract if it (a) is incurred specifically for the contract, (b) can be distributed to relevant contracts in reasonable proportion to the benefits received, or (c) is necessary to the overall operation of the business, even though a direct relationship to any particular cost objective cannot be shown.

The allocation of indirect costs is based on the particular circumstances involved. The buyer should question allocations when any of the below arise:

- Any substantial difference occurs between the cost patterns of work under the contract and the supplier's other work
- Any significant change occurs in the nature of the business, the extent of subcontracting, fixed asset improvement, inventories, volume of sales and production, manufacturing processes, or the supplier's products
- Indirect cost grouping developed for a supplier's primary location is applied to off-site locations. Separate cost groupings for costs allocable to off-site locations may be necessary to permit equitable distribution. For example, landscaping of the corporate headquarters should not be allocated to overhead costs for a remote site.

Use of these cost principles is recommended in determining the allowability of costs in the negotiation and administration of cost incentive and reimbursement contracts as described in Chapter 13. They also should be used in the evaluation and negotiation of cost in fixed-price type contracts when arriving at a total price.

CONCLUDING REMARKS

Cost analysis is a technique for evaluating the fairness and reasonableness of a price by analyzing individual elements of cost such as labor, material, indirect costs, and profit. Ideally, prospective suppliers will supply the data required for such an analysis. If they are unwilling to supply the required data, it may be necessary to consider them nonresponsive and deal with another potential supplier. If, on the other hand, it is essential that the buyer deals with a supplier who is unwilling to furnish the required cost data, it may be necessary to develop a cost model which predicts the likely cost structure.

Experience at Polaroid has shown that the development of the trust and collaboration underlying a true sharing of cost data is a process which requires patience and perseverance. But the end result is a relationship between the professional buyer and the seller's staff which assures that the resulting prices are fair and reasonable to both parties and result in maximum value received.

Having completed our overview of the principles of cost analysis, we now address the relationships between cost, volume, and profit.

ADDITIONAL REFERENCES

"Annual Statement Studies," Robert Morris Associates, 1616 Philadelphia National Bank Building, Philadelphia, PA, 19107. This organization publishes key ratios for 348 different industries.

"Industry Norms and Key Business Ratios," Dun and Bradstreet, One Diamond Hill Road, Murray Hill, NJ, 07974-9931.

"Labor Costs Special Report," USPS, No. 517-780, February 16, 1984, (Vol. 152, No. 7, Sec. 1), Standard & Poor Corp., 300 W. Chester Street, Ephrata, PA, 17522. An excellent report for the percent of labor costs to sales by major firms and industries.

Chapter 9

Cost-Volume-Profit Analysis

The professional buyer, when preparing for negotiations, needs to understand how the supplier's profit is affected by changes in quantity and contract cost elements.

Assume that you have requested and received the following price quotations for a unique chemical which is produced in the supplier's facilities. The price was requested at three possible volumes. The quotes were $1,375,000 for 500 tons; $1,650,000 for 1000 tons; and $1,925,000 for 1500 tons.

Now, assume that you

- need to estimate a price for 750 tons
- need to determine the effect of different levels of operations on the supplier's profit
- have contracted for 1,000 tons at $1,650 per ton. Subsequently, you want to issue a follow-on order for another 1500 units during the same production year. You need to estimate the supplier's cost and a reasonable price. And,
- have entered into a contract for 1,500 tons. You need to terminate the run after 400 tons are produced.

An understanding and analysis of the supplier's cost-volume-profit relationship provides answers to these and related questions.

COST BEHAVIOR PATTERNS

Costs can be classified based on their behavior as production volume changes. Costs may be fixed, variable, or semivariable as production volume changes in the short run. The short run is a period too short to permit facilities expansion or contraction that might change the overall production relationships.

Fixed Costs

Fixed costs remain relatively consistent on a total basis as production volume is varied over the short run. Examples of fixed costs include fire insurance, depreciation, rent, and property taxes. While total fixed costs remain constant over the range of production, the fixed cost per unit will change as volume changes.

Variable Costs

Variable costs vary in direct proportion to changes in the activity level over narrow ranges of output. For simplicity these costs are treated as being *constant* on a *per unit basis* over a relevant range of volume. The sophisticated buyer recognizes that the linearity assumption is not always valid.

For a cost to be "variable" it must vary *with something*. That "something" is the activity base. The popular activity bases are units produced and units sold. A few variable costs commonly encountered are listed below:

- Direct material
- Direct labor
- Variable portion of manufacturing
  - Variable indirect materials
  - Lubricants
  - Supplies
  - Setup time
  - Variable indirect labor

- Selling and administrative costs
  - Salesperson's commissions (buyer should object on repeat business)
  - Clerical costs (invoicing)
  - Freight

Semivariable Costs

Semivariable costs vary directly, but less than proportionally, with volume. Examples of semivariable costs include supervision, rental of machines, and electricity.

Total Costs

Total cost is, of course, the sum of all costs—fixed, variable, and semivariable. Graphically, total cost resembles semivariable cost.

ANALYSIS OF COST AND VOLUME DATA

The buyer can analyze total cost and volume data by assuming total cost is part variable and part fixed. This technique allows a systematic analysis of the cost-volume-profit relationships.

The buyer can analyze a supplier's cost structure using the three quotes given at the beginning of this chapter. This is done by estimating total costs, fixed cost, and variable costs for the unique chemical.

The supplier's total selling prices (TP) are plotted for the three volumes (Figure 9.1). Next, the buyer subtracts an allowance for profit (estimated to be 10 percent of cost) to estimate the seller's total cost (TC) for the three volumes. These estimates are plotted on the graph in Figure 9.2. Next, the buyer draws a straight line which best fits the three total cost points. The point at which this line intersects the y axis (the point at which the supplier's output is zero) provides an estimate of the supplier's fixed cost ($1,000,000). The variable cost (VC) component of total cost for the quoted volumes of production is estimated by subtracting fixed cost (FC) from the total cost (TC) at that level of output as shown in Figure 9.2.

As seen in Figure 9.2, total fixed costs are constant, and variable costs are directly proportional to an activity base (say the vol-

Figure 9.1   Total Price: Unique Chemical

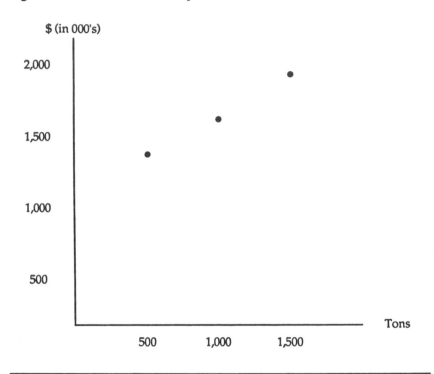

ume of production) within some relevant range over the short run. Total costs (TC) are equal to the sum of total fixed costs (FC) plus total variable costs (VC).

Algebraic Analysis

Variable cost per unit is equal to the difference in the total cost divided by the difference in the volumes at any two points, respectively.

$$VC_u \quad = \frac{TC_2 - TC_1}{Vol_2 - Vol_1} \tag{1}$$

Figure 9.2   Price, Total Cost, Fixed Cost, and Variable Cost

	500 tons	*1,000 tons*	*1,500 tons*
Price	$1,375,000	$1,650,000	$1,925,000
Profit (assume 10% of Total Cost)	125,000	150,000	175,000
Total Cost	$1,250,000	$1,500,000	$1,750,000
Fixed Cost (from graph)	1,000,000	1,000,000	1,000,000
Variable Cost	$ 250,000	$ 500,000	$ 750,000

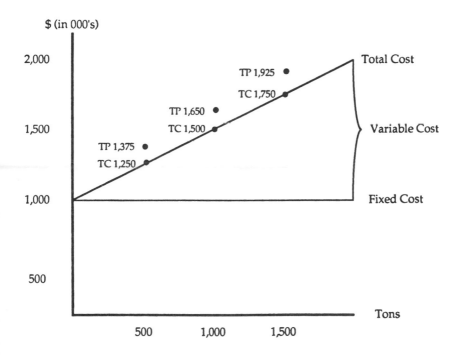

Copyright © 1990, Burt, Norquist, and Anklesaria.

$$\text{Substituting: } VC_u = \frac{\$1,500,000 - \$1,250,000}{1,000 \text{ tons} - 500 \text{ tons}}$$

$$= \$500 \text{ per ton}$$

where,

TC = total costs
FC = total fixed costs
VC_u = variable cost per unit
Vol = volume of production

By deriving the variable cost per unit (VC_u), the buyer can calculate the total fixed costs (FC).

$$FC = TC - VC_u(\text{Vol}) \tag{2}$$
$$FC = \$1,500,000 - \$500 (1,000)$$
$$FC = \$1,000,000$$

Thus, the general equation for the unique chemical is:

$$TC = \$1,000,000 + \$500 (\text{Vol})$$

Now, the buyer can predict the total cost at production volume of 750 tons as follows:

$$TC = \$1,000,000 + (\$500 \times 750)$$
$$TC = \$1,375,000$$

This $1,375,000 can also be estimated using Figure 9.2. For example, plot the point representing 750 tons on the x axis. Now draw a vertical line up to the total cost curve (TC). Next draw a horizontal line to the y axis. This point ($1,375,000) represents the total cost at a volume of 750 tons. The good buyer/analyst usually accomplishes both a graphic and algebraic analysis of the cost-volume relationship to increase confidence in the solution. This technique has wide application. It allows a buyer to take available data (Annual Reports, SEC 10-k Reports, past purchases at volumes, bids requested at different volumes) and estimate fixed and variable costs. The resulting knowledge frequently can be used to support an argument for a lower price.

COST-VOLUME-PROFIT RELATIONSHIP

So far, the discussion has developed the basic total cost equation where the total cost is equal to the total fixed cost plus the total variable cost:

$$TC = FC + VC_u(Vol) \qquad (3)$$

By adding profit to both sides of the equation, we can derive the cost-volume-profit relationship:

$$Profit + TC = FC + VC_u(Vol) + Profit \qquad (4)$$

Profit plus total cost equals revenue (sales) when the entire production volume is sold. Therefore,

$$Revenue = FC + VC_u(Vol) + Profit \qquad (5)$$

This represents the basic cost-volume-profit analysis equation. Many problems involving the nature and behavior of cost, volume, and profit can be solved by using equation (5).

Changes in revenue (sales) normally vary directly and proportionally to changes in volume of production if all units produced are sold and price remains constant. In the chemical example, revenue per unit changes with the unique product. When the buyer wants a low volume, a higher unit price must be paid since the total cost must be covered.

Pricing in a Competitive Market

The buyer now is in a position to answer the questions raised at the beginning of the chapter:

1. What should the price be for 750 tons of the chemical?

    Previously it has been determined that total cost (TC) for 750 tons is $1,375,000.

    Price = TC + Profit
         = $1,375,000 + .10 ($1,375,000)
         = $1,512,500

2. What is the effect of different levels of operations on the supplier's profit?

For the unique chemical (that is, one which is customized for the buyer) it is assumed that profits will be 10 percent of the supplier's total cost of operations.

3.   You contracted for 1,000 tons at $1,650 per ton. You now desire to issue a follow-on order for another 1,500 tons during the same production year. You need to estimate the supplier's cost and a reasonable profit.

The supplier's fixed costs of $1,000,000 were covered in the initial contract. Accordingly, you need cover only its incremental (additional) variable cost of $500 per ton and profit. (Again, assume profit = .10)

Price for the additional tons = 1,500 x $500 + .10
                                                       (1,500 x $500)
                                              = $825,000

4.   You entered into a contract for 1,500 tons. You need to terminate after 400 tons are produced.

In this situation, you first determine what might have been a reasonable price if your original contract had been for 400 tons.

    TC   = FC + VC (Vol)
             = $1,000,000 + ($500 x 400)
             = $1,200,000
    Price = TC + .10 (TC)
             = $1,200,000 + .10 ($1,200,000)
             = $1,320,000

A buyer would explore how the fixed costs will be absorbed because of the capacity released. The buyer will start at $500 per ton x 400 tons or $200,000 and then offer to pay any reasonable costs plus profit. These costs might include costs that have been incurred in anticipation of production and delivery of the balance of the order. The settlement would probably not exceed $1,320,000.

REVENUE LINE EXAMPLE

When a product sells on the open market against competition, the revenue line normally represents a constant price per unit. A new example (bicycles) is now introduced for analysis. Consider a single product manufacturer who builds 50,000 bikes in accounting period one at a total cost of $6,000,000 (A) and 60,000 bikes in accounting period two at a total cost of $6,800,000 (B). This information is shown in Figure 9.3.

Figure 9.3   Cost of Bicycle Manufacture

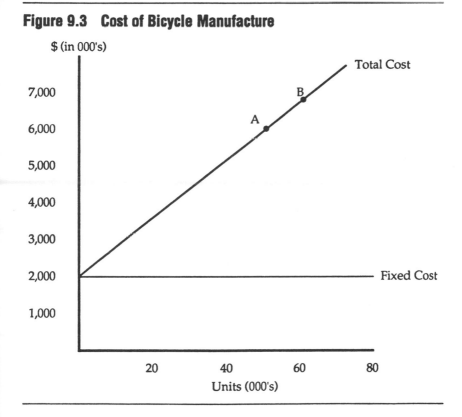

Breakeven Point

Assume the bikes are priced at $125 each. Then the revenues at different volumes of production (and sales) are as follows:

Volume	Unit Price		Revenue
0	$125	=	0
20,000	125	=	$ 2,500,000
40,000	125	=	5,000,000
60,000	125	=	7,500,000
80,000	125	=	10,000,000

A revenue line can be drawn on Figure 9.3, producing a graph of both cost and revenue data. Figure 9.4 illustrates the concept. Notice that the revenue line and the total cost line intersect at 44,444

Figure 9.4   Breakeven Point: Bicycles

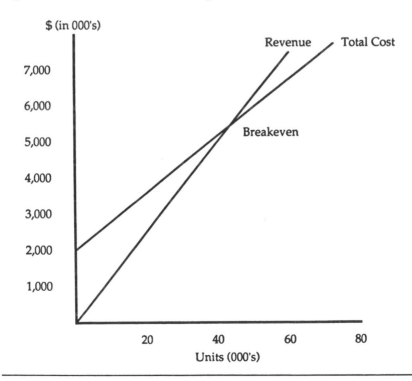

units and $5,555,555. The point at which the revenue is equal to the total cost is called the breakeven point. It is also the point at which there is no profit or loss. Thus, if the supplier sells more bikes than 44,444 at $125 each, a profit is made. If the supplier sells fewer than 44,444, a loss occurs.

Establishing Selling Prices

The buyer can calculate or graphically portray any business situation involving a single product over the short run with the cost-volume-profit (C-V-P) equation.

For example, assume that total fixed costs of $2,000,000 and variable cost per unit of $80 have been determined through prior analysis:

$$\text{Revenue} = FC + (VC_u)(Vol) + Profit \tag{5}$$
$$(Vol)(SP_u) = FC + (VC_u)(Vol) + P \tag{6}$$
$$(Vol)(SP_u) = \$2,000,000 + \$80(Vol) + P$$

The supplier can determine a target unit price for an item given a desired profit of $100,000 and a production volume of 55,000 by substituting as follows:

$$(55,000)(SP_u) = \$2,000,000 + (\$80)(55,000) + \$100,000$$
$$(55,000)(SP_u) = \$2,000,000 + \$4,400,000 + \$100,000$$
$$SP_u = \$6,500,000/55,000$$
$$= \$118.19$$

Given the same data, the target breakeven price, for any given volume, say 55,000 units, can be calculated as follows (remember that the breakeven point is defined as the point where revenues equal total costs and profit is 0):

$$\text{Revenue} = FC + VC(Vol) + Profit \tag{5}$$
$$(Vol)(SP_u) = FC + (VC_u)Vol + P$$
$$55,000(SP_u) = \$2,000,000 + (\$80 \times 55,000) + 0$$
(the breakeven price):
$$SP_u = \$116.36$$

In order to determine the effect of different levels of operations on the supplier's profit, take equation (5):

Revenue = FC + VC (Vol) + Profit   (5)
and derive
Profit = Revenue - FC - VC (Vol)   (7)

If revenue from the sale of 80,000 units is $10,000,000, fixed
costs are $2,000,000; and variable cost is $80 per unit.

Profit = $10,000,000 - 2,000,000 - ($80 x 80,000)
       = $1,600,000

INCREMENTAL COST ANALYSIS: THE CONTRIBUTION APPROACH

Once the buyer has separated costs into fixed and variable elements,
he or she uses what is now popularly referred to as "incremental
cost analysis" or "contribution analysis." Incremental cost analysis
involves estimating the effects of decision alternatives. These analyses apply to both dealing with suppliers and the make portion of
make-or-buy analyses. This approach focuses on the changes in total
costs and total revenues that result from changes in such variables as
price, cost, profit, or volume of production.

For example, a supplier might have to decide whether to accept
an order that will generate $15,000 in additional revenues when
costs are estimated as follows:

Cost Element	Full Cost
Labor	$ 1,500
Material	6,000
Manufacturing Overhead (100% of direct costs)	7,500
Total Manufacturing Costs	$15,000
General and Administrative	
(10% of total manufacturing costs)	1,500
Total Costs	$16,500

The order appears to be unprofitable since the $15,000 in antic-
ipated revenues will not cover the total cost of $16,500. But suppose
there is idle capacity in the plant, such as machine tools that are not

producing anything. Further, suppose that acceptance of the order will add only $2,000 in overhead due to the added costs of utilities, supervision, and so forth. Suppose, also, that the order required no added general and administrative costs. Then, on an incremental cost basis, the figures will add up as following:

Cost Element	Incremental Cost
Labor	$1,500
Material	6,000
Manufacturing Overhead (Incremental)	2,000
General and Administrative	0
	$9,500

What appears to be a $1,500 loss on a full cost basis turns out to be a $5,500 contribution using incremental cost analysis.

Usually, procurement activities price end items on a full cost basis. In certain situations, however, incremental cost analysis leads to a more reasonable price decision than would a full cost analysis. Incremental cost analysis involves the concept of contribution income. Contribution income is revenue that exceeds the variable costs associated with a decision.

$$\text{Contribution Income} = \text{Revenue} - \text{Variable Cost}$$
$$CI = R - VC$$
$$CI = (\text{Vol}) (SP_u) - (\text{Vol}) (VC_u) \qquad (9)$$
$$CI_{unit} = SP_u - VC_u$$

Application of incremental pricing is a short-term strategy. Over the long term, if the company fails to cover all fixed costs and to show a profit, it cannot survive. However, in the short term, the company may use incremental pricing analysis to make decisions that appear uneconomical, based on full cost pricing. Consider our single product manufacturer of bicycles. It has fixed costs of $2 million and variable costs of $80 per unit. The firm had contemplated selling 50,000 units at $125 each. The firm has orders for 40,000 units at $125 each but finds it cannot sell an additional 2000 units at $125. However, it can sell them at $100 each. Should it do so? Based on the stated facts and not considering the alternative use of resources, an incremental pricing analysis would say, "Yes, sell them at $100." The contribution income will assist in attaining the company's long-range goal of survival. Therefore, the supplier would consider this a good business decision. Looking at the facts pertaining to this decision, one must analyze the effect of selling the additional 2000 units at $100 per unit.

$$CI= (Vol) (SP_u) - (Vol) (VC_u) \qquad (9)$$
$$CI= (2000) (\$100) - (2000) (\$80)$$
$$CI= \$200,000 - \$160,000$$
$$CI= \$40,000$$

This decision would result in a contribution of $40,000 over variable costs to apply toward fixed costs and profit. If the firm had no other production alternatives, it will be $40,000 better off if this decision is implemented than if it were not.

Under more favorable circumstances, incremental pricing can be applied to profit rather than cost. The incremental analysis concept and the C-V-P technique together offer a solution to pricing situations where there is a good chance that part or all of the supplier's fixed costs are already covered. Candidates for such situations and this type of analysis are incremental quantity buys, option quantities, and the make portion of make-or-buy analyses.

Incremental or Option Quantities

One of the issues facing you as the buyer in the opening section of this chapter was to assume that you entered into a contract for 1,000 tons of the unique chemical at $1,650 per ton. You now need to issue a follow-on order for another 1,500 tons during the same production year. You need to estimate the supplier's cost and a reasonable price. In this instance, it is likely that the price of the basic production run will be estimated by the supplier on a full cost basis and that the fixed costs will have been covered by the initial run. Generally, the supplier will price the option quantity on a full cost basis, even though the fixed costs are already covered. Such pricing will lead to windfall profits for the supplier. The time to obtain a price for optional quantities is during the initial negotiation, not after award of the contract.

The above examples are ideal to clearly illustrate the concept. Most suppliers make more than one product. Admittedly, it may be more challenging to discover the fixed and variable cost ratio in a multiproduct plant. But the potential for savings will make the effort worthwhile.

ESTABLISHING PRICING OBJECTIVES USING FINANCIAL DATA

Figure 9.5 contains the Income Statement of HART Inc. for the years ending December 31, 1986 to 1989. A buyer should be able to review these statements and arrive at a fair and reasonable price to offer the prospective supplier for a new or follow-on order. There are many details hidden beneath the numbers on the Income Statements. These include the depreciation charge, replacement charges, and so on. While depreciation for the year can be computed by comparing the total depreciation in successive Balance Sheets, a good analyst would look for more details available in a 10-k Report. However, a cursory glance at the Income Statement can provide sufficient information to arrive at a "ballpark" figure for negotiation.

The buyer should keep in mind that fixed costs can be viewed as being either *committed* or *discretionary*. Examples of committed fixed costs are depreciation on buildings and equipment, taxes on real estate, insurance, and executive salaries. Even if operations are interrupted, these costs will continue unchanged. Discretionary fixed costs arise from annual decisions by management to spend in certain fixed areas (dependent on the annual budget). Examples of these costs include advertising, research and development, and management development programs. The key factor to remember is that for discretionary fixed costs, management is not locked into a decision for more than a single budget period.

Unfortunately most buyers today are not aware of information sources available for obtaining financial data. Apart from annual and 10-k Reports, a buyer could consult a *Dun & Bradstreet Report,* especially for privately held corporations that are not required to

Figure 9.5   HART Inc. Income Statements for the Years Ended December 31st

(In $ Millions)

	1986	1987	1988	1989
Gross Sales	4,405	5,280	5,533	6,397
Cost of Goods Sold	1,987	2,439	2,543	2,970
Gross Profit	2,418	2,841	2,990	3,427
General, Selling, and Administrative Expenses	1,553	1,657	1,759	1,869
Operating Profit	865	1,184	1,231	1,558
Other Income	-	9	9	39
Net Profit Before Tax	865	1,193	1,240	1,597
Income Tax	432	596	620	798
Net Profit After Tax	433	597	620	799
Dividends	175	200	250	300
Retained Earnings	258	397	370	499
Sales in Units (Millions)	405	476	487	534

Note:
From 10-k Reports or estimating plant capacity and utilization.

print annual reports. *The Business Connection*, a product of *Dialog Information Services Inc.*, Palo Alto, California, is another useful source of financial and other information. The data base contains about 10 million items of information on products and industry information for public and privately held companies. If the company being analyzed is a subsidiary or division of a larger corporation, look up *Moody's Industrials* or the 10-k Report for product breakdowns.[1]

1.   Richard G. Newman and Joseph Scodro, "Price Analysis For Negotiation," *Journal of Purchasing and Materials Management*, Spring 1988: 8-14.

How can an analyst use the data in Figure 9.5? First, it helps to express all elements of cost as a percentage of sales (Figure 9.6).

First, one can evaluate the major trends. Note how the general, selling, and administrative expenses (GS&A) has been decreasing as a percent of sales from 1986 to 1989. This change has resulted in increasing operating profit, as the costs of sales have remained around 45 to 46 percent. Figure 9.5 shows revenues climbing sharply but GS&A moving much slower than revenues.

It is observed that the Cost of Goods Sold (COGS) represents about 46 percent of every sale dollar. COGS consists of material, labor, and factory overhead. Using information available on industry ratios (U.S. Department of Commerce, "Annual Survey of Manufacturers") the buyer can determine the ratio of material to Cost of Goods Sold. What one needs to observe is the relevant SIC code as used in Appendix E (see Chapter 8). For example, if the ratio of material to COGS for the industry that represents HART Inc. is 50 percent, then the buyer can reasonably assume that the material component is (50 percent of 46 percent) 23 percent. Using the same technique as in the Should Cost model in Chapter 8, the buyer can reasonably predict the labor component.

Figure 9.6   Worksheet Showing Percentage of Sales

	1985	1986	1987	1988
Gross Sales	100.00	100.00	100.00	100.00
Cost of Goods Sold	45.11	46.19	45.96	46.43
Gross Profit	54.89	53.81	54.04	53.57
GS&A	35.27	31.38	31.80	29.22
Operating Profit	19.62	22.43	22.24	24.35
Other Income	-	0.16	0.16	0.61
Net Profit before Tax	19.62	22.59	22.40	24.96
Income Tax	9.81	11.29	11.20	12.48
Net Profit after Tax	9.81	11.30	11.20	12.48
Dividends	3.97	3.79	4.52	4.69
Retained Earnings	5.84	7.51	6.68	7.79

Assume the material to labor ratio for this type of SIC code is 2.5. Using this information, the labor content in every sale would be (23 ÷ 2.5) 9.2 percent. Now the material and labor portion of COGS can be totaled. It is 32.2 percent. The remaining portion of COGS is factory overhead. This is 46 - 32.2 = 13.8 percent.

While material and labor are variable costs, there may be some fixed portion in factory overhead, for example, depreciation. A buyer can use the information available from 10-k Reports and other sources to remove the fixed charges in factory overhead. If not, the buyer can estimate the percentage using industry averages. In the example, if 80 percent of factory overhead is fixed, 20 percent is variable. Remember, in contribution analysis the buyer is more interested in the variable costs. Using the information in Figures 9.5 and 9.6 together with the industry ratios, the buyer can calculate the variable cost as follows:

Material	23.0%	
Labor	9.2%	
Factory overhead	2.8%	(20% of 13.8)
Total	35.0%	

General, selling, and administrative expenses are typically unaffected by follow-on orders. However, the buyer might concede a further 5 percent to cover processing, handling, and shipping costs. This brings the variable costs to 40 percent per sale dollar or a contribution of 60 percent (1-.40). If the supplier has excess (unused) capacity, a good buyer should be able to negotiate an option price starting out at about 40 percent of the quoted price, plus a fair and reasonable profit.

COST-VOLUME-PROFIT ANALYSIS WHEN PURCHASING SERVICES

At first, the preceding analysis may appear only marginally interesting to someone involved in the procurement of services. But the basic principles apply as equally to services as to production items.

There are two basic approaches to applying C-V-P to the procurement of services ranging from janitorial service to the development of software. Using the example of software, (1) the buyer can identify an acceptable unit of output (e.g., programs or subroutines or lines of tested code), or (2) use man-hours or man-days for key skills (e.g., systems analysts or programmers) as pseudo-outputs.

Either approach introduces some problems. But virtually all of these problems are conceptual; e.g., "We've never done it that way . . . we've never thought of it that way." The magnitude of software development procurements requires us to step up to the challenge of adapting proven production procurement techniques to this challenging area.

In the case of janitorial services for work on Saturdays, the incremental costs of labor with, say, a 50 percent overtime rate, plus the actual cost of material used, and a reasonable contribution to profit should still result in a lower total hourly cost. Buyers have successfully argued that fixed costs like rent, lease of equipment, depreciation, insurance, and other overhead costs have been absorbed with the firm's billings for regular hours.

LIMITING ASSUMPTIONS OF COST-VOLUME-PROFIT ANALYSIS

A buyer who uses C-V-P analysis should be aware of several limiting assumptions:

- Both revenues and costs behave in a linear manner only within relevant ranges.
- It is possible to accurately break up costs into their fixed and variable elements.
- There is no change in the sales mix.
- Inventories remain constant.
- Worker productivity and efficiency remain constant within the relevant range.

CONCLUDING REMARKS

The professional buyer, in preparation for negotiations, must understand how the supplier's net income is affected by changes in quantity and contract cost elements. He or she needs to know the relationships and the resulting behavior of cost, volume, and profit over the short-run time period. Specifically, the buyer wants to know how the additional volume resulting from his or her order will affect the supplier's total and unit costs.

In the next chapter, we will investigate the process of evaluating the direct cost elements of a supplier's proposal and business.

RECOMMENDED READING

Ray A. Garrison, *Managerial Accounting: Concepts for Planning, Control and Decision Making*, 3rd ed., (Plano, TX: Business Publications, Inc.)

Chapter 10

Analysis of Direct Costs

In many contracts, direct costs account for 35 to 60 percent of total costs. Equally important, direct cost dollars usually are the basis for allocating most of the indirect (overhead) cost. The direct costs of manufacturing labor, sometimes materials, and occasionally engineering labor serve as the basis for allocating overhead. Manufacturing overhead is often 150 percent or more of direct manufacturing labor costs. Engineering overhead rates may be even higher. Furthermore, general and administrative rates and profit rates traditionally are loaded as successive application of predetermined rates.

Accordingly, a change in direct cost can produce a much larger change in the price paid. For example, with a manufacturing overhead rate of 150 percent of direct manufacturing labor costs, a decrease in estimated direct labor costs of $100,000 would result in a decrease in total direct and indirect manufacturing costs of $250,000. (See Figure 10.1.) If the general and administrative costs were applied at a rate of 10 percent of total manufacturing costs, the $100,000 decrease in direct manufacturing labor costs would grow to a $275,000 decrease in total cost. Finally, if profits were estimated at 10 percent of total cost, the estimated price would decrease by an additional $27,500. Thus, in this illustration, a $100,000 decrease in estimated direct labor cost is reflected as a $302,500 decrease in estimated contract price. No other element of cost has this

---

Figure 10.1 Price Reduction Resulting from a 10% Reduction In Direct Labor Expense

	Baseline	*Labor Reduced 10%*
Direct material	$2,000,000	$2,000,000
Direct manufacturing labor	1,000,000	900,000
Overhead (150% of direct manufacturing labor)	1,500,000	1,350,000
Total manufacturing cost	$4,500,000	$4,250,000
G&A @ 10%	450,000	425,000
Total cost	$4,950,000	$4,675,000
Profit @ 10%	495,000	467,500
	$5,445,000	$5,142,500
Total Price Reduction:		$302,500

---

much leverage in terms of return on analysis effort. It is clearly most important to assure that every direct cost dollar proposed, especially direct labor cost, is fully justified.

NATURE OF DIRECT COSTS

The distinction between direct and indirect costs is hard to define, since there is no sharp dividing line, with costs of one type falling into the direct category and costs of another type falling into the indirect category. It is customary to categorize costs as direct when they have the following three characteristics:

- The cost is directly associated with the product. An example would be cost of the time of a machine operator who performs various machining processes on a forging and produces a component that will be part of a finished product. On the other hand, the work of the person who maintains the machines normally would be regarded as indirect labor.
- The cost is readily identified with the product.

- The cost is important enough to merit identification and measurement.

Whether costs of a particular sort are to be regarded as direct or indirect often may be a matter of arbitrary decision. The buyer must ensure that the supplier does not change a cost item to indirect when that is most advantageous at one point or in one phase of a contract, only to change over to direct as soon as it appears that to change would be to the supplier's advantage.

The rates at which overhead costs are added to the charges for direct cost are generally set by negotiation between the buyer and the supplier. The higher the rate proposed by a supplier, the more likely it is to attract attention and be subjected to scrutiny by the buyer. One way in which the supplier can keep overhead rates down and maintain a low profile in the overhead area is to classify as many costs as possible as direct costs. Consequently, there is a tendency for firms to treat various types of cost as direct, even though normally they have been treated as indirect. This action has a double effect toward decreasing overhead rates. First, it reduces the total sum that must be recovered by the firm as overhead costs; and second, it increases the base figure on which the appropriate overhead is charged. In such circumstances, the buyer should be sure to negotiate low overhead rates.

MATERIAL COST ANALYSIS

Material is usually about half of the total cost of a product. Appendix E (which can be used to develop cost models as described in Chapter 8) gives average material to direct labor ratios by industries.

Material cost control is approached in many ways. Analysis of requirements before and after the product is in production (Chapter 2) can increase quality and lower costs. Value engineering (Chapter 3) can lead to major cost savings during design. This is especially important in industries with a short product cycle. Early supplier involvement aimed toward reducing cost prior to production usually provides much larger dividends than seeking cost reductions after production has begun.

Alternative materials and even alternative suppliers have been a major source of cost reduction and will continue to be where the length of the product run justifies the work involved. Value analysis which can result in design improvements (Chapter 3) can also lead to lower material costs.

By working with a supplier to analyze yield losses and scrap losses, purchasing, quality and engineering can find ways to help the supplier improve his process control and reduce material costs (Chapter 15). Just as learning can result in fewer labor hours, learning by management, labor, and purchasing can reduce material costs as discussed later in this chapter.

DIRECT LABOR HOUR ANALYSIS

In analyzing labor cost estimates, the buyer must carefully review the labor hours and wages estimated for the job. If indirect expenses are allocated on the basis of labor hours, or labor costs, this review is especially important. If direct labor hours or wages are overestimated or underestimated, overhead amounts will be similarly affected, and the error will be multiplied accordingly. Direct labor costs plus labor overheads are usually a large part of the total cost estimate and frequently represent a substantial segment of the costs that are directly controllable by the supplier. For these reasons, the buyer must document the basis for labor estimates.

In reviewing the hours and wages proposed, the buyer must recognize that there are patterns in the incidence of various types of labor. At the start of the program or contract, there may be a heavy input of design and production engineering effort. As these efforts peak and then decrease, tooling and setup efforts increase. After tooling and setup efforts peak, machining and assembly labor become predominant. At the end of the contract effort, practically all work is being done by assembly and final test labor. In evaluating direct labor hours, one must determine if the estimate is based on proper planning and reasonable labor efficiencies. These determinations will affect the buyer's evaluation of both hours and wages proposed.

Although subject to some differences in practice, direct manufacturing labor is that which produces a change in the purchased material, can be readily identified with the product, and will be large enough to merit identification and measurement. However, quality control labor may be a significant part of some factory direct labor.

When analyzing labor costs, a buyer should pay particular attention to the impact of the following on the supplier's quoted price:

- The learning curve
- Allowances for rework (steady state)
- Variations in geographical location
- Variation in skills

  (i) Individual wage rates
  (ii) Labor category rates
  (iii)Departmental rates
  (iv)Plantwide rates

- Variation with time

Learning Curves[1]

In many circumstances, labor and supervision become more efficient as more units are produced. The learning curve (sometimes called the improvement curve) is defined as an empirical relationship between the number of units produced and the number of labor hours required to produce them. Production managers can use this relationship in scheduling production and in determining manpower requirements for a particular product over a given period of time. Buyers can use the relationship to analyze the effects of production and management "learning" on a supplier's unit cost of production.

Traditionally, the learning curve has been used primarily for purchases of complex equipment in the aircraft, electronics, and other highly technical industries. Recently, its use has spread to other industries. The learning curve is useful in both price and cost

---

1. This section of the chapter is from *Purchasing and Materials Management: Text and Cases* (Fifth Edition) by Donald W. Dobler, David N. Burt, and Lamar Lee, Jr. The material is used with the permission of the authors and their publisher, McGraw Hill Publishing Company.

analysis. It is probably most useful in negotiations, as a starting point for pricing a new item. In addition to providing "buyer's insurance" against overcharging, the learning curve is also used effectively by government and commercial buyers in developing (1) target costs for new products, (2) make-or-buy information, (3) delivery schedules, and (4) progress payment schedules for suppliers.

The Cumulative Curve and the Unit Curve

In practice, two basic forms of the learning curve exist. The first curve, "the cumulative average cost curve," is commonly used in price and cost analysis. This curve plots cumulative units produced against the average direct labor cost or average labor hours required per unit for all units produced. The second, "the unit or marginal cost curve," is also used in labor and cost-estimating work. The unit curve plots cumulative units produced against the actual labor hours required to produce each unit. Figure 10.2 illustrates and compares the two types of curves.

Selection of one of these two learning curve techniques tends to be based on an organization's past experience. Ideally, whether one should use a cumulative or a unit curve is a function of the production process itself. Some operations conform to a cumulative curve, others conform to the unit curve. The only way to know which to use is to record the actual production data and then determine which type of curve best fits the data. The relationship is strictly an empirical one.

Target Cost Estimation

If a new product is custom-made to unique specifications, what should be paid for the 50th item? The 500th item? Obviously, costs should decline—but by how much?

Analysis of the learning curve provides an answer. Cost reductions and estimated prices can be obtained merely by reading figures from a graph.

The learning curve is a quantitative model of the commonsense observation that the unit cost of a new product decreases as more units of the product are made because of the learning process. The manufacturer, through the repetitive production process, learns how

Figure 10.2 Comparison of a Cumulative Average Learning Curve and a Unit Learning Curve

Direct Labor Hours

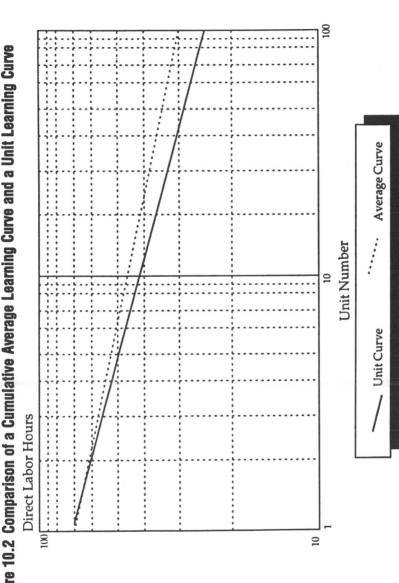

Unit Number

Unit Curve   Average Curve

Appreciation is expressed to Professor Charles Teplitz of the University of San Diego for Figures 10.2–10.5.

to make the product at a lower cost. For example, the more times an individual repeats a complicated operation, the more efficient he or she becomes, both in speed and skill. This, in turn, means progressively lower unit labor costs. Familiarity with an operation also results in fewer rejects and reworks, better scheduling, possible improvements in tooling, fewer engineering changes, and more efficient management systems.

Suppose a buyer knows that it took a supplier 100 hours of labor to turn out the first unit of a new product, as indicated in Figures 10.3 and 10.4. The supplier reports that the second unit took 80 hours to make, so the average labor requirement for the two items is 180 ÷ 2 = 90 hours per unit. The production report for the first four units is summarized in Table 10.1.

Observe that the labor requirement dropped to 74 hours for the third unit and to 70 hours for the fourth unit. Column 4 shows that the average number of labor hours required for the first four units was 81 hours per unit. Investigation of the learning rate shows the following relationships:

- As production doubled from one to two units, the average labor hours required per unit dropped from 100 to 90, a reduction of 10 percent.

- As production doubled from two to four units, the average labor hours required per unit dropped from 90 to 81, a reduction of 10 percent.

Figure 10.3 indicates that the same learning rate continues as production of the new item increases. Each time production doubles, the average labor requirement for all units declines by 10 percent. Thus, the product is said to have a 90 percent learning rate, or a 90 percent learning curve. Note that this is based on the cumulative average learning curve phenomenon. The basic point revealed by the learning curve is that a specific and constant percentage reduction in the average direct labor hours required per unit results each time the number of units produced is doubled. It is an established fact that specific learning rates occur with reasonable regularity for similar groups of products in many different industries.

Figure 10.3 A 90 Percent Cumulative Average Learning Curve

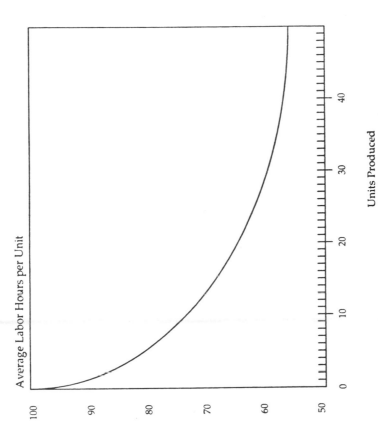

Figure 10.4 The 90 Percent Cumulative Average Learning Curve of Figure 10.3, Plotted on a Log-log Grid

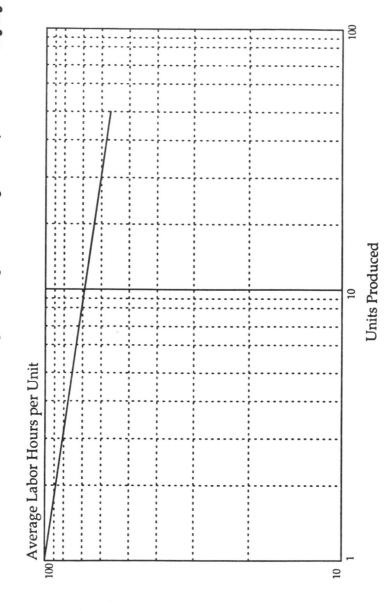

Table 10.1 Ninety Percent Cumulative Learning Curve Data

Unit Produced	Labor Hours Required	Cumulative Labor Hours Required	Average Labor Hours Required Per Unit
1st	100	100	100.0
2nd	80	180	90.0
3rd	74	254	84.7
4th	70	324	81.0

Studies made in the aircraft, electronics, and small electromechanical subassembly fields indicate that learning rates of 75 to 95 percent are typical. However, learning curves can vary anywhere within the practical limits of 50 to 100 percent. As more units are produced, the effect of a constant learning rate on unit costs gradually diminishes. After several thousand units, the absolute reduction in cost from learning becomes negligible. Note in Figure 10.3 how the curve flattens out as the number of units produced increases. This is why learning curve analysis is of greatest value for new products.

Different types of labor generate different percentages of learning. Assembly-type labor generates the most rapid improvement, and fabrication-type labor the least. Fabrication labor has a lower learning rate because the speed of jobs dependent on this type of labor is governed more by the capability of the equipment than the skill of the operator. The operator's learning in this case is confined to setup and maintenance times. In some situations, therefore, when a precise analysis is desired, a learning curve should be developed for each category of labor. Also, it should be noted that different firms within the same industry experience different rates of learning.

Most analysts prefer to plot the data for learning curves on log-log graph paper, as in Figure 10.4. The logarithmic scales on both the horizontal and vertical axes convert the curve of Figure 10.3 into a straight line (because a log-log grid plots a constant rate of change as a straight line). The straight line is easier to read, and it also simplifies forecasting since a constant learning rate always appears as a straight line on log-log coordinates. To verify the fact that both graphs represent the same thing, look at the number of hours needed to produce 100 units in Figures 10.3 and 10.4; both figures indicate about 50 hours per unit.

Application of Learning Curves. Before applying a learning curve to a particular item, a buyer must be certain that learning does in fact occur at a reasonably constant rate. Many production operations do not possess such properties. Gross errors can be made if a learning curve is misapplied; therefore, buyers must be alert to the following problems.

Nonuniform Learning Rates. Learning curve analysis is predicated on the assumption that the process in question exhibits learning at a reasonably constant rate. Direct labor data from such a process should plot in a straight line on a log-log grid. If a straight line cannot be fitted to the data reasonably well, the learning rate is not uniform and the technique should not be used.

Low-Labor Content Items. Continued learning occurs principally in the production of products entailing a high percentage of labor. The learning opportunity is particularly high in complex assembly work. On the other hand, if most work on a new item involves machine time, where output tends to be determined by machine capacity, there is little opportunity for continued learning in direct labor. The buyer should look for learning in overhead items like inspecting, materials management, and purchasing.

Small Payoffs. Obtaining historical cost data to construct a learning curve entails much time and effort, particularly when a supplier uses a standard cost-accounting system. Therefore, learning curve analysis is worthwhile only if the amount of money which can be saved is substantial.

Incorrect Learning Rates. Learning varies from industry to industry, plant to plant, product to product, and part to part. Applying one rate just because someone in the industry has used it can be misleading. Intelligent use of learning curves demands that learning rates be determined as accurately as possible from comparable past experience.

Established Items. If a supplier has previously made the item for someone else, a buyer should not use the learning curve, even if the product is nonstandard and new to the buyer. Since most of the learning has already been done on previous work, any additional cost reduction may well be negligible.

Misleading Data. Not all cost savings stem from learning. The economies of large-scale production spread fixed costs over a larger number of output units, thus reducing the unit cost of the item. However, this phenomenon has nothing to do with the learning curve.

An Example of Learning Curve Application: The Cumulative Average Curve. The following simplified example shows a basic application of the cumulative average learning curve concept in labor cost analysis and contract pricing.

> The ABC Corporation has purchased 50 pieces of a specially designed electronic component at $2,000 per unit. Of the $2,000 selling price, $1,000 represents direct labor. An audit of product costs for the first 50 units established that the operation is subject to an 80 percent cumulative average learning curve. What should ABC pay for the purchase of 350 more units?

Solution

1. Using log-log paper, plot 50 units (on the horizontal axis) against $1,000 direct labor cost on the vertical axis (see Figure 10.5).

2. Double the number of units to 100 on the horizontal axis and plot against a labor cost of $800 (80 percent as high as the original $1,000 cost).

3. Draw a straight line through the two cost points. The line represents an 80 percent learning curve, constructed on the basis of labor costs data for the first 50 units of production.

4. Locate 400 units on the horizontal axis (the total expected production of 50 original units plus 350 new ones). Read from the

Figure 10.5 Estimating Labor Cost for the New Contract

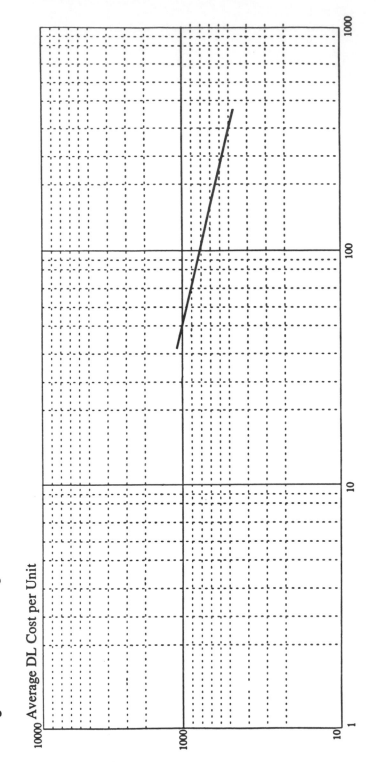

Average DL Cost per Unit

Units Produced

curve the labor cost of $510. This is the average expected labor cost per unit for the total production of 400 units.

5. To find the labor cost for 400 units, multiply 400 x $510, the direct labor cost per unit. The total is $204,000.

6. Subtract the labor paid in the original order to determine the labor cost of the new order of 350 units. Hence, subtract $50,000 (50 x $1,000) from $204,000. The answer is $154,000, the labor cost which should be paid for the new order of 350 units: $154,000 ÷ 350 units = $440 per unit labor cost, as compared with the original $1,000 per unit.

7. Now determine the cost for materials, overhead, and profit on the 350 units. (All should be lower on a per unit basis.) Add this figure to the labor cost determined in step 6 to obtain the total price ABC should pay for the additional 350 units.

An Example of Learning Curve Application: The Unit Curve. The preceding application dealt with the use of a cumulative average learning curve. To illustrate the application of a unit learning curve, consider the following hypothetical situation.

Suppose a manufacturer receives an order to produce 100 units of a new product. If the first unit to be produced requires ten labor hours and the second unit requires eight labor hours, it is obvious that a learning effect is indeed in place and may be at an 80% rate. To test this, time units four, eight, and sixteen. Compare the observations to the theoretical rate shown in Figure 10.6 for an 80% rate of learning on an item which required ten hours to produce the first unit.

Obviously, the difference or amount of labor hour reduction is not constant. Rather, it declines by a continually diminishing amount as the quantities are doubled. But the rate of change or decline is found to be a constant percentage of the prior cost because the decline in the base figure is proportionate to the decline in the amount of change.

Learning does not happen automatically; *it must be encouraged.* A study of jute manufacturers in Bangladesh shows that over a 26-

Figure 10.6 Unit Curve Concept (80% Learning Curve)

Units Produced	Labor Hours per Unit at Indicated Unit Number	Difference in Labor Hours per Unit at Doubled Quantities	Rate of Change (%)	Slope of Curve (%)
1	10		20	80
2	8	2.0	20	80
4	6.4	1.6	20	80
8	5.12	1.28	20	80
16	4.096	1.024	20	80
32	3.277	.819	20	80

year period, there was significant productivity growth during start-ups. But over time, productivity declined instead of increasing at a slower rate (as learning curve theory predicted).[2] Whether we like to admit it or not, many suppliers have been conditioned to believe that, within certain limits imposed by market competition and possible substitutes, the higher the cost, the greater the profit. (This cost-plus mentality is especially prevalent in government contracting and in some service industries.) Thus, it is common to encounter suppliers who argue that no learning on the part of labor, management, or purchasing will result during work under the proposed contract and that labor and material costs will not decrease (on a unit basis) as work proceeds.

The professional buyer must examine each situation on its merits. If he or she is satisfied that learning *will* take place, then it may be necessary to apply learning rates from similar situations or from texts on the subject when establishing the negotiation objectives for labor and for materials. Table 10.2 portrays typical rates of learning for representative activities.

---

2. Kibris and Tisdall, "International Comparison of Learning Curves and Productivity" *Management International Review* (Germany) Vol 25:4 (1985): 66-72.

Table 10.2 Typical Basic Learning Slopes[3]

	%
Job Shop	95
Sheet Metal Stamping	92
Wire Preparation	90
Job Machining	88
Electronics Sheet Metal	87
Electronics Ship Assembly	85
General Subassembly	83
Major Aircraft Assembly	80

Dexterity on the part of individual workers is only one of the reasons for improvement in the usage of labor hours per unit of production. Changes in workers' environment, morale, the flow process, work simplification, design and work setup, run times and yields may all contribute to improvement (or to disimprovement), but such changes are generally induced by management functions or developed by employee participation teams. The term "learning curve" is a misnomer, and terms like improvement curve, cost or time reduction curve, or experience curve more accurately describe the process. However, the term "learning curve" has become so widely used that it is appropriate to use it here. But when using it, one must understand that it represents the learning of the firm and is not specifically isolated to the learning of individuals. Especially attractive candidates include the following:

- Nonmechanized assembly operations
- A continuous process with constant effort to reduce labor hours
- Mechanized operations where learning brings higher run times and yields
- "State of the art" items. The many engineering changes that are characteristic of such items seem to contribute to the overall process of improvement or learning

[3]Phillip F. Ostwald, *Cost Estimating for Engineering and Management* (Englewood Cliffs, NJ: Prentice-Hall, 1974).

With each change in model, the learning curve phenomenon tends to repeat itself. That is, when a production program is completed for a particular model and a new production is set up for a similar but new model, it cannot be expected that the first unit of the new model will continue where the old model left off. Rather, it can be expected that the labor hours to be used for the first unit of the new model will behave as unit one of a new production run and learning will begin anew.

Allowances for Rework—Steady State

Careful analysis should be made of the supplier's estimate for rework. Historically, a significant portion of rework costs were attributed to defects in incoming materials at each level of the value chain. But through the application of modern quality techniques, particularly total quality commitment (TQC), the defect rate on incoming materials at all levels of the value chain should drop significantly. Just as progressive firms expect (and, if need be, assist) their suppliers to implement modern quality techniques, they should insist that their suppliers demand (and assist) their own suppliers to do so in turn. The implementation of TQC within the supplier's operation will further reduce the supplier's rework costs.

Variations in Geographical Locations

Wage rates for the same work vary widely with geographical location. (See the Should Cost model development in Chapter 8.) This variation results from the supply and demand position in relation to a particular trade, the strength of the particular trade organization, the cost of living in the area, and other similar factors. It is important for the buyer to ensure that the wage rate stated in the proposal is the one that applies in the location in which the work will actually be done.

Information on wage rates paid to different trades in different locations is published by the Department of Labor (Employment and Earnings Report) and by various state and local agencies. The buyer's first action should be to compare the wage rates proposed by the prospective supplier with those given in the published tables.

Differences should be explained and justified by the supplier, or its rates should be adjusted.

Variations in Skills

Both the nature and degree of the skill required have an important bearing on the wage rate. Generally, as the degree of skill required increases, the period of training is longer and the wage rate is higher.

A proposed wage rate should not be agreed to unless it is consistent with the value of the contract effort involved. If the work is routine assembly that could be done satisfactorily by assemblers, a wage rate for a higher skill level (fitters) is not appropriate.

It is evident that considerations of this sort require the buyer to have a considerable knowledge and appreciation of the methods of production that the supplier plans to use and the nature of supplier facilities and equipment. At an early stage in the analysis, the buyer should set out to acquire this knowledge. The question of whether a particular operation calls for the work of individuals with particular skills is one on which the buyer may often need advice from a specialist, such as an industrial engineer.

The performance of a contract frequently entails the employment of individuals in numerous skills with varying wage rates. Several methods may be used to propose the required variety of wage rates. These include proposing wage rates for specific individuals, for labor categories, or for departmental or plantwide average rates.

Rates

Individual Wage Rates. Individual wage rates may be used when the project requires extraordinary skills that in turn demand extraordinary wages. Even though singling out expensive personnel may be a fair method of estimating cost, the approach is acceptable only if the supplier uses the individual rate method on all other business, including situations where the required skills and wages may be lower than average. A buyer of professional services should be particularly cautious since some accounting or legal firms are known to bill at rates applicable to partners or seniors for work that is being performed by juniors or law clerks.

Labor Category Rates. Use of rates developed by labor category is found primarily in estimating engineering labor requirements. Such a classification system is necessary because of the wide variations in labor rates by the various categories and because each project usually requires a particular combination of engineering expertise rather than a *pro rata* share of all levels.

Departmental Rates. For this method to be valid, work done within each department should require effort from the various skills in proportion to the manpower available in that department.

Plantwide Rates. Plantwide rates are usually used by organizations producing a limited number of products that pass through all or most departments during manufacture. If each department of the activity contributes to every job roughly in the same proportion as the number of personnel in each department, an average wage rate for the plant might then be applied fairly to the total labor hours.

It is important that departmental and plantwide average rates be derived by averaging the wage rates of the various labor categories. To determine this average, the various labor categories must be weighted by the number of individuals to whom they apply.

If labor contracts are renegotiated during the period of the contract, it is likely that wage rates will be increased, and this may substantially affect contract costs. The supplier will project from the current wage rates to an estimate of the future wage rates and consequently include these additional anticipated costs in its proposal. The buyer has no option but to attempt similar projections to determine whether the wage rates that the supplier estimates are fair and reasonable. However, the buyer should negotiate that actual rates will be used whenever they are lower than the estimated ones. (This situation may require the use of an economic price adjustment clause, as described in Chapter 13.)

MATERIAL COST CONTROL

What a company calls direct material in a proposal will usually depend on its accounting and estimating practices. The data a company uses to estimate direct material costs will also depend on those same practices. Most of what is normally included as direct material will have been purchased from outside sources. Some of the materials may have been produced in other plants, divisions, or organizations of the supplier.

Suppliers' Material Costs Should Experience Learning

When applied to material, the theory of the learning curve predicts that the cost of material required to produce any doubled quantity decreases at a constant rate. The constant rate is usually less than rates of improvement experienced for labor. Material improvement curve slopes of 90 to 95 percent are common. A number of factors explain why the experience curve–cost-estimating relationship should work on material costs.

- The supplier usually finds more efficient ways to use the raw stock to eliminate scrap as he or she gains experience with the material.

- The rate of generating rejects should decrease as the workers become more familiar with the product.

- The supplier's and his or her suppliers' purchasing functions should obtain lower prices with additional buys.

- The supplier's purchasing people should discover sizes of raw stock that are more suited to the specific manufacturing process, thereby reducing scrap cost.

- Many purchased materials have much value added in terms of labor expended by subcontractors. These items should decrease in cost due to learning.

Careful analysis should be made of the quantities of incoming materials estimated to be required for the manufacture of the firm's requirements. With the application of modern quality techniques, particularly statistical process control (SPC), both incoming defects and the production of items which will not meet quality standards can be significantly reduced from pre-SPC days.

Pre-production Costs

Occasionally, there may be a sound reason for setting aside a portion of pre-production costs for allocation to later procurements of additional quantities of items. An agreement to defer any amount of pre-production costs should be worked out carefully so that it does not result in an unintended advantage to a supplier. For example, in a competitive situation, suppose supplier A quotes on the basis of deferring a substantial portion of estimated start-up costs, and all other potential suppliers quote on the basis of full allocation of this expense to the first contract. Then, supplier A would be in an advantageous position for the initial contract unless the deferred cost were identified and all suppliers were placed on a comparable basis for evaluation purposes. When pre-production costs are deferred and agreements are made on the treatment of these costs, a detailed record must be made by the buyer of the amount involved and the intent of the parties. This record will guide those who inherit the responsibility for later pricing actions.

When negotiating a follow-on contract, the buyer should not include in the pricing any deferred basic engineering or tooling identified as pre-production costs without assurance from the original buyer that such consideration has been anticipated and previously agreed upon.

Tooling Costs

As discussed here, tooling refers to special tooling that consists of jigs, dies, fixtures, and test equipment used in the production of end items and does not include machines, perishable tool items, or small hand tools.

There should be an inverse relationship between the amount of tooling and the number of labor hours expended per unit of product. It is extremely important that the supplier plan to use adequate tooling to minimize labor hours, but avoid tooling in excess of the needs of present and reasonable predictable future purchases.

Analysis of tooling is much like the analysis of any other cost. It requires evaluation of material, with special recognition of the fact that many suppliers purchase all or a significant part of their basic tooling requirements. It also requires analysis of the labor hours, labor rates, and overhead rates applied to tooling.

The possibility of future competition can be maintained if the buyer pays for and owns any special tooling and/or test equipment.

Owning the tooling and test equipment gives us the ability to move them elsewhere if necessary. A strike or unreasonable price increase, a fire or a quality problem might lead the buyer to want to move the contract. The decision to own the tooling and/or test equipment, versus paying for it as part of the cost of each individual part, is a major one. The above considerations make buying the tooling with the right to move it the preferred alternative for the firm doing the buying. In effect, by assuming the risk associated with owning the tooling, the buyer gains flexibility and lower unit cost.

CONCLUDING REMARKS

Direct costs are doubly important: they frequently amount to 35 to 60 percent of a supplier's costs, and they usually are the basis for allocating most indirect (overhead) costs.

Labor and materials are the two primary components of direct costs. Each requires extensive and careful analysis. Both labor and materials are subject to learning or improvement. Accordingly, the professional buyer should expect to see reductions in these direct costs as production proceeds.

Special test tooling and special test equipment costs also require careful attention. In most cases, the buyer is advised to pay for these items and take title to them.

We now turn our attention to the area of indirect costs.

Chapter 11

Analysis of Indirect Costs

Indirect costs are a major component of most proposals. Figure 11.1 depicts the results of a DOD study on this subject. Indirect costs were found to be about 36 percent of total costs. Yet, if direct material costs are excluded, indirect costs were about 64 percent of the remaining costs generated in the manufacturing plants included in the study. A special report in the June 6, 1988 issue of *Business Week* entitled "Productivity Paradox" indicates that general overhead frequently accounts for 50 to 55 percent of production costs.[1]

Indirect costs are known by many names, including overhead and burden. Indirect costs cannot practically be assigned directly to the production or sale of a particular product. In accounting terms, they are not directly identifiable with a specific cost objective. Costs are not considered as being identifiable with a specific cost objective when they are incurred for the benefit of two or more cost objectives or when it is impractical to trace them to a specific cost objective. A direct cost of a minor dollar amount may be treated as an indirect cost for reasons of practicality. After direct costs have been determined and charged directly to the contract or other cost objective as appropriate, indirect costs are those remaining to be allocated to the various products or services.

---

1. Portions of this chapter are based on the Armed Services Pricing Manual.

Figure 11.1 Indirect Cost Percentage

Total Cost

Inplant Cost
(excluding materials)

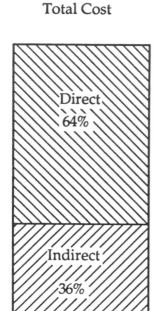

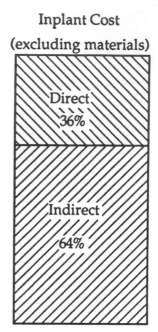

FOUR CHALLENGES

The buyer, when negotiating overhead, is confronted with four major challenges:

- How much should the supplier's indirect costs be in absolute terms?
- How accurate is the supplier's forecast of likely business activity?
- How should allowable indirect costs be recovered by the supplier?
- What proportion of the indirect costs should be allocated to the buyer's purchases?

ALLOWABLE INDIRECT COSTS

When addressing the question of how much the supplier's indirect costs should be in absolute terms, the buyer is concerned with the necessity and reasonableness of the cost. Is it necessary to have one supervisor for each three employees? Is it necessary and reasonable that corporate executives be provided with $70,000 automobiles and chauffeurs? This area is extremely challenging for two reasons:

- Most individual costs are based on precedence
- When a cost buildup approach to pricing is employed, the supplier has little or no incentive to control costs

Precedence

If the supplier has "always" employed one supervisor per three employees, it is challenging to question the associated expense. If corporate executives have always had luxury cars and chauffeurs, it is even more challenging to question this expense. But, the professional buyer does challenge these and similar indirect costs.

Incentives

If the supplier is in a sole source or in a preferred position, or if the supplier operates in an industry where cost buildup pricing is the norm (construction and defense), there frequently is little or no economic incentive to minimize indirect costs. (This is especially true during the proposal stage.) In fact, in many instances, the incentive may be to increase costs since every extra dollar of costs means an additional 6¢ or 8¢ or 10¢ of profit.

A Rule of Thumb

When reviewing questionable expenses, the buyer should ask, "How would I feel if this expense were held up for public scrutiny?"

ACCURACY OF SUPPLIER'S FORECAST

When allocating the buyer's share of overhead expenses, the supplier has an inherent incentive to forecast its business activity very conservatively. Table 11.1 portrays the buyer's share of indirect costs under two scenarios: a conservative forecast and the level of activity which the buyer believes to be realistic for the supplier in question.

These data demonstrate that the seller has incentive to be conservative when projecting future business activities in an effort to have the buyer absorb as much indirect cost as possible. Being aware of this phenomenon, the professional buyer must develop a realistic forecast of the seller's business activities for the period under discussion.

RECOVERY OF INDIRECT COSTS

Recently, on questioning a salesman requesting a 6 percent price increase, a Polaroid buyer indicated that the overhead charges were excessive. The salesman explained that despite less R&D being used, "you get 20 percent of our overhead because you are 20 percent of our sales." The buyer's offer to lower overhead by cutting purchases in half brought about a reduction in overhead and no price increases.

There are several legitimate bases for recovering indirect costs. This section looks at how such costs are grouped, at their composition, at the allocation approaches, at selection of the appropriate recovery base, and at the rate of application.

Table 11.1 Individual Costs under Two Forecasts

	Conservative Forecast	Buyer's Forecast
Total Forecasted Sales	$10,000,000	$15,000,000
Buyer's Volume	5,000,000	5,000,000
Buyer's Share	50%	33.3%
Indirect Costs	$4,000,000	4,500,000
Buyer's Dollar Share of		
Indirect Costs	$2,000,000	$1,500,000

Grouping of Indirect Costs

The seller accumulates indirect costs by logical cost groupings. Each grouping should be made to permit distribution of the indirect costs. The four most commonly found are material overhead, manufacturing overhead, engineering overhead, and general and administrative expenses (G&A).

Material overhead includes the costs related to the purchase, transportation (incoming), receiving, inspection, and handling and storage of materials.

Manufacturing overhead, also known by terms such as manufacturing expense or factory burden, embodies all items of production cost except direct materials, direct labor, and other costs. The component elements of factory overhead consist of several major categories of expense, such as listed below:

- Indirect labor, consisting of supervision, inspection, maintenance, custodial, and other personnel who are not charged directly to a product or operation
- Costs associated with indirect labor, such as social security and unemployment taxes, vacation pay, shift and overtime premiums, and group insurance
- Indirect supplies, such as small tools, grinding wheels, janitor supplies, and lubricating oils
- Fixed charges, including depreciation, insurance, rent, and property taxes

Engineering overhead includes the cost of directing and supporting the activities of the engineering department. Not all companies departmentalize engineering. Some use a single, plantwide rate for manufacturing and engineering (this opens an opportunity to a buyer who is sourcing an item that is already designed to reduce an overhead allocation). When there is separate identification, the efforts charged against engineering overhead are not unlike those charged against manufacturing overhead. These are, for example, indirect labor (both supervisory and support), costs associated with labor, indirect supplies, and fixed charges (such as depreciation).

General and administrative expenses (G&A) includes the expenses of a company's general and executive offices, the cost of such staff services as legal, accounting, public relations, financial and similar functions, and other miscellaneous activities related to the overall business.

Allocating Indirect Costs

To determine the cost of a contract or product, it is necessary to allocate indirect costs to that cost objective. This allocation is accomplished by using an indirect cost rate for each indirect cost pool. The rate is established by selecting an appropriate base on which to prorate the indirect costs and taking the ratio of the indirect cost pool dollars to that base. The examples that follow illustrate rate development.

$$\frac{\text{Engineering pool dollars}}{\text{Engineering direct labor hours}} = \frac{\$5,000,000}{1,000,000} = \frac{\$5 \text{ per engineering}}{\text{direct labor hour}}$$

$$\frac{\text{Manufacturing pool dollars}}{\text{Manufacturing direct labor dollars}} = \frac{\$8,000,000}{\$2,000,000} = 4.0$$

or, 400% of manufacturing direct labor dollars

$$\frac{\text{General and administrative dollars}}{\text{Total manufacturing costs}} = \frac{\$1,000,000}{\$20,000,000} = .05$$

or, 5% of total manufacturing costs

The basis used for the allocation of indirect costs differs between firms, depending on a particular firm's accounting system and operations. In general, the base that is used for allocating indirect cost should have the following characteristics:

- It should produce a rate that will result in an equitable allocation of the indirect costs

- It should be applied consistently from year to year and from cost objective to cost objective
- It should be in accordance with generally accepted accounting principles and the particular cost-accounting standards applicable in the circumstances

In evaluating the recovery rates for indirect costs, the buyer should be careful in making judgments about the magnitude of a particular rate. One often hears the expression: "That rate is too high." This conclusion can be dangerous because a rate merely represents the relationship between one number and another. It has relevance only to what is in those numbers. An overhead rate of 90 percent can be too high, and one of 200 percent too low, depending on what is in the base and what is in the overhead pool.

To evaluate the reasonableness of overhead rates, the buyer cannot just look at the rate. The buyer must consider the indirect costs in the overhead pool and the appropriateness of the overhead allocation base.

Selecting the Overhead Recovery Base

A supplier may use a number of different bases for recovery of indirect costs including the following:

- Sales
- Contribution margin
- Cost input (cost of goods manufactured including direct material, direct labor, other direct costs, and applicable overhead)
- Total cost incurred (cost input plus general and administrative expense)
- Prime cost (direct material, direct labor, and other direct costs)
- Processing or conversion cost (direct labor and applicable overhead)
- Direct labor dollars
- Direct labor hours
- Machine hours
- Usage
- Unit of product
- Direct material cost

From the buyer's standpoint, the base used to recover indirect costs is one of the two most important considerations in evaluating indirect costs. The other consideration is the reasonableness of the indirect dollars in the pool. The base or bases used to recover indirect costs will determine the amount of indirect costs to be charged to a contract or product. Tables 11.2 and 11.3 show the impact of five different recovery approaches on five products.

Five Income Statements have been developed (Tables 11.2(a)-11.2(e)) from the information contained in Table 11.2. Take a close look at the profit, total cost/unit and the profit/unit. You will see how these numbers change for each product depending on the basis of allocating overhead. Table 11.3 compares profit as a percent of sales for the five allocation methods.

Table 11.2   Information on Five Product Lines

Product	#101	#201	#301	#401	#501	Total
Sales (in '000) units	100	150	200	150	200	800
Unit selling price ($)	5	2	1	4	3	
Sales (in $'000)	500	300	200	600	600	2200
Direct labor hours	5000	5000	2000	10000	8000	30000
Machine hours	200	300	325	100	75	1000
Direct materials (in $'000)	300	150	50	250	350	1100
Direct labor (in $'000)	50	75	10	115	150	400
Discretionary fixed costs (advertising, sales promotion, salaries, engineering, research, etc. in $'000)						220
Committed fixed cost (depreciation, property taxes, insurance, interest, etc., in $'000)						180
Total overhead (in $'000)						400

Table 11.2(a) Productwise Income Statement

(in $'000)
(overhead allocation based on sales dollars)

Product	#101	#201	#301	#401	#501	Total
Units	100	150	200	150	200	
Sales	500	300	200	600	600	2200
Direct labor and material	350	225	60	365	500	1500
Manufacturing contribution	150	75	140	235	100	700
Allocation of overhead	91	55	36	109	109	400
Profit	59	20	104	126	-9	300
Total cost/unit ($)	4.41	1.87	0.48	3.16	3.05	
Profit/unit ($)	0.59	0.13	0.52	0.84	-0.05	
Profit/Loss in % of sales	11.8	6.7	52.0	21.0	(1.5)	

Table 11.2(b) Productwise Income Statement

(in $'000)
(overhead allocations based on direct labor hours)

Product	#101	#201	#301	#401	#501	Total
Units	100	150	200	150	200	
Sales	500	300	200	600	600	2200
Direct labor and material	350	225	60	365	500	1500
Manufacturing contribution	150	75	140	235	100	700
Allocation of overhead	67	67	26	133	107	400
Profit	83	8	114	102	-7	300
Total cost/unit ($)	4.17	1.94	0.43	3.32	3.03	
Profit/unit ($)	0.83	0.06	0.57	0.68	-0.03	
Profit/Loss in % of sales	16.6	2.7	57.0	17.0	(1.2)	

Table 11.2(c) Productwise Income Statement

(in $'000)
(overhead allocation based on machine hours)

Product	#101	#201	#301	#401	#501	Total
Units	100	150	200	150	200	
Sales	500	300	200	600	600	2200
Direct labor and material	350	225	60	365	500	1500
Manufacturing contribution	150	75	140	235	100	700
Allocation of overhead	80	120	130	40	30	400
Profit	70	-45	10	195	70	300
Total cost/unit ($)	4.30	2.30	0.95	2.70	2.65	
Profit/unit ($)	0.70	-0.30	0.05	1.30	0.35	
Profit/Loss in % of sales	14.0	(15.0)	5.0	32.5	11.7	

Table 11.2(d) Productwise Income Statement

(in $'000)
(overhead allocation based on direct labor dollars)

Product	#101	#201	#301	#401	#501	Total
Units	100	150	200	150	200	
Sales	500	300	200	600	600	2200
Direct labor and material	350	225	60	365	500	1500
Manufacturing contribution	150	75	140	235	100	700
Allocation of overhead	50	75	10	115	150	400
Profit	100	0	130	120	-50	300
Total cost/unit ($)	4.00	2.00	0.35	3.20	3.25	
Profit/unit ($)	1.00	0.00	0.65	0.80	-0.25	
Profit/Loss in % of sales	20.0	0	65.0	20.0	(8.3)	

Table 11.2(e) Productwise Income Statement

(in $'000)
(overhead allocation based on manufacturing contribution)

Product	#101	#201	#301	#401	#501	Total
Units	100	150	200	150	200	
Sales	500	300	200	600	600	2200
Direct labor and material	350	225	60	365	500	1500
Manufacturing contribution	150	75	140	235	100	700
Allocation of overhead	86	43	80	134	57	400
Profit	64	32	60	101	43	300
Total cost/unit ($)	4.36	1.79	0.70	3.33	2.79	
Profit/unit ($)	0.64	0.21	0.30	0.67	0.21	
Profit/Loss in % of sales	12.8	10.7	30.0	16.8·	7.2	

Table 11.3   Profit as a Percent of Sales

Overhead Allocation Method	#101	#201	#301	#401	#501
A - Sales Dollars	11.8	6.7	52.0	21.0	(1.5)
B - Direct Labor Hours	16.6	2.7	57.0	17.0	(1.2)
C - Machine Hours	14.0	(15.0)	5.0	32.5	11.7
D - Direct Labor Dollars	20.0	0.0	65.0	20.0	(8.3)
E - Manufacturing Contribution	12.8	10.7	30.0	16.8	7.2

Think of the variation in pricing a buyer could encounter depending on the base used to allocate overhead. This is why a buyer should always question overhead allocation!

Despite the logical attractions of using various overhead pools and various allocation bases, it is advisable to use few pools and few bases. Consideration generally is given to (a) the factors obviously associated with the individual products on jobs (for example, direct materials, direct labor), (b) necessary clerical costs and effort in application, and (c) difference in final results.

The calculation, application, and appraisal of some of the more frequently used bases follow. In calculating the recovery rate, the numerator in the equation is always the total pool dollars to be allocated.

Bases of Manufacturing and Engineering Overhead. Allocation bases usually associated with manufacturing, engineering, and comparable indirect pools include a variety of options.

Direct Labor Hours. The formula for this base is as follows:

$$\frac{M + E \text{ pool dollars}}{\text{Total direct labor hours}} = \text{Dollars per direct hour}$$

This method is easy to understand and apply. It is useful when labor is the main cost element. However, this method ignores variations in the skills used. If the work being bought involves low skilled labor, then too much overhead is being allocated. On the other hand, if the work involves principally high skills, less overhead will be allocated.

Machine Hours. In this case the formula is as seen below:

$$\frac{M + E \text{ pool dollars}}{\text{Machine hours}} = \text{Dollars per machine hour}$$

This method assigns indirect cost to each machine hour. This method is fair to the buyer when the indirect costs are related more closely to machine operations than to direct labor.

Direct Labor Dollars. The formula for this method is as seen below:

$$\frac{\text{M + E pool dollars}}{\text{Total direct labor dollars}} = \frac{\text{Percentage of indirect cost}}{\text{per direct labor dollar}}$$

The recovery rate is similar to direct labor hours except the hours are weighted according to the wage rate structure. If the variances in wage rates are small, the results from either method will be almost identical. But if the wage rates used are low, the allocation is lower to the product under direct labor hours. From a clerical viewpoint the direct labor dollar base is usually the simplest to apply. It also is the most convenient base for many firms.

Manufacturing Contribution

The contribution approach to cost allocation is one of the most effective methods for helping management to evaluate performance and make decisions. The formula used for this base is below:

$$\frac{\text{G\&A pool dollars}}{\text{Contribution dollars}} \times 100 = \frac{\text{Percentage of allocable cost}}{\text{per dollar of contribution}}$$

This approach frequently is used in a company where there are certain less profitable products or divisions. In Table 11.3, Product #501 is nonprofitable when costs are allocated on the basis of sales dollars, direct labor hours, and direct labor dollars. However, Product #501 contributes $100,000 toward fixed costs and profit. With a lower burden of overhead such as shown in Table 11.2(e), wherein the overhead allocation is based on manufacturing contribution, product #501 shows a 7% margin of profit on sales (i.e., .21/3.00).

If the product is an unusually profitable one, the buyer will be absorbing too much overhead and should object. If the product being bought is a marginal one, this method is in the buyer's favor, and he or she may want to leave it alone.

Unit of Product. The formula for this method is below:

$$\frac{\text{M + E pool dollars}}{\text{Number of production units}} = \text{Dollars per unit of production}$$

This simple method will be advantageous if the units being purchased are above the average in value and disadvantageous if the units are below the average in value. It provides satisfactory results for manufacturing a single product in large quantities or a few units of similar products. This base is not suitable for indirect cost recovery when production is diversified and a number of sizes, grades, or styles are made.

Prime Costs. Prime costs normally include direct labor and direct material costs. The formula is below:

$$\frac{M + E \text{ pool dollars}}{\text{Prime costs}} \times 100 = \frac{\text{Percentage of indirect cost}}{\text{per dollar of prime cost}}$$

The method involves combining all elements of direct cost as a base. It may be appropriate in cases where direct labor and material costs are relatively constant, where there is a narrow line of similar products, and where material handling costs are a significant part of the indirect pool dollars.

Bases of General and Administrative Expenses. The following bases are usually associated with general and administrative pools, including corporate home office expenses.

Cost Of Goods Manufactured. Such costs include direct labor, direct material, other direct costs, and applicable overhead. The formula is below:

$$\frac{G\&A \text{ pool dollars}}{\text{Cost of goods manufactured}} \times 100 = \frac{\text{Percentage of indirect}}{\text{cost per dollar of}}$$
$$\text{manufacturing costs}$$

This is one of the most frequently used bases for recovering general and administrative expenses. It presumes that the indirect costs are proportional to manufacturing cost in the time period involved.

Processing or Conversion Costs. These include the cost of direct labor and applicable overhead expenses. The formula for this base is below:

$$\frac{\text{G\&A pool dollars}}{\text{Processing or conversion cost}} \times 100 = \begin{array}{l}\text{Percentage of indirect} \\ \text{cost per dollar of pro-} \\ \text{cessing or conversion cost}\end{array}$$

This base is similar to the cost of goods manufactured base except that direct material costs are excluded. Including direct material costs in the base would result in an unreasonable allocation of costs to those products with high direct material content.

ESTIMATING INDIRECT COSTS

Normally, a company will project indirect costs for each period of operation so that a fair share of these costs may be applied to each item produced during this period. The volume of business, the direct activity bases for indirect costs, and the indirect costs themselves are estimated. Indirect cost rates then are developed from the estimates of the indirect costs and associated bases. Each of these estimates affects the projected rates. *The most critical factor, however, is how well the firm forecasts its future level of operations (volume),* because this is the basis for allocating indirect costs.

If the firm's estimate of its volume is too low, its indirect cost rates usually will be overstated. If the company prices using a cost buildup approach, the result will be to overprice the items produced. Conversely, if a too-high volume is estimated, the company's rates usually will be understated. Either situation is undesirable from the buyer's point of view.

Functional Organization. Indirect costs are incurred for the performance of specific functions. To a buyer, the reasonableness of indirect costs depends on the costs per unit of each function and on the necessity for or value of that function. A buyer's evaluation of the need for a function should come before the evaluation of the cost to perform that function. The evaluation of indirect costs must always be accomplished within the framework of total cost evaluation. Analysis of indirect functions is helped by a detailed understanding of how the company is organized.

Rate of Application

After a firm has determined what its overhead rate should be for the accounting period, it will use that rate in estimating unit costs for the period. As a matter of fact, estimates rarely equal incurred costs.

As discussed previously, since indirect costs cannot be assigned to any particular unit or lot of production, there usually are problems associated with recovering indirect costs. Assume, for example, that a company is producing a single product. The firm estimates that it will produce 1,000 units. At this volume, manufacturing indirect costs will be $1 million. Manufacturing overhead is estimated to be $1,000 per unit ($1,000,000/1,000 = $1,000 per unit). It is this estimated $1,000 per-unit rate that will be applied to the direct cost base throughout the cost-accounting period.

For the moment, assume that the firm's indirect costs were all fixed at $1 million and 1,000 units are made. Then, applied costs will equal the $1,000,000. However, if the firm produced fewer than 1,000 units, indirect costs would be underapplied. Similarly, if more than 1,000 units were produced, indirect costs would be overapplied. An estimation can result in windfall profits or losses, neither of which is a desirable state.

EVALUATING OVERHEAD PROPOSALS

Overhead evaluation is obviously important in determining price reasonableness through cost analysis. The professional buyer needs to be able to verify the allowability of costs and cost behavior.

To conduct this evaluation, historical data are required. The larger the dollar value of the procurement, the more information the buyer should try to obtain. A five-year base of overhead history is desirable, if it can be obtained. (See Table 11.4.) It is desirable to use constant-year dollars to eliminate the effect of inflation.

What if the supplier had the manufacturing overhead base and pool history shown in Table 11.4 and estimated 19X9 production at 690,000 direct labor hours?

Using this history, the buyer can construct a scatter diagram such as the one shown in Figure 11.2. Overhead base estimates

Table 11.4 Manufacturing Overhead History

(Constant Year $s)

Year	Volume (in direct labor hours)	Manufacturing Overhead Dollars	$/Hour
19X4	702,000	7,420,000	10.57
19X5	681,000	7,280,000	10.69
19X6	664,000	7,270,000	10.95
19X7	717,000	7,500,000	10.46
19X8	736,000	7,530,000	10.23
Total	3,500,000	37,000,000	10.57
Average	700,000	7,400,000	

serve as a measure of the forces that drive overhead pool changes. In this case the supplier estimate is found to be reasonable. Based on the graphic analysis, manufacturing overhead for 19X9 will be approximately $7,360,000.

The use of this approach assumes that fixed and variable cost relationships remain relatively constant over the periods considered. It further assumes that these same relationships will remain valid for the period or periods being estimated. If the firm has purchased facilities and equipment, the fixed versus variable cost relationships probably will change. Then this type of analysis may be invalid. The same is true if such changes are expected during the periods being estimated. If the supplier states that such changes have occurred, the buyer should ask for evidence of the changes.

Also, when using this method of analysis, the buyer must remember that the historical data will reflect inflation over the years. Adjustment to constant year dollars is difficult because of the numerous types of labor and material contained in these accounts. As long as the overall rate of inflation is relatively low, its effect will be minimal. However, a significant change in the rate of inflation could affect the estimate.

Figure 11.2 Manufacturing Overhead History

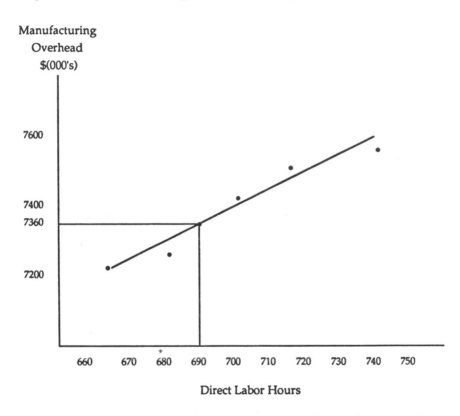

Manufacturing
   Overhead
     $(000's)

Direct Labor Hours

CONCLUDING REMARKS

Indirect costs are a major component of a supplier's price. When a buyer employs cost analysis to arrive at a price which is considered fair and reasonable, it is necessary to investigate the reasonableness of proposed overhead costs. Three issues then are of key importance: (1) the supplier's projection of overhead costs for the period of the contract, (2) the realism of the supplier's forecast of business activity during this period, and (3) the reasonableness of the supplier's basis for allocating his or her overhead costs.

Having completed our analysis of direct and indirect costs, we turn our attention to the issue of profit.

RECOMMENDED READING

Ray A. Garrison, *Managerial Accounting: Concepts for Planning, Control and Decision Making*, 3rd ed., (Plano, TX: Business Publications, Inc.)

Chapter 12

Profit Analysis

Most enterprises have two major interrelated goals: survival and profitability. Survival depends on profit, which is the difference between sales revenue and product cost. Without profit, the company cannot buy more modern equipment or modernize buildings or raise additional working capital. On the other hand, too much concentration on profit without consideration of risk can endanger the firm's ability to survive. Going after the "big gain" can cause firms to accept more and more risk until they are too overextended when a major shift occurs in the market or economy.

Business managers, therefore, must consider both potential risk and potential profit when evaluating an investment possibility. They expect higher profit for higher risk just as an individual investor would. The business manager's evaluation of profit versus risk could be likened to an individual's consideration of whether to invest in stocks or put money in a savings account at a local bank. Stocks offer a higher potential return than a savings account, but they also offer more risk. The value of stock can increase tremendously or drop to almost nothing, while a savings account is designed to grow slowly but safely. Some firms, like some individuals, may opt for the potential of more profit and accept greater risk. Others may accept less profit with a lower risk. However, no rational investor would knowingly accept both high risk and low profit.

Profit does not concern procurement professionals in a truly competitive market. The price of an item is set by the marketplace. Suppliers in such markets not only must consider estimated cost and desired profit, but also the price at which the item can be sold. At any given price for a competitive item, more efficient firms will realize a larger profit simply because they have lower costs. Firms that cannot operate profitably will leave the industry, and new firms will enter. The amount of profit realized by the firm depends on its ability to control and reduce costs.

Where a competitive environment exists, cost analysis of proposals is unnecessary. However, where no competitive market exists, cost analysis and profit analysis are essential. The constraints imposed on cost and profit by the marketplace are no longer present. Properly applied, cost and profit analysis encourage efforts toward more effective and economical contract performance. Profit analysis should recognize effective supplier effort and the risk involved in a given contract or program. *Concentration solely on negotiating the lowest possible profit, using historical averages, or application of some arbitrarily determined percentage to the total product cost does not motivate effective and economical performance.*

PROFIT PRINCIPLES

Several principles of profit analysis require consideration in an effort to stimulate effective and economical contract performance and attract good suppliers:

- Motivate suppliers to undertake more difficult work requiring higher skills by rewarding those who do so.
- Allow the supplier an opportunity to earn profits commensurate with the extent of the cost risk assumed.
- Motivate suppliers to increase their productivity by rewarding those who do.
- Highly reliable (dependable) suppliers deserve above average profits.
- Higher profits generally are necessary on jobs requiring highly skilled personnel.
- A higher profit is justified for a supplier who consistently turns out exceptionally reliable technical products.

- A firm which manufactures to another firm's design specification should receive a lower profit than one which has developed its own specification.
- Profit tends to be a function of current supply and demand patterns.
- Profit rates applicable to overtime costs should be lower than those applied to regular labor costs.

WEIGHTED GUIDELINES METHOD[1]

The weighted guidelines method of profit analysis, when properly applied, rewards suppliers with profits commensurate with the circumstances of each contract. With this method of profit analysis, various profit weights are applied to various costs projected to be incurred by the supplier.

The weighted guidelines method of profit analysis is a technique for analysis and the establishment of the profit objective. While the weighted guidelines method should be applied to larger procurements only, familiarity with its principles allows the professional buyer to improve his or her negotiating skills and the pricing of all negotiated procurements.

Discussion with the supplier of the evaluation factors considered in setting the profit objective is quite proper. However, experience has shown that no separate agreement should be specifically reached on the exact amount of profit included in the negotiated price. Total profit dollars should not be negotiated apart from total cost. This is particularly important in the incentive-type contracts discussed in Chapter 13, where sound negotiation technique requires simultaneous agreement on the interrelated elements of target cost, target profit, and share arrangement, which, when taken together, make up the pricing arrangement. The professional buyer is not

---

1. This section is loosely based on the 1984 version of the Armed Services Pricing Manual. It is the authors' belief (and that of many defense industry pricing professionals) that the presented methodology is both more understandable and more logical than current versions prescribed in government directives.

drawn into a piecemeal agreement on target cost, then target profit, then share arrangement, and finally profit limits or price ceilings.

The development and use of the weighted guidelines method is best illustrated through the use of an example. Assume that a buyer is completing cost analysis of a supplier's proposal to develop and build an alpha-beta prototype. Even though there is considerable cost uncertainty, the buyer prefers to use a firm fixed-price contract. Past experience indicates that the supplier is dependable, produces a highly reliable product, and achieves above average productivity through the employment of conscientious employees and managers.

Cost Analysis of Supplier Effort

The first section of the weighted guidelines method evaluates the technical resources and skills, as well as supplier management, required to perform the work covered by a particular contract. This is done through analysis of the expected supplier effort expressed in dollars. (This is the $ Base Column of Table 12.1.)

Profit Ranges

The second step in the weighted guidelines method is to develop the possible allowable profit ranges for the various cost elements. The profit weight ranges shown in Table 12.1 are based on DOD experience with weighted guidelines during the 1970's and 1980's. They are introduced as a starting point for developing your own ranges.

The prescribed weight ranges for direct materials are lower than the ranges for other cost inputs because direct material costs normally represent the lowest investment by the supplier of resources *per cost dollar*. The maximum weight of subcontracted items is slightly higher than for other direct material. Under subcontracts, the prime contractor is responsible for design, specification development, and other development efforts not required for other material. The sourcing, pricing, and administration of subcontracts normally require more effort than does the procurement of commodities.

Table 12.1 Weighted Guidelines Profit Objectives

Cost Element	$ Base	Profit Weight Ranges			Weight Assigned (for this example) (percent)	Profit/Fee Base X Weight (for this example) $
		Mfgr	R & D	Ser-vices		
		(in percentages)				
Materials						
Subcontracted Items	$1,000,000	1-5	1-5	1-5	3	30,000
Purchased Parts	500,000	1-4	1-4	1-4	2	10,000
Raw Material	200,000	1-3	1-3	1-3	2	4,000
Standard Commercial Items	300,000	1-2	1-2	1-2	1	3,000
Interdivisional Transfers	0	1-4	1-4	1-4		
Engineering						
Direct Labor	200,000	9-15	9-15		11	22,000
Overhead	300,000	6-9	6-9		7	21,000
Manufacturing						
Direct Labor	300,000	5-9	5-9		8	24,000
Overhead	400,000	4-7	4-7		5.5	22,000
Services						
Direct Labor				5-15		
Overhead				4-8		
General Mgt (G&A)	100,000	6-8	6-8	6-8	8	8,000
Total Effort	$3,300,000					144,000
Cost Risk	$3,300,000	0-8	0-7	0-4	6[1]	198,000
Capital Employed[2]		16-20				
Other Factors[3]	$3,300,000	0-4	0-4	0-4	2	66,000
						$408,000

1. The example is for a fixed-price contract involving considerable cost uncertainty.

2. "Capital Employed" will be used only if depreciation expenses for plant and equipment required to perform this contract are *not* included in Manufacturing Overhead.

3. Dependability of supplier, reliability of products, productivity, skill level of personnel involved, production to own specs, and so on.

Assigning Weights

The third step is to assign weights for the cost elements which were developed through cost analysis. The first principle of profit analysis is to motivate suppliers to undertake more difficult work requiring higher skills and reward those who do. The profit weights assigned should measure the quality, character, and value of the labor and materials which the supplier must employ to deliver the product required by the contract. The more technical or managerial skill required to perform the contract, the higher the overall weight assigned in this area.

Materials. The analyst's consideration of the appropriate weight to assign individual types of material requires an evaluation of the managerial and technical effort applied by procurement to increase economy and effectiveness under the contract. Selection of the appropriate weight from each range should be based on answers to such questions as those below:

- How many orders and suppliers are there?
- Are established sources available, or will it be necessary to develop new sources?
- Are materials readily available, or will it be necessary to develop new sources?
- Are materials readily available in the market, or will the supplier have to develop a source which will have to design the item and/or product to extremely tight tolerances?
- Will materials be acquired through routine order or complex subcontracts?
- What managerial and technical efforts will be required to administer a subcontract and to increase competition?

Obviously, if the material procurement task involves few orders and suppliers, the management task will be less complex than if there were many. In the same light, dealing only with established sources requires less research and source evaluation than developing new sources. Purchasing a complex item involves greater source qualification and product inspection than purchasing a routine item.

Likewise, complex cost contracts involve considerably more effort than fixed-price purchase orders.

Considering the potentially wide range of effort, interdivisional transfers at cost are evaluated by individual components of cost, such as material, labor, and overheads. The ranges and evaluation criteria used are the same as for materials furnished by outside suppliers.

Labor. Analysis of labor includes evaluation of the comparative quality and level of the talents, skills, and experience to be employed. Issues which the buyer should consider include the following:

- the diversity of scientific and engineering specialties required
- the need for engineering supervision and coordination
- the variety of manufacturing labor skills required
- the supplier's manpower resources

The Relationship between Cost and Profit

This phase of the profit buildup assumes a direct relationship between the effort required and the cost of getting that effort. In other words, more cost leads to more profit. At first glance this seems to reward the supplier who incurs high costs and to penalize the supplier who controls expenditures. This is not the case. In developing the cost objective, cost analysis is used to identify and trim costs that appear to result from ineffective management. Therefore, the cost objective should be a reasonable estimate of what the item should cost. By basing profit analysis on the cost objective, the buyer eliminated the possibility of rewarding a firm for cost inefficiency.

Cost Risk

This portion of the weighted guidelines method specifically relates to the second principle of profit analysis: allow the supplier an opportunity to earn profits commensurate with the extent of cost risk assumed. This factor can be critical to the reduction of costs applied to the total of the individual bases.

Risk Assumption and Type of Contract. Determination of the degree of cost risk assumed by the supplier is related to the selection of contract type as described in Chapter 13. The extremes of contract types are a cost-plus-fixed-fee level of effort contract, which requires only a supplier's best efforts to perform a task; and a firm-fixed-price contract for a complex item. A cost-plus-fixed-fee contract would reflect a minimum supplier assumption of cost risk, but a firm-fixed-price contract requires complete assumption of cost risk by the supplier. Normally, reward for risk by contract type would fall into the following percentage ranges:

Contract Type	*Percentage Ranges for Risk*
Cost-plus-fixed-fee	0 - ½%
Cost-plus-incentive-fee	1 - 2% on contracts with cost incentives only; 1½ - 3% on contracts·with multiple incentives
Fixed-price-incentive	3 - 5% on contracts with cost incentives only; 4 - 6% on contracts with multiple incentives
Fixed-price redetermination	4 - 6%
Firm-fixed-price	6 - 8%

These ranges may not be appropriate in all contract situations. For instance, a fixed-price-incentive contract that is closely priced with a low ceiling price and high incentive share may be tantamount to a firm-fixed-price (FFP) contract. In this situation, the buyer might determine that a basis exists for high confidence in the reasonableness of the estimate and that little opportunity exists for cost reduction without extraordinary efforts. On the other hand, a contract with a high ceiling and low incentive formula could be considered to contain features of a cost-plus-incentive-fee contract. In this situation, the buyer might determine that his or her company is retaining much of the contract cost responsibility and that the risk assumed by the supplier is minimal. Similarly, if a cost-plus-incentive-fee contract includes an unlimited downward (negative) fee adjustment on cost control, it could be comparable to a fixed-price-incentive contract. In such a pricing environment, the buyer may determine that the supplier is accepting a greater amount of cost responsibility than is typical under a normal cost-plus-incentive-fee contract.

Cost Risk of Overrun. Although the percentage profit range is normally established considering the supplier's acceptance of cost risk, the exact weight assigned within that range is established by considering the risk of overrun. The risk of overrun is directly affected by two factors:

- the complexity of the task assumed
- the reliability of the cost estimates for the task assumed

The willingness of a supplier to accept more difficult contracts must be rewarded. There is little difficulty in building the one thousandth production unit when it is just like the first nine hundred ninety-nine units. On the other hand, development of a new item that approaches the state-of-the-art involves substantial task complexity. Within a given profit range, add-on production would receive a lower profit rate, and a complex development contract would receive a higher rating.

Reliability of the cost estimate relates to the confidence the buyer has in the estimate and the likely difference between the estimate and final cost. Confidence in an estimate is influenced by many things, such as the preciseness of the statement of work, the existence of historical cost information, the time period covered by the proposed contract, the adequacy of the estimating methods, the judgment and abilities of the estimators, and the decisions of management. These factors also are elements considered in cost analysis and selection of the pricing arrangement. Thus, cost analysis, pricing arrangement consideration, profit analysis, and setting of price ceilings, when applicable, are all closely interrelated.

The buyer will have good insight into the supplier's acceptance of cost risk when comparing the supplier's estimate with the buyer's objective. If the buyer is confident that the final cost will approximate his or her objective (within plus or minus three percent, for instance), and if the supplier is willing to contract on a firm-fixed-price (FFP) basis, the buyer can conclude a willingness by the supplier to accept a high degree of cost responsibility. On the other hand, if the supplier's estimate is 20 percent higher than the buyer's objective, and the buyer, after re-evaluation of his or her own estimate, is satisfied that it is realistic, then it appears that the supplier is reluctant to accept any cost risk. The weight assignment in the first case may indicate a high-risk situation. (This valuation may need to be modified during negotiations. The higher the negotiated costs, the lower the risk in the situation, and the lower the profit warranted within the appropriate percentage range for cost risk.)

The buyer must remember that when firming up a letter contract, a contract change, or any other unpriced action where costs have been incurred, there is virtually no cost risk associated with the already incurred costs. Therefore, these incurred costs should be assigned a 0 percent cost risk weighting. Additionally, the "to go" portion (the estimate to complete) may be of less risk than if there were no performance experience and should be assigned a weight below the normal ranges. However, if actions by the buyer's company have caused the late definitization of the letter contract, equity may require this circumstance to be considered in the profit objective for cost risk.

Capital Employed by Supplier

This element recognizes the investment risk associated with the facilities used in performance of the contract. This element is considered only when depreciation expense is *not* included in manufacturing overhead. The profit base for this element is facilities capital employed.

The normal profit range is 16 percent to 20 percent of capital employed. For existing facilities, the normal range is between 16 percent and 18 percent, for new facilities, 18 to 20 percent. The 16-20 percent is prorated if the contract is for a fraction of a year and/or requires only a portion of the facilities and equipment capacity. The key factors in evaluating risk and selecting a profit weight for capital employed include the following:

- Age of the facilities
- General purpose or special purpose nature of equipment
- Undepreciated value of facilities
- Relationship between the facility's remaining depreciation life and the length of the contract

Other Factors

The purpose of this area of the weighted guidelines is to reward the supplier for unusual efforts in the area of dependability, contribution to product, and reliability of product and encourage such efforts in the future.

A reduction of costs can reduce the profit shown for Total Effort in Table 12.1. In order to mitigate the profit opportunity loss caused by productivity gains, a special "reward" may be included under other factors. This element provides an element of flexibility. It allows us to reward suppliers who are exceptionally dependable, who invariably produce highly reliable products, who employ exceptionally highly qualified personnel, who produce to their own design specifications, and so on.

Examples. Three examples with solutions are presented in order to give the reader a better understanding of the Weighted Guidelines Method.

Production Contract Example

Problem:

After detailed cost analysis and negotiations with the Alpha-Beta Electronics Co. for production of an Alpha-Beta-developed module, the following costs appear realistic:

Materials	$10,000,000
Engineering (modification for our modules) Direct Labor Overhead	 100,000 100,000
Manufacturing Direct Labor Overhead	 2,000,000 1,000,000
G&A	150,000
Capital Employed (depreciation expense is not included in overhead, and contract will last one year)	1,000,000

The risk involved is considered to be relatively low, since the project calls for modification of an existing product and then its production. The contractor is extremely dependable and considered highly productive. His products are highly reliable.

What is a realistic profit fee in dollars? In percent of total costs?

Solution:

		Assigned Weight	Profit Fee ($)
Material	$10,000,000	2%	$200,000
Engineering			
Direct Labor	100,000	12%	12,000
Overhead	100,000	7%	7,000
Manufacturing			
Direct Labor	2,000,000	7%	140,000
Overhead	1,000,000	6%	60,000
G & A	150,000	7%	10,500
Total Effort	13,350,000		429,500
Cost Risk	13,350,000	3%	400,500
Capital Employed	1,000,000	18%	180,000
Other Factors	13,350,000	4%	534,000
Profit Objective (in dollars)			$1,544,000

Profit Objective (in %) $1,544,000 / $13,350,000 = 11.57%

R&D Services Example

Problem:
You are processing R&D Services for a gamma delta transponder. Based on a number of factors, you have entered into detailed negotiations with the Gee Wiz Electric Company. Following is a synopsis of the costs which appear to be reasonable:

Materials	$ 25,000
Engineering	
Direct Labor[1]	200,000
Overhead	200,000
G&A	20,000

The potential contractor is very dependable and considered to be very productive. He employs an excellent group of R & D personnel. What profit or target fee do you recommend?

Solution:

		Assigned Weight	Profit Fee ($)
Materials	$ 25,000	4%	$ 1,000
Engineering			
Direct Labor	200,000	12%	24,000
Overhead	200,000	8%	16,000
G&A	20,000	7%	1,400
Total Effort	$445,000		42,400
Cost Risk[2]	445,000	0%[3]	—
Independent Development	445,000	2%	8,900
Other Factors[4]	445,000	2%	8,900
Price Objective (in dollars)			$ 60,200
Price Objective (in %)		$60,200 / $445,000 = 13.53%	

1. This is the most likely cost outcome for engineering labor. Costs for this item could go as low as $140,000 or as high as $260,000.
2. Cost risk will depend greatly on the type of contract employed. With a firm-fixed-price there is great risk. With a cost reimbursement contract, there is virtually no risk.
3. Assumes Cost-Plus-Award-Fee contract.
4. Dependability, productivity, skill of personnel, etc.

Services Contract Example

Problem:

You are a senior buyer in the G.F. Computer Company with primary responsibility for the procurement of software. You are engaged in the procurement of a development effort for a sophisticated program which will aid in the operation of small- and medium-sized procurement offices.

You have followed your corporate procurement guidelines to the "T" and are in the process of determining a target fee for the Hold Em Up Software Company (HEUS), the supplier with whom you have been negotiating. The following target costs appear to be realistic:

Direct Labor	
Programmers	$300,000
System Analysts	100,000
	400,000
Overhead (125%)	500,000
G&A	50,000

This is a new firm which formed around five members of Peachstone Software Designers. HEUS has hired a number of skilled programmers and analysts. You are satisfied that the firm will be able to meet your specifications. The cost estimates for this type of programming and systems work are ±25 percent.

a. What will be your target fees if you enter into a cost reimbursement contract?

b. What would be your target objective if you were to enter into a firm-fixed-price contract?

Solution:
Question a.

Services		Assigned Weight	Profit Fee ($)
Direct Labor	$400,000	12%	48,000
Overhead	500,000	6%	30,000
G&A	50,000	7%	3,500
Total Effort	950,000		81,500
Cost Risk	950,000	0%[1]	—
Profit Objective (in dollars)			$81,500

Profit Objective (in %) $81,500 / $950,000 = 8.58%

Question b. Same except we would allow a significant amount for risk, e.g., 8%.

Cost Risk	$950,000	8%	76,000
			$157,500

$157,500 / $950,000 = 16.58%[2]

1. No risk under cost reimbursement contract.
2. This assumes that actual cost will be equal to target costs. If costs grow, the profit rate will be much smaller.

CONCLUDING REMARKS

Most professional buyers agree that profit should vary with the situation. To date, most efforts to vary profit with the procurement situation have been highly subjective. The weighted guidelines approach advanced in this chapter introduces a more objective element into the establishment of profit rates for negotiated contracts. Making the calculations helps a buyer evaluate the profit component in relation to the requirements being put on the supplier.

As we have noted, profit is, or should be, a function of contract risk. This, in turn, is a function of the type of contract compensation arrangement, the subject of our next chapter.

Chapter 13

Contract Compensation Arrangements

A wide selection of contract compensation arrangements is necessary to provide the flexibility needed for the procurement of a large variety of supplies and services. The compensation arrangement determines (1) the degree and timing of the cost responsibility assumed by the supplier, (2) the amount of profit or fee available to the supplier, and (3) the motivational implications of the fee portion of the compensation arrangements.

The buyer has a range of compensation arrangements designed to meet the needs of a particular procurement. At one end of this range is the firm fixed-price contract where the supplier assumes all cost responsibility and where, therefore, profit and loss potentials are high. At the other end of this range is the cost-plus-fixed-fee contract where the supplier has no cost risk and where fee (profit) is fixed, usually at a very low level. In between these two extremes are numerous incentive arrangements that reflect a sharing of the cost responsibility.

CONTRACT COST RISK APPRAISAL

The degree of cost responsibility a supplier can reasonably be expected to assume is determined primarily by the cost risk involved. It is to the buyer's advantage to estimate this risk prior to negotiations. Since the majority of contracts are "forward priced," that is, priced prior to completion of the work, some cost risk is involved in each of them. The degree of cost risk involved will depend on how accurately the cost of the contract can be estimated prior to performance. The accuracy of the cost estimate and the degree of cost risk usually are a function of both technical and contract schedule risk. A buyer should insist on a fixed price unless (1) the risks will result in a contract with large reserves for contingencies that may or may not occur, or (2) the risks result in reliable suppliers refusing to agree to a fixed-price contract, or (3) the use of a fixed-price contract could lead to a significant loss for the supplier.

Technical Risk

Technical risk is that risk associated with the nature of the item being purchased. Appraisal of technical risk includes analysis of the type and complexity of the item or service being purchased, stability of design specifications or statement of work, availability of historical pricing data, and prior production experience. Analysis of technical risk in a complex system may include appraisals by a team from the requiring activity, engineering staff, and purchasing.

Technical risk is reduced as the item or service requirements, production methods, and pricing data become better defined and the design specifications or statement of work becomes more stable. Research and development contracts, in particular, have a rather high technical risk associated with them. This is due to the ill-defined requirements that arise from the necessity to deal beyond, or at least very near, the limits of the current technology (often called "state of the art").

Contract Schedule Risk

In addition to technical risk, schedule risk must be assessed in determining the supplier's cost risk. Preferred procurement practice calls for forward pricing of contract efforts. Forward pricing provides a baseline against which the buyer and the supplier can measure cost or price performance against the contract effort.

GENERAL TYPES OF CONTRACT COMPENSATION ARRANGEMENTS

Compensation arrangements can be classified into three broad categories: (1) fixed-price contracts, (2) incentive contracts, and (3) cost reimbursement contracts.

Fixed-Price Contracts

Under a fixed-price arrangement, the supplier is obligated to deliver the product called for by the contract for a fixed price. If, prior to completion of the product, the supplier finds that the effort is more difficult and costly than anticipated, it is still obligated to deliver the product. Further, the supplier will receive no more than the previously agreed-on amount. The amount of profit the supplier receives will depend on the actual cost outcome. There is no maximum nor minimum profit limitation in fixed-price contracts. A fixed-price arrangement is normally used in situations where specifications are well defined and cost risk is relatively low.

Incentive Contracts

Incentive contracts are employed in an effort to motivate the supplier to improve cost and, possibly, other stated requirements such as schedule. In an incentive contract, the cost responsibility is shared by the buyer and the seller. This sharing addresses two issues: (1) the desire to motivate the supplier to control cost and (2) an awareness that if the supplier assumes all or most of the risk when significant uncertainty is present, a contingency allowance will be required, thereby inflating the contract price. Incentive contracts are of two types: (1) fixed-price incentive and (2) cost-plus-incentive-fee. With a fixed-price incentive contract, the ceiling price is agreed to (or fixed) during negotiations. Under the cost-plus-incentive-fee arrangement, the supplier is reimbursed for all allowable costs incurred, up to any prescribed ceiling. In addition, the supplier receives a fee designed to motivate it to meet the buyer's cost and other stated objectives.

Cost-type Contracts

Under a cost-type arrangement, the buyer's obligation is to reimburse the supplier for all reasonable, allowable, allocable costs incurred and to pay a fixed fee. Most cost arrangements include a cost limitation clause that sets an administrative limitation on the reimbursement of costs. Generally, under a cost-type arrangement, the supplier is obligated only to provide its "best effort." Neither performance nor delivery usually are guaranteed. Cost-type arrangements are normally used when

- procurement of research and development involves high technical risk
- some doubt exists that the project can be successfully completed
- product specifications are incomplete, or
- high-dollar, highly uncertain procurements such as software development are involved.

SPECIFIC TYPES OF COMPENSATION ARRANGEMENTS

There are a number of specific types of compensation arrangements under each of the above categories:

1. Fixed-price compensation arrangements are as follows:
   - Firm fixed-price (FFP)
   - Fixed-price with economic price adjustment (FPEPA)
   - Fixed-price redetermination [FPR-prospective (P) and FPR-retroactive (R)]
2. Incentive arrangements are listed below:
   - Fixed-price incentive (FPI)
   - Cost-plus-incentive-fee (CPIF)
3. Cost-type arrangements are as follows:
   - Cost reimbursement (CR)
   - Time and material
   - Cost-sharing (CS)
   - Cost-plus-fixed-fee (CPFF)
   - Cost-plus-award-fee (CPAF)

The applicability, elements, structure, and final price computation for the various compensation arrangements are discussed in the following paragraphs.

Firm Fixed-Price Contracts

The most preferred contract type, if appropriate for the procurement, is the firm fixed-price contract. A firm fixed-price (FFP) contract is an agreement to pay a specified price when the items (services) specified by the contract have been delivered (completed) and accepted. The contracting parties establish a firm price either through competitive bidding or negotiation. Since there is no adjustment in contract price after the work is completed and actual costs are known, the cost risk to the supplier can be high.

A FFP contract is appropriate in competitive bidding where the specifications are definite, there is little schedule risk, and where competition has established the existence of a fair and reasonable price. A FFP contract also can be appropriate for negotiated procurements if a review reveals adequate specifications and if price analysis establishes the reasonableness of the price.

As previously stated, under a FFP contract there is no price adjustment due to the supplier's cost experience. Because the supplier has all cost responsibility, the actual outcome will show up in the form of profit or losses. Therefore, the supplier has maximum incentive to control costs under a FFP contract. If the supplier incurs expenses beyond the buyer's obligation, the seller must find the required funds elsewhere. Conversely, if the supplier reduces costs, all savings contribute to the supplier's profit. This dollar-for-dollar relationship between expenditures and profit is the greatest motivator of efficiency available. A FFP contract has only one contract compensation arrangement element: total price. Although negotiations may involve the discussion of costs and profit, the contractual document reflects only total price. This structure can be seen in Figure 13.1, which depicts a FFP contract for $20,000.

In this example cost is shown as the independent variable (x-axis), and profit, since it is a function of cost, as the dependent variable (y-axis). The graph depicts the one-to-one relationship between costs and profit by showing that as costs increase $1, profit decreases $1.

Figure 13.1 Firm Fixed-Price Contract—$20,000

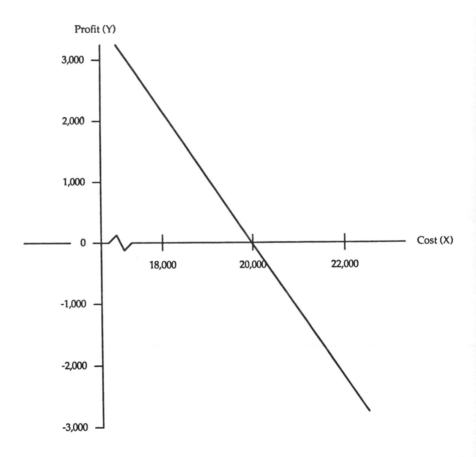

Computing the final price in a FFP-type contract is a simple matter. If a $20,000 firm fixed-price contract were negotiated, on contract completion the supplier will receive $20,000 whether costs were $15,000 or $25,000 or any other amount.

It should be noted that a fixed price does not always stay fixed. A supplier who is losing money *may* request and get some relief, if the following apply:

1. The customer in some way has contributed to the loss.
2. The customer badly needs the items and other suppliers are not willing to provide them at the established price.
3. The supplier has unique facilities and time is too short to do anything but to get the product at an increased cost from the initial supplier.

As discussed in Chapter 2, early supplier involvement (ESI) with a decision to rely on one supplier during and after development results in many benefits based on the early matching of process and product. But ESI may result in cost overruns and higher costs if the supplier can't perform at the fixed price due to unforeseen (usually technical) reasons. It should be recognized that when a supplier fails to perform under a fixed-price contract and the buyer is forced to turn the business into a cost-plus type of contract, the supplier has damaged its chance for future business with the customer and other potential customers. The buyer, on the other hand, can use the prospect of continued future business to keep the price well below what the supplier's leverage of the moment might appear to allow.

Variations of the FFP contract have been developed to meet special circumstances. One such variation is the FFP level of effort contract. This arrangement calls for a set number of labor hours to be expended over a period of time. The contract is considered complete when the hours are expended, although normally a report of findings is also required. The FFP level of effort contract is appropriately used when the specification is general in nature and when no specific end item (other than a report) is required. This arrangement is most frequently used for research and development efforts under $100,000 and "get our foot in the door" consulting contracts.

Fixed-Price with Economic Price Adjustment Contracts

Fixed-price with economic price adjustment (FPEPA) contracts are used to recognize economic contingencies, such as unstable labor or market conditions which would prevent the establishment of a firm fixed-price contract without a large contingency for possible cost increases for labor and/or materials. A FPEPA contract is simply a FFP contract that includes economic price adjustment clauses. Such provisions are common when purchasing items containing precious metals.

Economic price adjustment (EPA) or escalator/de-escalator clauses provide for both price increases and decreases to protect the buyer and supplier from the effects of economic changes. If such clauses were not used, suppliers would include contingency allowances in their bids or proposals to eliminate or reduce the risk of loss. With a fixed contingency allowance in the contract price, the supplier is hurt if the changes exceed its estimate, and the buyer will overpay if the increases do not materialize.

An economic price adjustment clause may be used for fixed-price type arrangements resulting from both competitively bid and negotiated contracts. Price adjustments normally should be restricted to contingencies beyond the control of the supplier. Under a FPEPA contract, specific contingencies are left open subject to an EPA clause, and the final contract price is adjusted, depending on what happens to these contingencies. Where cost pass-through or escalator clauses cover specific materials and/or labor, the buyer should be sure that the price increase does not occur until the higher cost material is used or until the labor contract increase takes effect.

The use of economic price adjustment clauses varies with the probability of significant price fluctuations. Their use also increases when purchasing strategy favors early supplier involvement, longer term contracts, fewer supplies, and more single source suppliers. An economic price adjustment clause should recognize the possibility of both inflation and deflation in determining price adjustments. Further, labor and material costs subject to economic adjustment must reflect the effects of learning on both labor and material costs. It takes considerable purchasing skill to use economic price adjustment clauses successfully. Decisions must be made on what items to include and what is the best index for each item (See Appendix F). Attention must be given to controlling the use of economic price adjustment clauses and auditing their implementation.

The cost elements to adjust are high-value raw materials, specific high-value components, and direct labor. In rental agreements, real estate taxes are subject to escalation on a direct pass-through basis. The professional buyer generally should oppose including costs within the supplier's control such as development, depreciation, fixed expenses, other overhead items, and profit in the base subject to escalation.

In selecting indexes for price adjustment clauses, the following rules are suggested:

- Select from the appropriate BLS category
- Avoid broad indexes by use of the lowest level which includes the item
- Develop a weighted index for materials in a product
- Select labor rate indexes by type and location
- Define energy indexes by fuel type and location
- Analyze the past history of each proposed index versus the actual price change of the item being indexed

Using a broad index can give strange results. One marketing executive (an amateur buyer) used the Producer Price Index (PPI) to adjust the purchase price of electronic apparatus, not recognizing the PPI consists of about 40 percent food and fuel with only 3 percent electronics input. Further, the electronic component index generally is a declining one based on the ratio of price to capability.

The details of the economic price adjustment clause must be thought through with various scenarios in mind. When will adjustments be made? Under what conditions can the contract be renegotiated? How will it be audited? By whom?

Fixed-Price Redetermination Contracts

These contracts provide for a firm fixed-price for an initial contract period with a redetermination (upward or downward) at a stated time during contract performance [FPR (prospective)] or after contract completion [FPR (retroactive)]. The FPR (prospective) is usually used only in those circumstances calling for quantity production or services where a fair and reasonable price can be negotiated for initial periods but not for subsequent periods. The FPR (retroactive) is used in those circumstances where, at the time of negotiation, a fair and reasonable price cannot be established and the amount involved is so small and the performance period so short that use of any other contract type would be impractical.

Incentive Arrangements

Firm fixed-price (FFP) and cost-plus-fixed-fee (CPFF) contracts are extremes of the range of contract compensation arrangements since in either case all of the cost responsibility falls on only one party. In between these two extremes are a number of contract arrangements where the cost responsibility is shared between the customer and the supplier. These are called incentive-type contracts.

Incentives are applied to contracts in an attempt to motivate the supplier to improve performance in cost, schedule, or other stated parameters. By far the most frequent application of incentives is in the area of cost control. However, this is not the only type of incentive, and the specific type of incentive applied depends on the desired outcome. For example, if the primary interest is in developing a high-performance read head, it would be logical to reward the supplier for development and production of a read head which exceeds the minimum specifications. If the same read head were needed to meet a crash development effort, schedule may be the basis of an incentive. For the same read head, funds may be a real constraint due to budgetary limitations, and a cost incentive would be attractive. If a combination of performance and cost objectives were of concern, a multiple incentive contract could be developed.

In this text, the discussion of incentive arrangements is limited to cost incentives. The focus will be on the two most frequently applied cost incentive compensation arrangements: the fixed-price incentive (FPI) contract and the cost-plus-incentive-fee (CPIF) contract. A general discussion of how a simplified incentive contract is structured precedes an analysis of the specific elements and structure of these two compensation arrangements. The elements of a simplified incentive contract include (1) the target cost, (2) the target profit, and (3) the sharing arrangement.

Target Cost. The target cost for an incentive contract is that cost outcome which both the buyer and the supplier feel is most likely for the effort involved. The target cost should be based on costs that would result under "normal business conditions." Although the target cost is thought to be the most likely, it is recognized that the probability of the supplier's final costs being equal to the target cost is low. After all, if there were a high probability that the target cost would equal the final cost, a firm fixed-price contract would be appropriate. The target should be that cost point where both parties agree that there is an equal chance of going above or below the target.

Target Profit. In addition to a target cost, a target profit is developed. The target profit in an incentive contract is a profit amount that is considered fair and reasonable, based on all relevant facts as discussed in Chapter 12.

Allocating Costs Above or Below Target. Since an incentive contract recognizes that the target will most likely *not* be met, a method of allocating cost increases above or decreases below target is necessary. The method is a sharing arrangement that reflects the sharing of the cost responsibility between the buyer and the supplier. This arrangement should reflect the cost risk involved as evidenced by the magnitude of potential increases and decreases for the specific effort.

How is the magnitude of a potential cost increase or decrease established? It is developed through an assessment of possible cost outcomes, based on varying circumstances a supplier might face during contract performance. In addition to developing a target cost and profit outcome, the parties establish cost outcomes and associated profits for a "best case" and a "worst case" situation. The best case cost outcome is referred to as the most optimistic cost (MOC) point, and its related profit is referred to as the most optimistic profit (MOPr) point. The worst case cost outcome is referred to as the most pessimistic cost (MPC) point, and its profit is referred to as the most pessimistic profit (MPPr) point.

The difference between the target points and the most optimistic points provides the buyer with the magnitude of a potential cost decrease. The difference between the target points and the most pessimistic points provides the buyer with the magnitude of a potential cost increase. One normally would not expect these magnitudes to be equal, since the potential for things to go wrong is usually higher than the potential for things to go better than expected. Another way of looking at the magnitude of potential cost increase is that it provides an estimate of the cost risk a supplier faces if the target cost is not met. This cost risk and the supplier's assumption of this risk is reflected in the sharing arrangement.

An Example. The example below shows how an incentive contract is structured. The following cost and profit outcomes were agreed on by the buyer and the seller:

	(in thousands)
Target cost (TC)	$1,000
Target profit (TPr)	80
Most optimistic cost (MOC)	800
Most optimistic profit (MOPr)	120
Most pessimistic cost (MPC)	1,300
Most pessimistic profit (MPPr)	30

Computing of the final payment under an incentive arrangement is more complex than under either a FFP or CPFF contract. Under an incentive arrangement, the supplier's profit will be adjusted to reflect performance in the cost area. If the supplier has incurred costs above target, the target profit will be decreased by the supplier's share of the cost above target cost. Conversely, if the supplier's costs are below target, its profit is increased. The final price outcome (cost plus profit) would then be the final cost plus the supplier's share of the cost savings or cost increase. The steps used

Figure 13.2 Incentive Arrangement

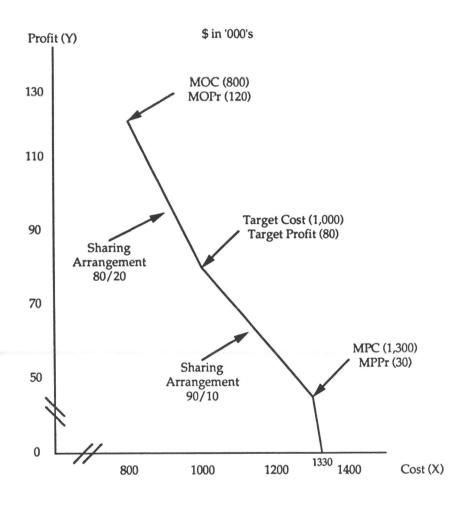

Profit (Y) $ in '000's

MOC (800)
MOPr (120)

Target Cost (1,000)
Target Profit (80)

Sharing
Arrangement
80/20

MPC (1,300)
MPPr (30)

Sharing
Arrangement
90/10

Cost (X)

Note:
The first number in the sharing arrangement (e.g., 80) refers to the buyer's share of the savings below target cost and to the buyer's share of additional costs above target cost. The second figure (e.g., 20) refers to the seller's share.

to compute the final price in an incentive arrangement are shown below.

Fixed-Price Incentive Contract

The FPI contract is like an incentive contract, except that a ceiling price is included, limiting the customer's total price obligation. Computing the final price is also similar to the computation for an incentive contract. However, the final amount the supplier will receive is limited by the ceiling price. For example, assume that on contract completion, an audit finds that the supplier incurred $1,400,000 in reasonable, allowable, allocable costs. Given the following elements of the FPI contract, what final payment would the supplier receive?

Final cost	$1,400,000
Target cost	$1,000,000
Target profit (TPr)	$80,000
Overrun sharing arrangement	90/10
Underrun sharing arrangement	80/20
Ceiling price	$1,330,000

The buyer computes the final price as follows:

1. Target cost - final cost = overrun/underrun cost (Δ)
   $1,000,000 - $1,400,000 = -$400,000

2. Δ x contractor share = overrun/underrun profit (π)
   - $400,000 x .10 = -$ 40,000

3. π + TPr = computed profit
   - $40,000 + $80,000 = $40,000

4. Computed profit + final cost = computed price
   $40,000 + $1,400,000 = $1,440,000

Because this is a fixed-price incentive contract with a ceiling price, the buyer must compare the computed price to the ceiling price. In this case the computed price is greater than the ceiling price; therefore, the supplier would receive only the ceiling price of

$1,330,000. The fixed-price nature of the FPI contract requires the buyer to ensure that the final amount paid to the supplier does not exceed the ceiling price.

Cost-Plus-Incentive-Fee Arrangements

CPIF contracts combine the incentive arrangement and the cost-plus-fixed-fee arrangement. Under a CPIF arrangement, an incentive applies over part of the range of cost outcomes. The fee structure resembles a cost-plus-fixed-fee contract at both the low-cost and high-cost ends of the range, as shown in Figure 13.3. Thus, if cost were $800,000 or less, the fee would be $120,000. If cost were $1,400,000 or more, the fee would be $20,000.

The diagram shows a CPIF arrangement that is structured and based on the following negotiated cost and fee outcomes:

Target cost	$1,000,000
Target profit	70,000
Optimistic cost	800,000
Optimistic and maximum profit	120,000
Pessimistic cost	1,400,000
Pessimistic and minimum profit	20,000
Sharing below target (customer/supplier)	75/25
Sharing above target (customer/supplier)	87.5/12.5

A cost-plus-incentive-fee arrangement is used in those circumstances where the cost risk warrants a cost-type arrangement but where an incentive can be established to provide the supplier with positive motivation to manage costs. CPIF arrangements are most suitable for advanced development efforts and for initial production runs. In these circumstances, risk may be too high to warrant use of a fixed-price arrangement or a FPI arrangement, but not high enough to require a CPFF arrangement to get a reliable supplier.

The CPIF contract is structured very similarly to the FPI compensation arrangement. Cost and fee outcomes are established for target, most optimistic, and most pessimistic points. These cost and fee outcomes are used to establish the sharing arrangement for cost decrease and increase situations. The difference between the struc-

Figure 13.3 CPIF Arrangement

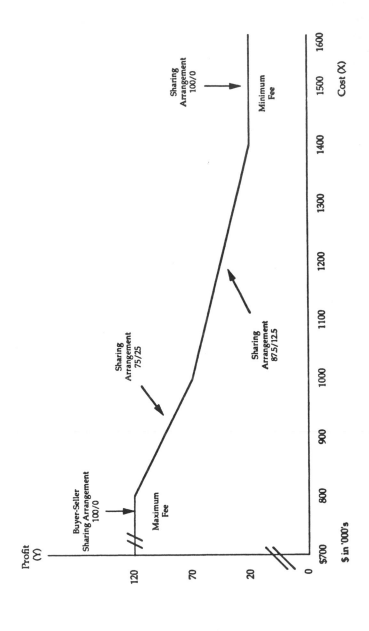

ture of the FPI and CPIF arrangements is that under the CPIF arrangement, the contract converts to a CPFF contract at both the most optimistic and the most pessimistic fee points.

The computation of the final price to be paid to the supplier on contract completion follows the same steps as in the fixed-price incentive arrangement. However, in a CPIF contract a comparison is made between computed fee and minimum and maximum fees prior to the calculation of the final price. For example, using the CPIF contract structured in Figure 13.3, the buyer would compute the final price, based on a final cost (FC) of $700,000 as follows:

Target cost	$1,000,000
Target profit	$70,000
Maximum fee	$120,000
Minimum fee	$20,000

1. Target cost - final cost = cost savings
    $1,000,000 - $700,000 = $300,000

2. Cost savings x supplier share = supplier's share of cost savings
    $300,000 x .25 = $75,000

3. Savings fee + target fee = computed fee
    $75,000 + $70,000 = $145,000

Since there is a maximum limitation on fee, a comparison is made between the computed fee and the maximum fee. In this case, the supplier receives only the maximum fee, $120,000.

4. Final cost + maximum fee = final price
    $700,000 + $120,000 = $820,000

The CPIF contract is an incentive arrangement that converts to a CPFF contract at both the maximum and minimum fee points. This type of contract provides the supplier some incentive to control cost outcomes in the area over which the sharing arrangements apply, called the range of incentive effectiveness.

Cost-Plus-Fixed-Fee Arrangements

Under a cost-plus-fixed-fee (CPFF) contract, the buyer agrees to reimburse the supplier for all allocable, allowable, and reasonable costs that may be incurred during the performance of the contract. Moreover, the buyer agrees to pay the supplier a fixed number of dollars above the cost as the fee for doing the work. The fee changes only when the scope of work changes. Under the CPFF the supplier has no incentive to reduce or control costs.

The contractual elements of this arrangement include an estimated cost and a fixed fee. The estimated cost represents the best estimate of the customer and the supplier for the work involved. The fixed fee is the amount of fee the supplier will receive regardless of cost outcome. Because the supplier has no cost risk under a CPFF contract, the profit potential is low. For example, in federal government CPFF contracts, the maximum amount of fee, based upon estimated cost, is set by 10 USC 2306(d) as shown below:

Kind of Contract	Maximum Fee
Research & Development	15% of estimated cost
Architect & Engineering	6% of estimated cost
All others	10% of estimated cost

The buyer should remember that the final cost should be audited. Purchasing departments spend hours negotiating the right to inspect the actual invoices for material and the hours worked. Many, however, don't conduct an appropriate audit. It is a good use of time to look at the details even though one might not expect to find any inappropriate charges. The knowledge gained will often prove helpful in future negotiations.

Computing the final payment due the supplier under a CPFF contract is simply a matter of adding the incurred costs (assuming that an audit has found them to be reasonable, allowable, and allocable) to the fixed fee. In the case of a CPFF contract with an estimated cost of $1,000,000 and a fixed fee of $50,000, some possible final contract price outcomes are shown below:

	(in thousands)			
Final cost	$800	$900	$1,000	$1,200
Fixed fee	50	50	50	50
Price to be paid to the supplier	850	950	1,050	1,250

The buyer must remember that in a cost-type contract, the limit is on the fee, not on total customer obligation. Obviously, the CPFF-type contract should be used only when the buyer cannot get a more favorable arrangement or when the presence of great uncertainty and risk would result in inclusion of a large contingency in a firm fixed-price contract. The CPFF contract also is appropriate in circumstances where the technical and schedule risk is so high that the cost risk is too large for the supplier to assume. This type of contract is designed chiefly for use in research or exploratory development when the uncertainty of performance is so great that a firm price or an incentive arrangement cannot be set up at any time during the life of the contract.

Cost-Plus-Award-Fee Arrangements

Cost-plus-award-fee (CPAF) contracts are a relatively new approach to compensating suppliers. The FPI and CPIF contracts have been found useful in motivating a supplier in various areas, including cost, schedule, and performance. However, there are times when the buyer may wish to motivate the supplier to perform in areas that are not susceptible to the quantitative measurement, such as management, responsiveness, and creativity.

The Award Fee. The CPAF contract provides for a base fee and for an additional fee amount (award fee) that may be awarded, in whole or in part, based upon periodic evaluations of ongoing supplier performance. A CPAF arrangement does not include predetermined targets and automatic fee adjustment formulas. The amount of award fee earned, if any, is a judgmental determination made unilaterally by the customer. This award fee amount is *not* subject to conventional disputes procedures, adjudication, or arbitration. Such a contract requires a high level of integrity and trust on the part of both buyer and seller. Experience has shown that the individuals responsible for determining the size of the award fees to be paid for any period have been objective and that the fees awarded have been reasonable.

The Base Fee. The base fee under a CPAF arrangement should be limited to 3 percent of estimated target cost. This compensates the supplier for factors such as management and investment commensurate with the level of performance categorized as the minimum acceptable. The award fee is the amount available to reward the supplier for performance above minimum performance in the areas described by the evaluation criteria. The total amount should be allocated by the established evaluation periods. Where appropriate, larger portions may be assigned to the more critical performance and evaluation periods.

The total fee available (base fee plus award fee) should not exceed the limitations established for CPFF and CPIF contracts as shown earlier. The amount the supplier receives in total payment will be the sum of the reasonable, allowable, allocable costs, the base fee, and the amount of the award fee awarded by the customer. The determination by the customer is made based on a negotiated award fee plan that includes categories for evaluation, criteria to be applied, and timing of evaluation periods.

Cost Reimbursement

Under a cost reimbursement (CR) contract, the customer agrees to reimburse the supplier for all allowable and allocable costs incurred in performance of the contract, but no fee is paid. Cost allowability is determined in accordance with appropriate procurement policies and procedures, cost-accounting standards, and any specific provisions of the contract. Because of the no-fee feature, this arrangement has limited appeal. Generally, its use is restricted to either research contracts with educational institutions or contracts providing facilities to suppliers. It is also typical of management consulting contracts, but the word *cost* is misleading since the hourly or daily rate is often three to five times the salaries of the consultants assigned and obviously includes overhead and substantial profit.

Cost-Sharing

Under a cost-sharing (CS) arrangement, the customer agrees to reimburse the supplier for only a predetermined portion of the allowable costs of contract performance. The supplier agrees to absorb a part of the cost of performance in the expectation of subsequent compensating benefits. Such benefits might include an enhancement of the supplier's capability and expertise or an improvement of its competitive position in the marketplace. An example would be where a software firm develops a specialized program for a customer for 5 percent of the cost but retains the right to sell the software to other firms.

Most cost-sharing arrangements are designed for the procurement of basic and applied research. The amount of cost participation by the supplier will vary in accordance with a number of factors, such as character of the research effort, profit or nonprofit status of the organization, potential application of results to other research activities, and commercial applicability.

Cost participation by educational institutions and other not-for-profit or nonprofit suppliers normally should be within a range from 1 percent to 20 percent of total direct and allocated indirect costs. Cost participation by commercial contractors could range from as little as 1 percent to more than 50 percent of the total contract cost. Whatever cost-sharing arrangement is negotiated, the point is that participation is intended to serve the mutual interest of the customer and contract performers to assure the efficient use of resources for the conduct of research projects.

Time and Materials

Time and material (T+M) contracts are used to buy labor at a fixed and specified hourly rate that includes direct labor, indirect costs and profit, and materials at cost. They are designed for situations where the amount or duration of work cannot be predicted and, as a result, where the costs cannot be estimated realistically. They frequently are used to buy repair and overhaul services.

Under a T+M contract, the supplier can increase indirect cost absorption and profits by expending additional hours of direct labor.

T+M contracts also may be abused if the supplier uses lower-graded labor than was priced out in the hourly rate. This may benefit the supplier in two ways. First, it provides a favorable differential in rates. Second, less-skilled laborers may take more hours to perform the job. These potential hazards make it necessary to administer T+M arrangements closely to insure that the supplier exercises proper control and restraint.

The T+M supplier should be reimbursed for the cost of materials plus certain other stated costs. Reasonable and allocable material-handling costs may be included in the charge for material at cost if they are clearly excluded from the fixed hourly labor rate. Subcontract costs should be limited to the amount actually paid to the subcontractor. The costs arising from the letting, administration, or supervision of subcontract performance should not be paid since they are included in the overhead covered by the hourly rate.

There are three reasons for limiting payment for material at cost, without a provision for profit or fee. First, profit for the contract is provided in the hourly rate. Second, this approach avoids a markup on a cost not under the buyer's control. Third, when time and materials are used to buy maintenance and overhauls, the buyer usually wants the supplier to repair rather than replace. To the extent that this is economical, the absence of a provision for profit on materials makes replacement a less-attractive alternative for the supplier.

PURCHASING RECURRING REQUIREMENTS

Large quantities required over long periods of time normally are purchased on an annual (or longer-term) basis. Such purchase orders and contracts can have many benefits: lower prices, additional services performed by the supplier (e.g., locating inventory points at or near the customer), assured sources of supply, and protection against unjustified price increases. In addition, the buyer's work load is reduced, allowing him or her to devote efforts to other areas. Most recurring requirements for production materials are negotiated on an annual basis (frequently with the escalation provision previously described). If substantial start-up costs are involved—whether for equipment, training of personnel, or other reasons—then a multiyear contract may be appropriate. With a multiyear contract, capital investment costs are amortized over the life of the contract with a provision for payment of unamortized costs in the event of early termination by the buying firm. Several of the more commonly employed approaches to different demand patterns (timing) are described next.

Definite Delivery (Quantity and Time) Contract

This is the ideal type of contract for purchasing recurring requirements, based on maximum certainty on the part of the purchaser and supplier. Prices are negotiated based on definite quantities for delivery on specified dates. The resulting advantages are as follows:

- The same or lower unit prices can result as when all deliveries are made at one time, since the total quantity is set, and yet the supplier will be paid as shipments are made.
- Less material handling is required. The material can move from the loading dock to the machining or assembly area, eliminating the move from the dock to the warehouse.
- Inventory carrying costs are reduced.
- Pressure on the customer's cash flow is reduced as a result of spreading payments over the contract period.

Definite Quantity, Indefinite Time Contract

When total quantities required for a period of time are known, but production schedules cannot be planned, it is recommended the contract be for a known quantity at given unit prices and lead times with a provision that delivery will be scheduled on an "as required" basis.

Systems Contracts, Systems Purchasing, or Demand Contract

Such contracts call for the purchaser to order all requirements for an item (or class of items) from the supplier, usually at stated prices and lead times. This type of contract frequently is used to purchase maintenance, repair, and operating (MRO) supplies. When used to buy standard items, the supplier provides either a catalog of all items to be supplied with a price for each item or the firm's standard catalog with a discount applying to the prices shown. This approach makes it possible for authorized company personnel not in purchasing to obtain supplies at negotiated prices immediately and directly from the supplier. The time saved by purchasing personnel is another benefit. At the end of the contract period, there is no obligation to purchase any remaining inventory since nothing is special.

Indefinite Quantity Contract, Blanket Orders, and Corporate Agreements

Such contracts provide for the delivery of indefinite quantities between designated low and high quantities at agreed-to prices and lead times. These contracts tend to result in unit prices somewhat higher than when known quantities are involved. However, these prices are significantly more attractive than if the items are purchased on several purchase orders as required.

Price Indexing

Price indexing contracts may be used when purchasing recurring requirements of capital equipment and commodities whose prices are extremely unstable. (See Appendix F.) Delivery lead times are established together with a provision that the price is the indexed price in effect on the date of shipment. The buyer can gain significant savings by negotiating the date of shipment. Price index figures are available on a monthly basis from the U.S. Department of Labor, Bureau of Labor Statistics. (See page 375.)

Many firms now employ their material requirements planning (MRP) system to make calls against these various types of contracts. The daily or weekly MRP printouts are sent directly by mail, by fax, or by electronic data interchange to the appropriate supplier, who treats the printout as a delivery order. This allows purchasing personnel to focus their attention on more profit-saving areas than placing delivery orders.

CONCLUDING REMARKS

A buyer can, in most instances, enter into a firm-fixed-price contract even when significant cost risk is present. But if risk is high, the buyer usually will experience either of two equally unsatisfactory results: (1) the contract price will include a large contingency or (2) the supplier could incur a loss. The possibility of a loss may result in (1) reduced quality in an effort to minimize the loss, (2) a request to renegotiate, (3) refusal to complete the work, (4) insolvency resulting in the loss of a good supplier, or (5) a "grin and bear it" approach.

The selection of the contract compensation arrangement to be used for a specific contract is an important determination. The selection must be based on the cost risk involved and the circumstances surrounding the procurement. The compensation agreement selected must result in a reasonable allocation of the cost risk and should provide adequate motivation to the supplier to assure effective performance. In addition, the compensation arrangement selected must be compatible with the supplier's accounting system.

It is the authors' observation that sound application of these compensation methods will significantly reduce expenditures when cost risk is present.

We are now in a position to use the tools of cost, price, and profit analysis in the vital area of negotiations. This topic is discussed at length in the next chapter.

RECOMMENDED READING

Richard G. Newman, "Validation of Contract Compliance under Systems Contracting," *Journal of Purchasing and Material Management,* Summer 1985: 14-21.

Chapter 14

Negotiation

Negotiation is the process of fair and businesslike bargaining between buyers and sellers aimed at a sound agreement on price and all other contract terms. Negotiation and competitive bidding are the major methods of arriving at the price paid in private business. Competitive bidding involves an invitation or request for bids, bid evaluation, and award to the responsible bidder whose bid is most advantageous, considering price and other factors.

In the private sector, the buyer frequently negotiates with some of the bidders. The practice of negotiating after receiving bids should *not* be misused in an effort to force prices down. Buyers who do this soon do *not* receive the potential supplier's lowest price offer on the initial proposal. Instead, suppliers play the buyer's game by submitting higher initial bids, hoping to "win" in the subsequent negotiations. Frequently, a higher acquisition price results than had the buyer earned a reputation as one who plays the competitive bidding game fairly.

On the other hand, professional buyers *do* undertake discussions with the supplier with the lowest acceptable bid in an effort to reduce the supplier's costs and thereby its price. The practice of discussions after bid opening is especially desirable when bids are difficult to compare. Such discussions frequently result in lower costs and price. The reasons are

- better understanding of the requirement,
- elimination of contingency costs,

- customer revisions,
- agreement to use alternative materials, and
- related suggestions by the supplier.

Competitive bidding usually results in a fair and reasonable price and is appropriate when the following conditions apply:

- The specifications are so clear that prospective suppliers may estimate their costs with a high degree of precision. If the specifications are unclear, prospective suppliers may protect themselves from uncertainties by submitting bids or quotations that include extra dollars for contingencies. Or, they may submit bids which will not cover the cost of producing the desired level of quality. Price renegotiations, conflicts, or "corner cutting" (resulting in quality problems) are the likely results.
- The amount of money involved is sufficient to offset the administrative expense involved in competitive bidding.
- There are many potential suppliers, and several of them will be willing to price competitively.
- There is enough time for competitive bidding. Developing requests for bids, mailing, opening the resulting bids, and evaluating them requires considerable time. Additionally, adequate bid preparation time must be afforded to the firms from whom bids are being solicited.

WHEN TO NEGOTIATE

Negotiations can reduce areas of uncertainty (and contingency pricing) and should be used:

- When there is a chance material prices will rise. The supplier may have included a contingency large enough to offer protection under most conditions. The use of negotiation allows the two parties to tailor an escalation provision that gives the buyer the prospect of a significant reduction in total expenditure through the assumption of some of the seller's risk.
- When the buyer is concerned about the relative emphasis placed on price, quality, timeliness, and service. Competitive

bidding requires that minimum standards be established for all requirements, leaving price alone to vary. In many instances, the buyer may be willing to pay now for earlier delivery. On the other hand, a lower price might be obtained provided the buyer accepts a later delivery. Where trade-off situations may be present, negotiation is the way to arrive at a contractual agreement.

- When quality is of concern. Negotiation usually lays a better foundation for obtaining the desired quality. Negotiations result in a far better understanding on *all* terms and conditions than does competitive bidding.

- When there is considerable uncertainty about the amount of engineering effort, quantity of materials, or labor required. Discussions between buyer and seller may be able to reduce or eliminate the uncertainty in these areas. If not, and if the dollar amount involved is significant, then one of the alternatives to a firm-fixed-price contract described in Chapter 13 may be appropriate.

- When a supplier must make or purchase special purpose tooling or test equipment. Questions of cost allocation and ownership frequently arise in such situations.

- When the buyer's requirements may be subject to numerous changes. If prospective suppliers recognize the likelihood of numerous changes, there is a good chance that they will "buy in" by submitting unrealistically low prices. This low-price proposal is submitted with the expectation of "getting well" or even gouging the buyer on the anticipated changes. It is far sounder to negotiate with two or three prospective suppliers and develop workable procedures with the chosen supplier for dealing with such anticipated changes.

- When the internal customer has only one supplier in mind because of previous experience, a very specific requirement, or even a friend at that supplier. Under such a condition, the professional buyer must be a skilled negotiator; both internally and externally, to prevent the seller from taking advantage of the situation.

THE NEGOTIATING TEAM

Usually the buyer can do the negotiating job alone or with limited help from the requiring activity. However, for complex procurements, the negotiation should not be a "one-person show." The buyer should call into being a negotiating team to help define requirements, discuss strategy, and prepare for negotiations. The team usually lasts until the contract has been negotiated and awarded and then is disbanded. The supplier usually does not see the entire team. The actual negotiation must be done by a small group that has no "loose cannons" who say inappropriate things. Members of this small team must know how to negotiate together.

The Team Leader

In most circumstances, the buyer should be the negotiating team chief. He or she provides overall knowledge of the procurement situation and information on special contract clauses that may influence prices, past buys of the same or similar material or equipment, experience with the offeror or offerors, and similar factors. The buyer may or may not be the principal negotiator, depending on organization concepts, assignments, and obviously the skills available. Basically, the best person available should be named the principal negotiator. The following characteristics of an effective negotiator, as identified by researcher John Hammon, should serve as a guide when selecting the individual to be the principal negotiator:[1]

- Preparation and planning skill
- Knowledge of the subject matter being negotiated
- The ability to think clearly and rapidly under pressure and uncertainty
- The ability to express thoughts orally
- The ability to listen
- Judgment and general intelligence
- Integrity

---

1. The study and findings are reported by Howard Raifla in *The Art and Science of Negotiation* (Cambridge: The Belknap Press of Harvard University Press, 1982), 119-122.

- The ability to persuade others
- Patience and decisiveness

Other team members may include requesters, estimators, project engineers, price analysts, legal experts, operations specialists/engineers, and auditors.

Requesters, Estimators, and Project Engineers

These individuals are responsible for determining technical requirements, preparing the independent cost estimate, assisting the buyer in developing the evaluation criteria, evaluating the offeror's technical proposals, and assisting in the technical evaluation of the offeror's price proposals. As the individuals who determine what is required, they influence every aspect of the procurement process.

Price Analysts

A price analyst may be designated to assist and to make recommendations on pricing matters including establishing any requirements for submission by prospective suppliers of cost data, reviewing the data received for adequacy, determining the need for and obtaining pricing proposal review by other specialists, and combining available information with his or her own analysis into an objective position.

Lawyers

In the majority of firms, legal review is required for bilateral contracts over a specified dollar threshold. After all, if the contract is poorly drawn, the best negotiating efforts will be wasted. If specifications, terms, and conditions are not clear and binding on all parties, costly problems can develop later. Ideally, the specifications and proposed terms and conditions should be reviewed prior to release of the request for bid or proposal. Legal review can identify potential inadequacies and inconsistencies before they become a problem.

Operations Specialists/Engineers

Based on their professional knowledge and familiarity with a supplier's operations, these technical experts have information that can be used to build a cost and quality analysis of the supplier's proposal. Experts in production, quality, and manufacturing can provide evaluations of such areas as plant capacity, equipment capabilities, and engineering and production know-how.

Auditors

An auditor should be a member of the team when the forthcoming contract provides for access to the supplier's books and financial records. Frequently, this function must be performed by the buyer. However, an auditor can be an important contributor to the evaluation of the supplier's actual incurred and estimated costs. Any denial by the supplier of access to records or cost or pricing data that the auditor considers essential must be reported to the buyer. Furthermore, the auditor must advise the buyer and supplier if the supplier's financial methods, accounting system, or records are inadequate to produce valid support.

THREE KEYS TO SUCCESSFUL NEGOTIATIONS

There are three keys common to most successful negotiations:

- careful preparation
- proposal analysis and the establishment of realistic objectives
- skillful face-to-face problem solving

Preparing for Negotiations

There are seven aspects of preparation: (1) understanding the nature and context of the negotiation, (2) technical preparation, (3) price and cost analysis, (4) understanding the relative bargaining power of the parties, (5) the buyer's self-knowledge, (6) understanding the seller, and (7) purchasing research.

Nature and Context of the Negotiation. The buyer begins the preparation process by answering two important questions:

- Is this a one-time deal, or are continuing relations important?
- Is it possible to enlarge the pie to develop an integrative solution wherein both parties are better off?

Technical Preparation. The buyer should know the specifications, the production process involved, and their effect on cost and quality. The buyer need not understand all the technical ramifications of the item but should be be aware of its use and limitations, as well as its critical components. The nature of the item affects the price, quality requirements, methods of contract pricing, terms of the resulting purchase order or subcontract, and the bargaining position of the two parties.

The buyer should be aware of the procurement history of the item or similar items and any of the work that can or must be performed by other than the prospective supplier. The buyer should know the language and phraseology used in the particular industry. The buyer should be aware of prospective engineering problems and other areas of uncertainty that the seller is apt to encounter.

Available Price and Cost Data. Once there is an understanding of the item to be purchased, the buyer needs to study available price and cost data. The ideal situation is one in which there are adequate competition, historic price data, and a detailed cost estimate. As discussed in Chapter 7, when price analysis does not lead to a conclusion that the price is fair and reasonable, it generally is necessary to employ cost analysis. Ideally, it should be possible to begin cost analysis by comparing the prospective supplier's cost breakdown with that developed by the buyer's engineering department or with a buyer developed cost model. (See Chapter 8.)

Relative Bargaining Power. Several factors affect the buyer's and seller's respective bargaining power:

Seller's Need for the Sale. The more urgently the seller desires a specific order, the weaker his or her bargaining position becomes. The buyer can gain insight into the seller's position through a review of published data, Dun & Bradstreet reports, and the judicious use of preaward surveys.

Importance of Each Issue. How important is each issue to the buyer's side? To the seller's side? This information is important when developing trade-offs.

Buyer's Bargaining Position. What is the buyer's best alternative to an agreement? This analysis is overlooked by many negotiators. Yet, it is of crucial importance.

Seller's Perception of Its Bargaining Position. Does the seller perceive that it has the "inside track" for a particular order? If the seller realizes that it is the only or the preferred source, the seller's bargaining position is greatly enhanced. One of the greatest dangers in the use of a negotiating team is that nonpurchasing team members frequently disclose information on the presence or absence of competition to the seller. The seller's possession of such information can be devastating to the buyer's negotiating position. The existence (or even the appearance) of competition is one of the buyer's major negotiating strengths.

Adequate Lead Time. Inadequate procurement lead time weakens the buyer's bargaining position and results in an inability to obtain adequate competition (a buyer's best friend). It also allows the seller to cause delays during negotiations, secure in the belief that the buyer is under severe pressure to conclude an agreement. Conversely, the seller, or the seller's representatives, may be under time pressure. For example, it is 8:30 p.m. on the last day of the month, and the agency is one sale short of meeting the month's extra bonus quota.

Availability of Cost Data. Adequate cost data and the time and willingness to analyze them greatly assist the buyer in establishing realistic cost objectives and in obtaining a fair and reasonable price. Well-developed cost models are invaluable when supplier-furnished data are unavailable.

What Alternatives Does the Buyer Have? The answer to this question determines the buyer's power.

The Buyer's Self-Appraisal. "What skills do you bring to a negotiation? What preparation can increase your confidence, performance, and power?" Successful negotiators know themselves and their opponents; they understand the items to be purchased, and they are versed in the areas of accounting, business law, economics, human behavior, and quantitative methods. They are skilled in the techniques of negotiation and conference leadership. They are skilled planners, master strategists, and expert tacticians. They view issues and problems from the vantage point of the firm's well-being and not that of their department or their own individual needs. They excel in good judgment. They are among a firm's most valued employees and should be one of the most highly paid professionals.[2]

Knowledge of the Supplier and Its Representatives. The buyer can never know too much about the people with whom he or she is going to negotiate. The buyer should examine the supplier's past history and study the records of previous transactions with the supplier (both successful and unsuccessful). Frequently, more insight into people can be gained from their failures than from their successes. In the process of this research, the buyer is coming to understand the supplier's needs and behavioral patterns. This insight will be invaluable during the course of negotiations.

Is the seller internally monolithic, or are there conflicting factions which have to negotiate among themselves? How can this insight be used to develop an integrative solution? Will the seller's representatives have the authority to enter into a binding agreement without approval of the home office? If not, ratification may be used to squeeze out one more concession from the buyer.

Purchasing Research. The buyer should have the latest information available on the nature, character of the industry, and needs of the firm with whom he or she is about to negotiate. Visits to prospective suppliers give the buyer an opportunity to gain insight into the supplier's organization, capabilities, executives, and needs.

In addition, much useful information is available in published material including financial statements, published reports, press releases, advertising, governmental reports, Dun & Bradstreet reports, and speeches by officials of the firm.

The professional buyer's role is that of fire fighter, mediator, sometimes expediter, but most importantly, skilled negotiator. Much of the buyer's time is spent keeping orders flowing, negotiating, and dealing with suppliers and interested customers. The time available to gather detailed, thorough, and useful information is generally

---

2. Based on Donald W. Dobler, David N. Burt, Lamar Lee, Jr., *Purchasing and Materials Management: Text and Cases,* 5th ed. (New York: McGraw-Hill, 1990).

small. The buyer can and does stay informed on the general market in his or her area of responsibility—but by sheer pressure of other demands on his or her time, the buyer generally is not able to pursue the detailed information that only *MIGHT* be available.

To insure adequate preparation, Polaroid purchasing offers its buyers the assistance of former buyers who have developed expertise in purchasing research. These individuals specialize in tracking prices, developing economic scenarios, cost modeling, and searching for the best data bases. They help gather detailed data, general economic information, and the special considerations of the specific industry. Appendix D contains two examples of data provided to buyers by purchasing research at Polaroid.

The buyer who needs assistance meets with the researcher. The researcher, by asking incisive questions, sets the scope for a series of data base searches that enhance the buyer's knowledge of the supplier. The resulting insight gives the buyer negotiating leverage and clout.

The ideal background for conducting purchasing intelligence (purchasing research) includes

- a broad business education, preferably an M.B.A., with an undergraduate business or technical degree
- an avid reader and searcher for useful information
- an inquiring mind
- the ability to counsel buyers, not dominate them or take over their negotiations
- a positive attitude that allows the researcher to undertake a search when it is not clear that there will be any success, and
- an innovative attitude to expand the application of data base information.

A New Tool for Preparation: On-Line Data Bases.[3] The amount of business information being printed is beyond anyone's comprehension. But, with the advent of on-line data bases, the buyer has

---

3. This section is based on W. E. Norquist, "The Ultimate in Negotiation Preparation: On-Line Data Bases," in *Purchasing's New Frontiers* (Tempe, AZ: NAPM, 1988).

instant access to the most recent information as well as to historical data at a fraction of the time and cost needed for a library search. With a personal computer a buyer can have information at his or her fingertips.

There are more than 2,000 data bases available. To speed access, data bases like Dialog Information Services, which is traditionally used by professional researchers, are replacing their fairly difficult search sequences with simplified menus. It is now easier for buyers to use these tools. Other services that lead in subscribers and options are Dow Jones News Retrieval, CompuServe, The Source, and Prodigy. These services are wholesales, and each provides access to many individual data bases.

Purchasers can locate information including

- potential suppliers
- background information on a supplier including all the information published during a desired time period
- capacity, cost, and price information on raw materials and components
- financial data on suppliers and their competitors
- the state of current technology and potential technology
- labor rates, availability of raw materials, and new processes, and
- forecasts of economic, business, and market conditions.

Being fully informed "manually" is almost an impossible task, even though the buyer knows that in negotiations, business intelligence is power. Now that the information is available electronically, the buyer can greatly increase the knowledge he or she brings to any negotiation.

Polaroid procurement people have used Dialog to be better prepared for negotiations. Three examples of data bases used are listed below:

- MAGAZINE INDEX™. This is an on-line data base that covers 435 magazines. It has the complete text of more than 100 magazines published since 1983.

- The NEWSPAPER ABSTRACTS. This data base provides comprehensive indexing and abstracting for 19 major newspapers published since 1984.
- TS NEWSLETTER DATABASE. This data base contains the full text of over 100 of the specialized industry newsletters.

Purchasing professionals can support a cost containment effort with timely information such as price indexes, capacity utilization, and cost information. This information can be gained from such data bases. Appendix G describes how the professional buyer uses on-line data bases.

While databases are unequalled for retrieving historical information (information older than one day), other services now available can provide "current-awareness" information daily to keep buyers updated on developments in the companies or markets they need to be tracking. One "current-awareness" service used at Polaroid is called *First!* (Individual, Inc., 84 Sherman Street, Cambridge, MA), which has several advantages:

1. By responding to plain English requests from the user, *First!* removes the burden of learning various complex retrieval languages.

2. Such services continuously act as an agent on behalf of the user, seeking information from multiple news wires and electronic sources, delivering that information daily to the user's desk via fax or electronic mail. It can make the latest information available to buyers that are in organizations too small to have purchasing researchers available.

3. By taking advantage of new software technology which analyzes the topics and concepts within each article, the service called *First!* is able to identify those business and economic news items of greatest relevance to the buyer. This eliminates the cost and time associated with traditional search methods, which can pick up many stories of marginal interest.

4. *First!* becomes more intelligent at identifying relevant articles and can adapt to the buyer's evolving interests by re-

questing simple feedback as to which stories were most relevant. This eliminates the need for re-writing a complex search and forgives the user for not being exhaustive in describing their interests and target companies in the original search request.

5. The buyer's knowledge of current and very applicable information can be greatly enhanced at a cost equal to about 5 or 10 percent of a buyer's salary.

Initial Proposal Analysis and the Development of Objectives

The second key to successful negotiations involves the development of realistic negotiation objectives. If the buyer anticipated employing negotiations to arrive at an agreement on price, then the request for bids should require that supporting cost data be furnished with the supplier's bid and that the buyer will have access to such additional cost data as may reasonably be required. As discussed in Chapter 8, the time to establish these rights is when there is competition or the appearance of competition.

Technical analysis must be conducted to measure the proposal's satisfaction of the internal customer's technical requirements. In technical analysis, the proposal is compared with the evaluation criteria previously established by the negotiation team.[4]

At this initial stage, the analysis also addresses such areas as proposal trackability to support data, an evaluation of cost risk, and cost realism. Ideally, the buyer can obtain whatever data is required to make the price decision. As a practical matter, the buyer's analysis is limited chiefly by the value of the contract and the availability of relevant data.

Award without Another Round of Negotiation. Minor informalities or irregularities and apparent clerical mistakes may be resolved substantially as they would be under competitive bidding, and communications with offerors required to resolve such matters should not be considered additional negotiations.

---

4. John A. Carlisle and Robert C. Parker, in their provocative book, *Beyond Negotiation*, discuss the use of "mandate teams" to develop the negotiating objectives.

Competitive Range. When discussions, written or oral, are required, they should be conducted with all offerors in the competitive range. The competitive range is determined on the basis of price or cost, technical, and other salient factors and should include all proposals that have a reasonable chance of being selected for award.

Establishing Objectives. Several basic objectives are common to most negotiations:

- Agreement on the quality to be provided and procedures for ensuring this level of quality
- Agreement on timely delivery (including production schedules)
- Agreement on a fair and reasonable price (Note: if the agreement is to be part of a long-term, collaborative relationship, the price should include a profit objective adequate to allow the supplier to invest in appropriate R&D, process engineering, and equipment to remain price and technologically competitive.)
- Adequate control over the manner in which the purchase order or subcontract is performed (especially in the areas of quality, quantity, and service)
- A commitment for necessary cooperation
- A continuing relationship with competent suppliers

The proposal can be broken apart and its elements questioned to identify areas that must be explored in detail. The buyer assembles actual historical costs of performing the same kinds of tasks. The historic costs are the basis against which the buyer will measure the probable future costs of performance under the proposed contract. Caution must be employed to ensure that the historic costs were based on efficient operations.

Specific negotiation objectives should be established for all items to be discussed during the negotiation including the following, as applicable:

- All technical and quality aspects
- Types of materials and substitutes
- Purchaser-furnished material or equipment
- The mode of transportation and liability for claims and damage
- FOB point

- General terms and conditions
- Progress reports
- Production control plans
- Labor content and prices
- Overhead
- General and administrative expenses
- Profit
- Incentive arrangements (if other than fixed-price contract)
- Patent infringement protection
- Packaging
- Warranty terms and conditions
- Escalation provisions (if fixed price with escalation)
- Payment terms (including discount provisions)
- Patents
- Responsibilities of the purchaser

As appropriate, an acceptable range and target should be established for each item subject to negotiation. The range should be bracketed by a minimum and maximum position. The minimum position should be based on the outcome if everything during production were to work out favorably. The maximum position is based on the premise that virtually every action required by the supplier will require the utmost effort. The target position is the negotiator's estimate of the most likely outcome for any element being negotiated. It should be the point at which the prospects for overrunning the estimate are substantially the same as for underrunning it.

On critical procurements, the buyer also should establish what he or she believes to be the seller's range and target for any item of discussion. Understanding the needs and objectives of one's counterpart can facilitate the ensuing discussions.

Face-to-Face Problem Solving

Professional face-to-face problem solving is the third key to more successful negotiations. For major negotiations, this can be thought of as a four-phase process and may involve a buying team, not just a buyer. During the first phase, the buying team gains additional information and investigates any inconsistency between the prospective supplier's proposal and its position. During the second phase, the buying team reviews and revises its objectives and develops a tactical plan for obtaining its objectives. In the third phase, the buying team attempts to narrow or close the difference between the seller's and its own position. This is done through the use of logic and persuasion. In the majority of cases, agreement is reached in this phase. During the fourth phase, agreement is reached (or not reached) through compromise and hard bargaining.

Phase 1: Fact-Finding. Prior to face-to-face negotiations, the buying team will have analyzed all available information in an effort to determine the reasonableness of the proposal. When meeting with the supplier, the team should investigate any inconsistencies between the proposal and its supporting information. Detailed questions of a who, when, how, what, and why nature should be employed to pursue specific points. Any issues or disagreements should be defined precisely but *not* negotiated at this phase of problem solving. The fact-finding should continue until the buying team has a complete understanding of the supplier's proposal. Not only does the team come to understand the supplier's position, but also the supplier's strengths and weaknesses.

As buyers move from adversarial to collaborative relations, it becomes necessary to gain an understanding of the seller's, and any representative's, interests. The basic problem in a negotiation lies not in the differences of the buyer's and seller's positions, but in the conflict between their interests: their needs, desires, concerns, and fears. Information on the seller's interests is gained through the use of "why" questions. The buyer is attempting to understand the seller's interests. In response, the buyer or buying team should be willing to communicate its interests. Such communication provides the basis of a pie-expanding, integrative solution during Phase Three.[5] On completing the first or fact-finding phase, the buyer should call a recess.

Phase 2: Recess. During the recess the buying team, under the buyer's leadership, should analyze the strengths and weaknesses of

---

5. For information on the development of integrative solutions, see Roger Fisher and William Ury, *Getting to Yes: Negotiating Agreement Without Giving In* (New York: Penguin Books, 1981).

each party on each important issue. Target objectives and maximum and minimum positions should be revised as appropriate. The buyer desires to create a contractual climate that will encourage the supplier to control costs, while maintaining quality and making timely delivery. For instance, the team may have concluded that the work should be done for $275,000 but may also acknowledge that the final cost might be as low as $230,000 or as high as $300,000. When developing the cost objective, the team should consider this range and the probability of incurring each level of cost. The cost level selected as the buyer's objective should be the one the buyer (negotiation team) feels is the most likely to be incurred in performing the contract. An agenda should be developed. Strong and weak points should be identified. Any items or topics that should be avoided during the next phases should be noted. Items whose targets must be achieved during the negotiation should be identified. A list of items or objectives that would be nice to have, but that can be traded in return for something of more importance, should be established.

Next, the buyer should anticipate the supplier's likely strategy and tactics. The buyer should identify likely responses to all points and develop rebuttals. A good negotiator will anticipate all moves and countermoves. A good negotiator becomes intimately familiar with any points likely to be discussed during the ensuing negotiations. Experienced negotiators have had success with two finishing touches when preparing for the second and third phases of critically important negotiations: "murder boards" and "mock negotiations."

A **murder board** consists of senior purchasing, manufacturing, engineering, and quality assurance personnel. The buying team presents to the board its agenda and tactics for the forthcoming discussions. The murder board discusses, analyzes, and dissects the plan in an effort to uncover weaknesses.

Mock negotiations allow the negotiating team members to prepare for face-to-face discussions with the potential supplier by simulating the forthcoming negotiations. Senior members of purchasing and other suitably qualified members of management play the roles of the supplier's negotiating team members. A mock negotiation is conducted prior to entering the third and fourth phases.

Both murder boards and mock negotiations have the additional benefit of upper management becoming aware of the buying team's objectives and tactics. Negotiations have a way of escalating. Through the use of murder boards and mock negotiations, senior personnel are prepared, should they subsequently become involved in negotiations.

Before entering face-to-face negotiations, the buyer should hold a prenegotiation meeting with his or her team. The purpose is to discuss and develop a position on all important aspects and to agree generally on the role each team member will play during negotiations with the company. From time to time during a negotiation, team members may reach different conclusions because of different interpretations of matters discussed. The team members should be forewarned to avoid public disagreement. If controversy arises, the team should get together away from the prospective supplier's representatives to consult and give each member an opportunity to express his or her views. The buyer has the right and obligation to make the final decision, but should accept and use the help specialists can furnish. There cannot always be full agreement among all team members on the conclusions reached and the counteroffers made, but there should be a minimum of disagreement and no misunderstandings.

Phase 3: Narrow Differences. The buyer now takes the offensive. He or she defines each issue; states facts, conditions, and assumptions; and attempts to convince the potential supplier that the buyer's reasoning is sound. If agreement cannot be reached on an issue, the buyer may choose to state the objective and ask the supplier how to meet the objective. If agreement cannot be reached on one issue, it usually is best to move on to another agenda item. Frequently, discussions on a subsequent issue will unblock an earlier impasse. The buyer does not need to get the prospective supplier's separate agreement on an exact value for each cost element and profit. The buyer is concerned primarily with the reasonableness of the total price that ultimately is established.

To put this process into perspective, consider that both the buyer and the seller start negotiations with separate understandings of cost experience and forecasts of what it should cost to perform the work. From the supplier's point of view, the cost experience is factual and serves as the basis for cost data. Since cost experience is involved in price negotiations, the buyer should reach an understanding with the potential supplier about the facts on each significant cost element. However, *there well may be questions and differences of opinion on what the costs should be.*

The second factor, forecasts of what the work should cost, is essentially a matter of judgment about the prospective supplier's future performance in controlling and reducing contract costs and how likely some events are to occur. In evaluating forecasts, the buyer must reach conclusions about future events, consider probabilities, and weigh the cost impact of divergent actions. This requires the buyer depend on cost projections and trends and to assess how risks should be distributed, how much potential there is for cost reduction, and how to exploit this potential in the negotiation of price. These assessments may be unrelated to any specific cost element.

There are intrinsic reasons why the buyer and the supplier will differ in their views of future events. The buying team should work toward an objective that will require the supplier to exert effort to earn a fair profit. In doing this, the buyer tends to minimize the difficulties and the likelihood that unfavorable events will occur. On the other hand, the supplier can be expected to work toward achieving a negotiation objective based on the occurrence of many unfavorable events. The buying team frequently will not agree with the supplier's forecasts, and the supplier often will not agree with the buyer's. However, both forecasts should be founded on the same factual basis. Further, both parties should bargain in the understanding that the total of all forecasts is a sum of possibilities, not certainties, and they should recognize that a compromise of extremes may be necessary to reach a fair settlement.

During this third phase of negotiations, the techniques of mutual responsiveness—the process of adjusting concessions to each other's needs—can be employed. Mutual responsiveness avoids many of the problems of pure bargaining. It encourages the creation of new solutions, requires less time, creates less friction, and results in more congenial relations at both the personal and institutional levels than does bargaining.

As previously indicated, some firms are moving from adversarial to collaborative relations. During face-to-face negotiations within the concept of such relations, the focus becomes the identification of both parties' interests, their needs, desires, concerns, and fears, and then the development of an integrative solution which meets these interests. During traditional adversarial negotiations, most negotiators see their job as reducing the gap between positions. But negotiations within the context of collaborative relations focus on a broadening of the options available. This change of focus is enhanced by—even requires—trust on the part of both parties.[6]

Fisher and Ury prescribe four actions which facilitate the development of creative options:

- Separate the act of inventing options from the act of judging them
- Broaden the options on the table rather than looking for a single answer
- Search for mutual gains
- Invent ways of making decisions easy[7]

Perhaps the greatest difference between adversarial and collaborative negotiation tactics is what to do with the pie. Traditional negotiations seek to distribute a fixed pie. Negotiations within the context of collaborative relations seek first to enlarge the pie and then develop fair and acceptable procedures for distributing the enlarged pie.

In many negotiations, it is possible to reach a mutually satisfactory agreement in this phase. However, if such an agreement is not yet possible, it is necessary to employ bargaining.

Phase 4: Bargaining. Bargaining employs persuasion in moving an opponent toward one's position. Effective negotiators are aware of and employ many of the approaches described in marketing litera-

---

6. Carlisle and Parker document and demonstrate that the development of trust between the buying and supplying negotiating teams greatly facilitates the negotiation process and normally results in preferred customer-supplier relationships.

7. Fisher and Ury, *op. cit.* p. 62.

ture to achieve their objectives. Some specific negotiating techniques are described in the next section.

If persuasion fails, threats may be employed. For example, either party may threaten to break off negotiations. The buyer may threaten to take all his or her business elsewhere if the seller does not yield on a point. Or the buyer may threaten to develop alternative sources of supply or even to incorporate alternative materials. Before employing threats, one should consider their effect and the credibility of the person issuing the threat. The experienced negotiator does not bluff unless prepared to be called. Unsupportable positions should not be taken unless the buyer is willing to give them up if challenged.

Even when bargaining, the buyer and all members of the buying team should conduct themselves in an ethical manner. Distortions and misrepresentations, if detected, can disrupt or terminate the negotiation. Negotiation is not haggling or chiseling. It is an honest effort to arrive at a mutually acceptable agreement. The result of a negotiation should be an agreement that benefits both.

If either side leaves the negotiating table feeling that it has been unnecessarily abused, the stage has been set for future confrontations. An agreement reached in such a manner generally leads to future arguments, unsatisfactory performance, and the possibility of legal action.

SOME NEGOTIATING TECHNIQUES

Progress and Summaries

Avoid any attempts to sidetrack the meeting onto nonessential issues. Show progress. Use summaries to clarify understanding and to demonstrate progress.

The Use of Recesses

Recesses can be used as a tactical tool. They should be planned and executed carefully. Recesses may be used to get the members of the buying team back to functioning as a team. Do not call a recess when the potential supplier has made a strong point that cannot be refuted. Avoid revealing your weakness and proceed tactfully to the next issue.

Package Agreements

Sequential negotiations call for negotiation and agreement on all issues in turn. This approach will be much more likely to result in deadlocks than will the package approach. When a sequential agenda is followed, quid pro quo agreements are not practical.

The package approach calls for discussing individual issues with the objective of reaching agreement on each issue, if possible. If agreement on an issue is not feasible while discussing it in isolation, the needs of each party become recognized. These needs then can be dealt with in the context of an overall agreement with compromises on one issue receiving offsetting compromises on other issues. When all unresolved issues are negotiated together, such offsetting compromises or concessions are relatively easy to achieve.

New Suppliers

When a buyer and seller are entering into negotiations for the first time, it may be desirable to develop an agenda that calls for discussions on the least important issues first. This approach allows each party to feel out the opponent and make minor concessions in the hope of developing mutual trust. As mutual respect and trust develop, it will be possible to make progress on the more challenging items.

Discussions Away from the Bargaining Table

Many agreements are concluded away from the bargaining table. Informal communications conducted over lunch or cocktails may move a negotiation that appears headed for an impasse on to a successful conclusion. While considerable benefit may be gained from such discussions, the team members must recognize the social occasion for what it is: an extension of the bargaining table. The team members must conduct themselves accordingly.

Knowing When to Terminate Discussions

There are instances where one party is so stubborn or both parties are so far apart that no amount of persuasion or logic will result in an agreement. If the seller is being totally unreasonable, the buyer should consider terminating the negotiation. Such action may be in the face of demands from the requiring activity in the purchasing firm that an agreement be concluded on any terms. Such demands often are the result of failure, on the part of the requester, to allow adequate and realistic purchasing lead time and failure to consider the incorporation of competitively procurable materials into the item to be produced. The buyer should not enter into an unrealistic agreement in such circumstances.

Several benefits can result from the termination of negotiations. First, the open confrontation between buyer and the internal customer may be essential for the development of realistic discipline within the buying firm and adequate planning for future procurements. As a result, future procurements may enjoy the benefit of proper planning (lower prices, better services, more timely deliveries, etc.). Second, the break-off of negotiations may cause the seller to revise his or her estimate of the buyer's bargaining position and result in a greater willingness to enter into the give and take of true negotiations. Third, such action may move the negotiations to a higher (and, it is hoped, more reasonable) level in the seller's management. Frequently, the seller's representatives become emotionally involved in winning. Higher levels of management will tend to be less emotional and more aware of the implication of the loss of the order on the overall well-being of their firm.

Whenever possible, a well-prepared buyer tries to avoid the deadlock by being aware of the alternatives to a negotiated settlement and has considered the costs and timing involved. If excessive demands appear likely, a buyer should move quickly in anticipation of that and find possible alternatives before the negotiations start.

Perception of Power

Surprisingly large price concessions frequently result when a sole or single source of supply perceives that competition has entered the picture. A number of years ago, a buyer for a defense contractor used his firm's RFP form to gain the perception of power. The form had space available for three names and addresses of potential suppliers. The buyer had the sole source supplier's name shifted to the second position on the RFP, thereby creating the appearance of competition. The sole source's price came down by 20 percent when compared with previous bids.

Knowing When to Close

A seasoned and skilled negotiator knows when to close a negotiation. Premature efforts to close a negotiation are as bad as efforts to close too late. Once a point of agreement has been reached, close; don't keep talking. A timely summary will aid in determining if closure is possible. Say nothing that might confuse agreements already made. The agreement reached should be outlined in broad terms. Avoid introducing new issues that might result in reopening issues that have been settled.

Cross-cultural Negotiations

The negotiation principles that have been discussed apply in virtually all settings, but there are many nuances involved when dealing with people from other cultures. The following suggestions are based on the authors' own experiences doing business in other cultures and the experiences of several other purchasing and marketing professionals.

- Be sensitive to your opposites' culture. Read about their culture during the preparation phase. Ask questions of others who have experience negotiating with individuals of your opposites' culture. Obtain information on local circumstances in the country.

- Find out who your opposites are, who their families are, what their education is, and what makes them tick.

- Attempt to develop a personal rapport, a base of understanding, and a bank of goodwill.

- Be aware that in Europe, negotiations may take longer than in the United States. In Japan, negotiations may take even longer than in Europe. In both cases, the reason is the need of members of the seller's team to thoroughly assess the buyer in the context of a long-term relationship rather than in striking a deal on one project. The European or Japanese negotiating team *will* be less interested in just a one-time transaction than a serious *long-term* relationship.

- Be well prepared on all issues, especially technical ones.
- Conduct extensive price and cost analysis before the formal negotiation meeting. Do not expect your European counterpart to share with you a cost breakdown in the beginning of the relationship.
- Become familiar with applicable tax laws. Such knowledge can lead to significant price reductions.
- ROI, dividends, and profit as a percent of sales tend to be lower in many countries than in America. Consider this information during the objective-setting process.
- Obtain guidance from your controller on the issue of exchange rates and the likely costs or advantages of using a particular currency. Then negotiate the exchange rate as you would any other issue.
- Arrange issues in such a manner that your opposite can win his or her share of issues—possibly while you are winning the big ones.
- If possible, ensure that the head of the other team has the authority to reach agreement on behalf of his or her firm.
- The position of recorder is a powerful one. Be the recorder or appoint one from your team.
- Use the package approach of discussing each issue in turn, reaching agreement when possible, and finally developing an acceptable package addressing all issues.
- It is all right to be frank, open, and honest, but do not be too blunt. Be extremely cautious in being blunt during discussions. Most non-Americans are not accustomed to such an approach. It may be misunderstood and be disruptive.
- Recesses in the negotiation may be required to allow a team to gain approval of some proposal. But before such a break, an agreement must be reached on the topic to be discussed imme-

diately following the break. Otherwise, negotiations will become unnecessarily protracted.

- When negotiating in Japan, at times it may be necessary to convince the whole group whose activities will be influenced by the proposed transaction. Some Japanese companies include junior people as observers for training purposes and as recorders. It's important to recognize this situation when it exists.

- Americans tend to be uncomfortable with extended silences; the Japanese are not. They feel no compulsion to break a silence. An American's impatience or desire to "hammer out an agreement" results in breaking such extended silences, frequently yielding or compromising on the point being discussed. *A good negotiator will be content to allow the silence to run its course, rather than volunteering a concession in order to break the silence.*

- Unless the company has local representatives, it may be helpful to use a consultant who is experienced in the culture.

DEALING WITH AN INFLEXIBLE SUPPLIER

Thus far, the discussion has assumed that the supplier is responsive; willing to enter into constructive, problem-solving discussions; and willing to work toward a "win/win" agreement. But, what about negotiations with a sole (only one available) or single source (chosen one of many) supplier who says, "That's the deal: take it or leave it"?

Robert M. Benedict, in his forthcoming book, *Negotiating in the Real World of Purchasing and Engineering,* advocates the following action:

- Combine single sourced and nonsingle sourced requirements into one contract. The buying firm gains clout and, frequently, cooperation.

- Componentize—break out the item under discussion to determine if some or many of its components can be procured from responsive suppliers.

- Go back to the end user to determine if the supplier truly must be a sole source. Frequently, discussing the supplier's business practices with the internal customer results in pressure by the customer on the supplier to be reasonable and responsive. In other cases, the customer may revise the requirement to allow competitive sourcing from more responsive suppliers.
- After verifying a long-term need for the item, discuss the advantages of a long-term contract. The supplier knows that during a two- to four-year time frame its customer could design it out, retool, and/or qualify another supplier.
- Investigate the feasibility of making the item. To be effective, an actual study must be constructed with purchasing soliciting proposals for required equipment and materials. Internal customers and outside suppliers will transmit information on such activities to the recalcitrant supplier.
- If the supplier's demands cloud the financial attractiveness of the product or project, develop the appropriate analysis and share it with the supplier.
- Investigate the use of alternate materials.
- Point out to the supplier that inflexibility may (will) result in that supplier not being considered for future business of a competitive nature.
- Use a "long-term" supplier meeting which
  - > repositions the time frame (from short-term to a three- to five-year time period)
  - > escalates discussions from the buyer-salesperson level to directorial and vice presidential levels, and
  - > introduces the prospect of increased future business through a presentation by the buying firm's marketing team.

John Kappler, Vice President Finance and CEO, DUECO, a worldwide dealer in large equipment, offers the following levers to be used by the buyer who is negotiating with a difficult sole or a single source supplier.

- Does the supplier's corporate operating profit exceed your company's operating profit?
- Is there an unsettled warranty or other claim?
- Is the supplier blasé about below-standard service representatives?
- Is the supplier actively increasing its service capabilities?
- Have there been billing errors?
- Are there sufficient coordination meetings?
- Are there problems in the order-fill rate?
- Has the supplier reduced its investment in R&D?
- Does the supplier conduct technical development seminars for your company personnel?
- Has the supplier submitted a reasonable number of cost reduction recommendations?
- Are late deliveries a problem?
- Has the supplier introduced product improvements intended to reduce customer costs?

DOCUMENTATION[8]

It is essential to accurately document price reasonableness when required by law or when the purchase is a major one. Personnel turnover rules out reliance on memory. The value of contract files in succeeding procurements can make stand-alone documentation essential. These written memorandums should permit reconstruction of all significant considerations of the particular negotiation.

Documentation begins when the purchase request is received and continues through the life of the contract. Any contract action that may affect price, quality, or schedule must be documented. Documentation may take the form of file copies of correspondence or file memorandums.

Solicitations should specify the kind and extent of technical and cost information the supplier is asked to submit to support the pro-

---

8. This section is based on the Armed Services Pricing Manual.

posal. The information submitted by the prospective supplier is an important part of determining if the price is fair and reasonable.

Proposal Analysis Reports

The report should include the requested information to the extent available and relevant to the particular procurement. A cost analysis report or audit report also should identify the cost data reviewed and the influence of actual costs on the estimate or proposal.

Obviously, all analyses do not require the same detail or emphasis. However, they should answer two questions: What was analyzed? How was it analyzed?

Price Negotiation Memorandum

Except in bidding situations, the price negotiation memorandum (PNM) is the key in documenting price reasonableness. It tells the story of the procurement. Was negotiation required? What rationale was used for developing each position? If cost analysis was required, what were the supporting costs for the supplier's proposal, the buyer's objective, and the price negotiated?

As the permanent record of the decisions, the PNM charts pricing specifics from proposal through analysis and any necessary negotiation. It will be the source document if it becomes necessary to reconstruct the events of the procurement. The original buyer may not be around to help, so he or she should leave tracks that strangers can follow. To do this, the PNM must be specific as to the method and techniques of price or cost analysis used. It is not enough to say, "The proposal was reviewed in detail, and I have concluded that the price is fair and reasonable. Jonas Block, Buyer" or "The price of $50 per unit is fair and reasonable because it is $5 less than the last procurement. Betty Bliss, Buyer." The PNM should discuss the procurement situation, the proposal, the buyer's analysis, the basis for the negotiation objective, and tell why the price is considered fair and reasonable. The amount of detail will be determined largely by the complexity of the procurement and the requirements of the buyer's organization.

The PNM for large procurements requiring cost and price analysis should follow a six-section format. Each of these six sections of the PNM (subject, introductory summary, particulars, procurement situation, negotiation summary, and miscellaneous) is now described.

Subject. This is a memorandum for many readers with different orientations, so the subject, together with the introductory summary, should give the reader a complete picture of the negotiation. Information such as the supplier's name and location, the contract or purchase order number, and a brief description of what is being purchased should be included.

Introductory Summary. In the introductory summary, show the type of contract and the type of negotiation action involved, together with comparative figures of the supplier's proposal, the buyer's negotiation objective, and the negotiated result. Identify specifically the contract items included in the total figure shown as the negotiated amount.

Complete uniformity on the opening page accomplishes many things for many people. The purpose, objective, and negotiated figures shown must be truly comparable figures representing the same elements of work. If the scope has changed, suitable adjustments should be made. These changes should be explained in the memorandum with clarity such that the writer need not be there for others to understand and use the data.

Particulars. This section covers information on what is being bought and who is involved in the procurement. Specific items include the following:

- Contract or purchase order number, including supplemental agreement number if appropriate
- Complete name and location of the supplier
- Quantities and item description (if not covered in the introductory summary)
- Unit prices quoted and negotiated (if many, attach as a schedule)
- Dates and places of fact-finding, prenegotiation review, and negotiation
- Names and titles of participants in the prenegotiation review

- Names and titles of supplier and customer personnel in attendance, identifying the principal negotiators

Procurement situation. Discuss factors in the procurement situation which will affect the reasonableness of the final price.
These factors include those listed below:

- Outside influences and time pressures
- Delivery schedule or period of performance. Resolution of any differences between the schedule desired or required and that proposed by the offeror should be discussed here.
- The type of contract contemplated in the solicitation and the reason for any changes during negotiation
- Information on previous buys of the same or similar items including when, how many, schedule, unit or total price, and production rate. If prices were subject to adjustment in accordance with redetermination or incentive clauses, show both target and final prices.
- Factors influencing source selection
- Unique features of the procurement

Negotiation Summary. Include the supplier's contract pricing proposal, the buyer's negotiation objective, and the negotiation results tabulated in parallel form and broken down by major elements of cost and profit. The general rule is to portray the negotiation as it actually took place.

A summary tabulation, such as that in Table 14.1, gives a quick comparison of cost elements. It provides a thread of continuity from supplier proposal, to the buyer's objective, and to the amount considered negotiated. The paragraph reference column indicates where further documentation and discussion of that cost element may be found.

The following comments apply to the "Considered Negotiated" column in Table 14.1. The buyer may not have agreed with the supplier on all of the values for purchased parts, subcontractors, engineering, fabrication, and assembly labor, and so forth. However, as these and other costs were discussed with the seller—the buyer's

Table 14.1 Comparative Cost Summary

The supplier's proposal was reviewed by the buyer, pricing analyst, and the industrial engineer. Except as otherwise stated, our cost objective was based on the input of these individuals. Total price only was negotiated for this firm-fixed-price contract. No separate agreement was made with the supplier regarding the elemental cost and profit breakdown. Summarized below, by major elements of cost and profit, is a comparison of the supplier's proposal, our objective, and the negotiator's interpretation of the negotiated amount on each element.

	Supplier Proposed	Buyer Objective	Considered Negotiated	Paragraph Reference
Purchased Parts	$ 40,000	$ 40,000	$ 40,000	a
Subcontracted Items	250,000	200,000	210,000	b
Direct Engineering Labor	100,000	90,000	90,000	c
Engineering Overhead	150,000	135,000	135,000	d
Direct Manufacturing Labor	500,000	450,000	500,000	e
Manufacturing Overhead	400,000	315,000	350,000	f
G&A	144,000	123,000	132,000	g
Total Cost	$1,584,000	$1,353,000	$1,457,000	h
Return on Depreciated Value of Facilities and Equipment	63,400	54,000	58,000	
Profit	237,600	162,400	175,000	i
Total Price	$1,885,000	$1,569,400	$1,690,000	

objective gave them values. As the buyer negotiated, ideas about some of those values in the objective changed and with that, the objective also changed. When the buyer and seller finally shake hands, the buyer should know what the costs probably are going to be; these are the numbers put in the "Considered Negotiated" column.

The narratives referenced in the comparative cost summary and labelled (paragraph 'a' through 'i') would summarize treatment of each of the major elements in the prospective supplier's proposal.

If the negotiation is to firm up unpriced orders or otherwise agree to prices based in part on work that was authorized and started earlier, the buyer should show the trends of the data, segregate recurring and nonrecurring costs, indicate the percentage of physical completion of the contract, show actual costs incurred from inception to date, and if significant, show the supplier's current estimate to complete.

For initial price negotiations, particularly on government contracts, estimated profit is an integral part of the negotiation objective. The development of the profit objective for those negotiations should be discussed along with the cost objective. When the weighted guidelines method is used (as described in Chapter 12), the buyer should attach the "Weighted Guidelines Profit/Fee Objective" to the PNM. The rationale supporting assigned weightings should be shown in the body of the memorandum. When weighted guidelines are not used, the PNM should describe how the profit objective was developed.

In the private sector, buyers often maintain only sketchy files on their negotiations. A more complete record can make preparations for the next negotiation much easier. Complete records also make it easier to break in a new buyer. On the other hand, buyers must understand that "careless or excess" wording might be misread if the documentation becomes part of some legal suit.

Contract type. After a detailed description of the buyer's cost and profit thinking, the narrative should justify and explain the selection of contract type and the specific pricing arrangement on which agreement was reached, including any incentive arrangements.

CONCLUDING REMARKS

Many negotiations can be improved if the emphasis is on cost, not price. If cost analysis is appropriate, then the buyer can apply the tools and techniques introduced in Chapters 6 through 13 as the negotiations are prepared for and conducted. Obviously, good negotiations don't just happen. Like the tip of the iceberg, 90 percent of the effort and action is hidden from view.

It is our experience that most contract files, especially the record of negotiations, are inadequate. The files should allow a professional buyer or purchasing manager to understand and reconstruct what has taken place.

Now that the principles of pricing have been addressed, we return our attention to another key aspect of all-in-cost: quality.

RECOMMENDED READING

John A. Carlisle and Robert C. Parker, *Beyond Negotiation: Redeeming Customer-Supplier Relationships,* (Chichester, UK: John Wiley & Sons, 1989). Our favorite on how negotiations *should* be conducted!

Robert Axelrod, *The Evolution of Cooperation,* (New York: Basic Books, 1984).

Roger Fisher and William Ury, *Getting to Yes: Negotiating Agreement Without Giving In,* (New York: Penguin Books, 1983).

Chester L. Karrass, *Give & Take: The Complete Guide to Negotiating Strategies and Tactics,* (New York: Thomas Y. Crowell Co., 1974).

Ross R. Reck and Brian G. Long, *The Win-Win Negotiator,* (Escondido, CA: Blanchard Training and Development, Inc., 1985). A quick, easy, but significant step in the evolution of negotiation.

"Dialog, the Business Connection," Dialog Information Services, Inc., 3460 Hillview Avenue, Palo Alto, CA 94304. Phone 1-800-334-2564.

Howard Raiffa, *The Art and Science of Negotiation,* (Cambridge: The Belknap Press of Harvard University Press, 1982).

Chapter 15

Zero Base Pricing's Effect on Incoming Quality

Chapter 1 introduced the principle that there are two major areas which affect "all-in-cost":

- Acquisition price
- Avoidable in-house costs

These costs, in turn, are very much affected by actions taking place during the design and development process. The All-in-Cost Figure 1.5 is repeated as Figure 15.1 since it dramatically portrays the relationship between the requirements process, the acquisition price, and in-house costs.

Chapter 2 addressed the development of the "right" requirement with the "right" tolerances and the "right" specifications. Chapter 3, "Value Engineering/Value Analysis," described and discussed proven techniques which aid specification of the "right" material. Chapters 6 through 14 addressed key pricing tools which help the buying firm obtain the "right" price.

This chapter addresses the procurement system's responsibility for obtaining the "right" quality of purchased materials, recognizing that supplier quality problems arise from many sources, including

Figure 15.1 All-in-Cost

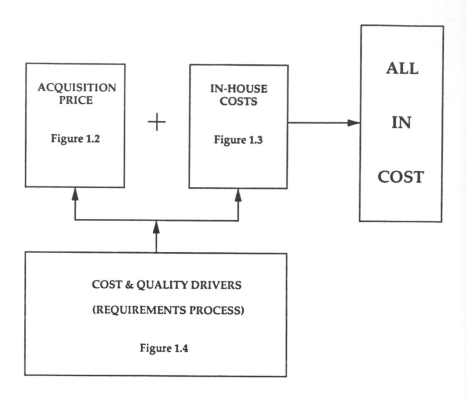

Copyright © 1990, Burt, Norquist, and Anklesaria.

the following: sudden schedule changes; insufficient teamwork among those who should be involved in new product development; designs which cannot be produced economically by suppliers; poor source selection; faulty pricing; insufficient attention to supplier management; reliance on inspecting "quality in" (in lieu of designing and building quality in); and a fairly pervasive belief that suppliers are adversaries, not partners.

ESTABLISHING REQUIREMENTS[1]

A marketing function, forecasting, plays a key role in procurement's ability to obtain consistently high quality incoming materials. For example, during the 1970's, the marketing department at a major computer manufacturer significantly underforecast demand for a new computer. Purchasing, using marketing's forecasts, contracted for the required components in the specified quantities. Demand exceeded forecast by more than 100 percent, thereby requiring purchasing to obtain additional components. Unfortunately, the additional required materials were not available soon enough from prequalified sources, so purchasing had to use less-preferred and even marginal suppliers. Not only were additional costs incurred, but quality problems increased drastically. Inspection, test, and rework costs all went up. Worse, a significant increase in field failures occurred. The firm's reputation and market share both suffered significant losses.

In a similar example, the marketing department at a major copier manufacturer grossly underforecast sales for a new model. As sales went up, the director of manufacturing ordered purchasing to "get the required volume . . . I don't care where." Once again, quality problems with incoming material resulted in additional inspection, test, and rework costs, and in significantly increased field failures. This manufacturer's reputation was so tarnished that, several years later, the firm still had not recovered its previous market share.

In another example, during the early 1970's, a major appliance manufacturer experienced several abrupt shocks to its production schedules. The impact of these shocks was in the millions of dollars. Of equal concern to management, product quality suffered. By 1980, management at this firm was committed to no more than two production output adjustments per product per year. Additionally, the firm shares information on these changes immediately with its sup-

---

1. Much of this material is from D. N. Burt's article, "Managing Product Quality through Strategic Purchasing," in the Spring 1989 issue of M.I.T.'s *Sloan Management Review*. The material is used with the permission of the Editor of the *Sloan Management Review*.

pliers. No schedule surprises eliminate a major source of supplier quality problems.

Purchasing departments frequently complain about the problems resulting from faulty forecasts and sudden schedule changes. Professional buyers must work with quality, marketing, production planning, and top management to create an awareness of the rate at which suppliers can increase production without compromising quality.

Buying to a higher schedule than the planned production schedule is one approach to assure quality parts in case of sudden schedule increases. Demand above that scheduled (reachup) can be met by manufacturing through the use of overtime and temporary help and inventoried materials. If it becomes apparent that the reachup schedule won't occur, purchases are reduced or suspended until the purchased parts inventory is reduced or eliminated. This approach results in increased carrying costs and increases the risk of obsolescence.

Just-in-time manufacturing minimizes obsolescence, inventory cost, and material movement. However, JIT is not free. In order to produce increased quantities on short notice under JIT, suppliers must have additional capacity available. The standby capacities requested should supply the anticipated reachup schedule. Assurance of this capacity may require that the buyer pay a standby charge. The buyer needs to sell his or her management on the possible need to pay these standby charges as a cost of doing business a better way (JIT) with both its tangible and intangible benefits.

The Design of New Products

Leading firms are working hard at eliminating territorial boundaries between the functions which should be involved in new product development. No longer are design and development the exclusive domain of design engineering. More and more, design engineering, reliability engineering, quality, manufacturing, finance, product planning, purchasing, and potential suppliers are involved in the development process. Representatives of these functions contribute their brains and experience up front . . . at the point where they have a major impact on performance, quality, and cost.

As discussed in Chapter 2, early during the design process, two or three carefully qualified potential suppliers should be invited to participate in the design of key nonstandard items to be out-sourced. These potential suppliers are told the function(s) to be performed, how the item is to fit into the larger system, together with the design objectives (size, cost, weight, reliability). The stakes are high for the potential suppliers since the winner normally is the single source of supply for the item for the life of the product in which it is used.[2]

While potential suppliers are developing their designs, they should simultaneously be conducting advanced quality planning in an effort to ensure that what is being designed will be producible *at the required quality*. This early emphasis on quality is critical to the objective of designing quality in (versus inspecting it in).

Selection of these potential suppliers should be a team effort. The potential supplier's design, quality plans, and price proposal are analyzed by all members of the design team. Price analysis, cost analysis, and negotiations are conducted by purchasing with appropriate assistance from other team members. The successful proposal must satisfy a balance of objectives: function, quality, aesthetics, and price.

During the design process, quality, purchasing and manufacturing personnel should review proposed design specifications and manufacturing plans. Quality *must* ensure that the quality called for by marketing is the quality that will result if the design is followed. For example, if the firm were developing a new camera, what temperatures, what humidity, what physical shocks, etc., should the camera be able to withstand? The buyer must work with the designer to ensure that the quality required in purchased material is obtainable at a reasonable cost. The buyer must ensure that the requirements are clear to the supplier and properly documented. Manufacturing should work with the designer to ensure that it can make or buy and assemble the product economically with minimum rework or scrap.

---

2. The buyer need not fear using a single source so long as the supplier qualification process is thoroughly executed. See Richard Newman, "Single Source Qualification," *Journal of Purchasing and Materials Management*, Summer 1988: 10-17.

To Make or Buy?

The purchasing department has valuable information to provide on the cost, quality, and availability implications of purchasing the materials and equipment required to make an item. Obviously, purchasing is in a position to provide similar information on the implications of buying the item.

Control of quality is one of the most commonly advanced arguments in favor of a "make" decision. Numerous people from top management, manufacturing operations, engineering, and even purchasing have been encountered who mistakenly believe that if "we do the manufacturing ourselves, then we won't have quality problems." This argument becomes even more questionable when the manufacturing is to be done by another division!

If a professional procurement staff *proactively* selects and manages its suppliers, then it normally should and will be able to purchase the right quality from outside suppliers. After all, who is going to be more responsive to the firm's quality needs: an outside supplier whose future is dependent on its customer's satisfaction, or an internal operation or sister plant? Further, an outside supplier who specializes in production of an item is far more likely to produce the desired quality than will an internal lower volume operation. This is especially true if the internal source is a start-up operation. The make-or-buy analysis is an extremely important activity. The decision to make or to buy is one of the most challenging and critical issues to confront management. Quality, cost, and timely availability and protection of the company's core technologies all must be considered, and considered objectively, during this analysis. The professional buyer is responsible for ensuring that objective information on the buying alternative is available to those conducting make-or-buy analyses.

SOURCE SELECTION AND PRICING

Source Selection and Quality Considerations

After the decision to purchase an item or service has been made, purchasing assumes lead responsibility for selecting the right source at the right price. Just as the development of a new product should be a team effort, so should source selection.

It is essential that a technically competent buyer review requirements before initiating sourcing activities. Requisitions for materials should not be accepted by purchasing until there are clear specifications or a plan to determine the TBD (to be determined) spec. Such action greatly minimizes quality problems. Philip Crosby, noted quality authority, says that at least half of the quality problems in purchased materials are caused by not clearly stating what the requirements are.[3] Progressive buyers increase incoming quality by working with their suppliers to reconcile specifications with the supplier's process capabilities before the design is completed.

Professional buyers prequalify new sources of supply (and may need to requalify known sources) to ensure that they have the technical, managerial, physical, financial, and attitudinal capability to meet their customer's quality and quantity requirements. This crucial activity frequently requires the involvement of members of the engineering, manufacturing engineering, production, quality, finance, and industrial engineering departments, with the buyer being the team chief. In addition to prequalifying suppliers for current requirements, they should be investigated for technological capabilities which may be required in the future.

Particular care should be taken with specifications being used to develop a new source of supply. A San Diego biotech firm recently selected a new source for a porous plastic disk used in a pregnancy test kit. The previous source had been providing satisfactory disks using the existing specification. The new source's price was 20 percent below that of the existing source. A material engineer qualified the new source, and a purchase order was issued. The quality control department inspected the first incoming lot and observed that the

---

3. James Gagne, "Quality Coaches," *CPI Purchasing*, March 1986: 64.

disks met all of the inspection criteria under the critical and major-defect classifications. However, 3 percent of the inspected discs exhibited surface irregularities. These parts were assembled into test units, and pregnancy tests were performed; all the units containing the defective part yielded a false-positive result. A review of the specifications revealed that the nonconforming parts were classified as a minor defect with an acceptable quality level of 4 percent. The disks met the specification, but the specification itself was inadequate. It had been adequate for the first supplier but not for the second one, whose purchased materials or processes were not the same.

In another example, a large manufacturer switched to an outside supplier for process materials previously made in-house. Material costs soon registered predicted savings. However, scrap losses soared as a result of incomplete specifications and ambiguous contract definitions. Fortunately, a well-integrated quality-loss reporting system focused management's attention on the problem, thus limiting the large losses that otherwise would have resulted.

The fact that finished product quality standards are met does not guarantee that component specifications are properly stated. A component may be using only part of the latitude allowed. A shift in process, supplier, or raw materials may cause final product failure.[4]

Collaborative Relations

Good suppliers are valuable resources. By helping customers with product development, value management, and timely delivery of the desired level of quality, they make a direct contribution to a firm's success.

Partnerships between industrial customers and their suppliers are replacing the adversarial relations of the past.[5] To the benefit of both parties, the focus has shifted from dividing the profit pie to increasing that pie. Good buyer-seller relations facilitate the buyer's

---

4. J. Reddy and A. Berger, "Three Essentials of Product Quality," *Harvard Business Review*, July-August 1983: 156.

5. D. A. Garvin, *Managing Quality, the Strategic and Competitive Edge* (New York: The Free Press, 1988), 140-144, 209-211. J. M. Juran, *Juran on Planning for Quality* (New York: The Free Press, 1988), 222-223.

efforts to gain superior quality performance, extra service, cooperation on cost reduction programs, and sharing of new technology, processes, and procedures.

Long-term partnerships allow and encourage suppliers to invest in better tools and equipment, better methods, and far more training. Supplier quality, cost, and flexibility (responsiveness) can improve dramatically as a result. The professional buyer has the primary responsibility for identifying candidates for such partnerships and taking the lead in developing and maintaining the relationships.

Accounts payable has a critical, but frequently overlooked, role to play in efforts to establish and maintain long-term collaborative relations. Prompt payment to suppliers greatly improves their desire to do business with and respect for their customer. Purchasing professionals educate accounts payable personnel on the role they play in the development and maintenance of collaborative relations. Such buyers also help accounts payable by resolving inconsistencies that occur between the purchase order, receiving documents, and invoices.

Price and Quality Considerations

Based on personal observations and interviews with dozens of buyers, it is apparent that most are "price" oriented. This results largely from management evaluating buyers on their ability to get the lowest price. Unfortunately, the lowest price frequently does not result in the lowest "all-in-cost" from the perspective of the firm's total cost of operations.

For example, until recently, buyers in the automotive industry were notorious for driving hard deals aimed at getting the lowest possible price. Quality problems on incoming materials resulted in lost productivity and shoddy finished goods. A 1982 article in *Business Week* quotes quality authority Joseph M. Juran: "The automakers turn the screws to the point where it's almost impossible to make money selling to the auto companies. So the vendors have to make it on spare parts in the aftermarket. That gives them a vested interest in failures, a miserable arrangement."[6] The best automotive

---

6. "Detroit Is Trying Harder for Quality," *Business Week*, November 1, 1982, 77. A special report.

buyers are still hard bargainers concerned with reducing the cost of the items they are purchasing. But they do this by motivating and even assisting their suppliers to become more efficient. This increased efficiency is the source of lower costs, with full recognition that quality *must* come first. The best buyers focus on all-in-costs of purchased materials, with the result that inspection costs, manufacturing problems, and defects in finished products have all been drastically reduced.

Procurement professionals responsible for negotiating prices recognize that in order for a supplier to provide the quality specified within a continuing relationship, the price must provide a competitive level of profit.

Both sides must feel that they have won if the basis for a lasting relationship is to be established. In addition many professional buyers have learned that granting price relief may be necessary to protect delivery and quality commitments when unexpected problems and costs are encountered.

MANAGEMENT OF THE ONGOING SUPPLY AGREEMENT

The procurement system's final area of responsibility for ensuring product quality is continual management of the relationship. Unfortunately, this area sometimes receives too little attention, resulting in avoidable quality problems and late deliveries.

Ensuring Understanding

The buyer-supplier relationship begins during source selection. Traditionally, purchasing authorities have advocated the use of competitive bidding for selecting sources, provided certain essential prerequisites are satisfied. Today, an increasing number of purchasing professionals use *competitive negotiations* to select sources of critical materials. This approach is used in large part to ensure that there is a good understanding by potential suppliers on all aspects (with emphasis on quality) of the requirements. Richard P. Baribault, former Vice President of Procurement for Aluminum Company of America, has stated, ". . . there has to be more open communication—information on needs and costs and quality—no more going out for three bids and simply taking the lowest evaluated bid."[7]

Negotiations are the optimal way to ensure clarity between the two parties and to establish sound agreements. By understanding the cost structure, the buyer can ensure that value is being received and costs are not at a level where quality will be compromised.

On critical procurements, purchasing must bring the key players from both the buying firm and the supplier together to ensure that there is a complete understanding on all terms and conditions of the contract. In addition, it is desirable to have any newly involved operations, quality, and design engineering personnel visit the supplier's facilities to better understand their counterpart's operations and needs.

Return visits by supplier personnel, even hourly operators, to the buyer's plant will help build an understanding of quality requirements. Such visits allow the supplier's team to see exactly how and when the product will be used. Not only do such visits increase the likelihood of receiving the desired quality, they also further the buyer's ongoing value analysis program.

Training

Xerox, Ford Motor Company, Tennant, Texas Instruments, and other progressive companies have learned that a relatively small investment in training their suppliers pays handsome dividends in the areas of quality, cost, and timeliness. These firms provide training of the suppliers' personnel in the areas of statistical process control (SPC), statistical quality control (SQC), design of experiments, total quality commitment (TQC), just-in-time (JIT), and other quality oriented topics.

Certification

Suppliers' production and quality systems must be reviewed, approved, and monitored in lieu of reliance on incoming inspection.

---

7. Paul Farrell, "For Buyers and Sellers, It's Not Business as Usual," *Purchasing World*, June 1984: 49.

Hewlett-Packard, for example, thoroughly reviews and inspects its suppliers' production and quality systems before authorizing production of a new item. All new items are subjected to rigorous testing and failure analysis. Several lots (shipments) of a new item are inspected and tested at the receiving plant. When the supplier has demonstrated that it consistently meets Hewlett-Packard's quality standards, the supplier is "certified" for the supply of the item. Certification means that Hewlett-Packard will rely on the supplier's quality system. Incoming inspection is replaced by reviewing the supplier's test results and conducting audits to maintain equipment calibration.

Polaroid employs similar procedures to ensure that it receives the specified quality of purchased materials. An example of a letter informing a supplier of its status as a certified supplier is contained in Appendix H.

Motivation

Just as in eliciting performance from individuals, the problem of supplier motivation can be approached in two basic ways: positive and negative reinforcement. Experiences like those below indicate that positive motivation is more successful.

Phillip Taddeau, Vice President for Procurement at Scott Paper Company, is quoted as saying, "One thing is for sure, we're not going to motivate suppliers in the traditional mode—short-term contracts, punishment, and negative rewards for suppliers."[8]

Several firms such as the Tennant Company of Minneapolis have adopted programs to stimulate supplier quality motivation through positive, ongoing communication and interaction. These programs include getting top executives from supplier companies to attend a daylong discussion on quality. Tennant's president even hosts these programs. At the end of the meetings, supplier executives are asked to commit to quality goals within several weeks. At Tennant, the supplier pledge reads as follows:

---

8. *Ibid*, 50.

We pledge to do our job right every time. It is our personal contribution toward zero defects and a statement of our commitment. Our individual efforts, along with those of all Tennant Company employees, will enhance our mutual overall continued success. Through our teamwork, Tennant Company and its customers, employees, and suppliers will benefit from this total quality commitment.

In addition to the initial management conferences, Tennant Company holds "celebrations" to review and renew employee and supplier commitments. These events, known as "Zero Defect Days," motivate suppliers to further cost reduction and quality improvement.[9]

Xerox takes a different but equally successful approach. Xerox's answer to improving supplier performance is to *raise* expectations. Xerox management believes that giving suppliers short lead times and accepting marginal-quality lots motivates the supplier to be a low-quality producer.[10]

In order to motivate outside suppliers and to make them aware of its quality objectives, IBM Raleigh holds one-day supplier quality awareness seminars. The supplier's chief executive officers and quality managers are asked to attend. These seminars stress three main points:

- Top level management commitment to zero defects (total conformance to requirements)
- Dependence on supplier quality improvements
- Motivation based on quality

The seminars include a tour of the IBM Raleigh facility. Suppliers are given an opportunity to see how their products are used and to obtain a feel for the difficulty, expense, and lost productivity resulting from nonconforming parts.[11]

---

9. "Getting Suppliers Involved in Purchasing Quality Improvement," *Purchasing World*, March 1986: 68-69.

10. "Expect More, Get More from Your Suppliers," *Purchasing World*, March 1986: 30-33.

11. W. E. Closer, "Objective: Zero Defect Suppliers," *Quality Progress*, November 1984: 20-22.

G. E.'s major appliance division successfully embraces a six-phase program of supplier motivation:

1. The biggest motivator of all is to be selected as the single source of supply for another period.

2. Successful suppliers are allowed (encouraged) to publicize their success.

3. Successful suppliers are encouraged to share their recognition with their employees. The employees are encouraged to continue their efforts to improve quality and productivity. Many suppliers reward their outstanding employees with a trip to Appliance Park to see how their products are used (and to visit nearby Churchill Downs, home of the Kentucky Derby).

4. G. E. Appliance provides speakers for suppliers' annual management reviews.

5. G. E. Appliance shares its business plans and data with its partners.

6. Each year, G. E. Appliance selects its 100 "best" suppliers. (These 100 are selected from the division's 12,000 suppliers.) This selection is based on a combination of service, responsiveness, value analysis suggestions, cost, and related factors. Each selected firm is invited to send its sales representative and CEO to attend the Division's Supplier Appreciation Day. Over 50 senior G. E. Appliance managers also attend. Each of the 100 outstanding suppliers receives a plaque acknowledging its status and contribution.

Packaging

The issue of packaging receives too little attention at many firms. Yet faulty packaging, or packaging which is incompatible with the many moves required for the material to arrive at the assembly plant or with the firm's material-handling equipment, frequently is the source of quality problems. The buyer should question the cost and adequacy of the incoming packaging. It pays to have a packaging engineer work with the supplier to determine or approve how incoming parts are packaged. A program to minimize disposal costs can also lead to lower all-in-cost.

Monitoring Quality

The firm must monitor and manage its suppliers' quality efforts on a timely basis. Monitoring may be done in one of several ways: physical inspection of material, certification programs, and monitoring the supplier's process control data. Suppliers whose performance is found to be unacceptable should be reviewed by the buyer and quality engineers. A plan should be formulated for such suppliers to bring their conformance to an acceptable level. Actions may include meetings with the supplier's management to review problems, visiting the supplier to agree on corrective actions, deciding that no new or additional business will be placed with the supplier, or finally, removing all business from that supplier. Every effort should be made to work with suppliers willing to improve quality. However, the buyer should not continue to do business with suppliers who cannot or will not meet the quality requirements.

Many firms have put their suppliers on notice that failure to meet quality standards will result in deletion of the supplier from the company's or division's list of eligible suppliers. A major defense contractor's efforts in this area are typical of the "get tough" attitude being adopted. This firm found significant quality problems in parts supplied to one of its divisions. Prior to introducing a supplier evaluation system, this division was experiencing an unacceptably high rejection rate on incoming materials. The division established a rating program for its suppliers based on the volume or dollar value of material supplied and the type and frequency of quality discrepancies noted on the products received. Each supplier was presented with an acceptable product quality level that he or she would have to maintain or face the loss of the firm as an account. Each supplier was advised of its known shortcomings. These were discussed and resolved in many cases. Within three years, 900 of the original 1,700 suppliers had been dropped, and those remaining picked up more business.[12]

12. D. N. Burt, *Proactive Procurement: The Key to Increased Profits, Productivity, and Quality* (Englewood Cliffs, NJ: Prentice-Hall, 1984), 209-211.

Provide Timely Feedback

It is surprising how few purchasing departments provide timely feedback to their suppliers. Yet such feedback is both a motivator and a source of essential information. At Hewlett-Packard, suppliers are rated quarterly on very critical items, semiannually on critical items, and annually on all other items. Ratings are based on technology, quality, responsiveness, dependability, and cost. The suppliers are provided feedback on their ratings and told where they stand relative to their competitors. Both technical and cost issues are addressed. Discussions may focus on process yields and the desirability of revising specifications or tooling to increase yields and lower unit costs. Quite obviously, this feedback spurs them on to improve these areas.

Supplier Data[13]

Obtaining and analyzing supplier quality data will dramatically reduce incoming inspection cost and improve quality. The buyer with quality engineering must identify the required data and make its timely submission part of the request for proposal and resulting contract. If this is not done beforehand, the supplier may ask for a price increase when data is requested later. After entering into contractual relations, the buyer must ensure that the required data arrives when specified, that it is properly evaluated and audited, and that a reference base is established. When a part is new or has been changed, the quality data should be analyzed immediately.

The buyer should request and be certain that the supplier's data is properly correlated with incoming inspection data or audits. If the supplier is certified, analyses must be conducted whenever the data are inconsistent or shifting. Frequently, pressure to reduce costs may result in the dropping of reviews of the supplier's quality data and the correlation audits. They remain dropped until a problem is found further downstream at a later date. Monitoring the supplier's quality data and conducting audits on incoming materials reduces the likeli-

---

13. Based on W. E. Norquist, "Improving Quality/Purchasing Teamwork," in *37th Annual Quality Congress Transactions* (Milwaukee, WI: A.S.Q.C.: 1983), 136-141.

hood of such quality problems and finds equipment correlation problems promptly.

Changes

The buyer should be the focal point for all communication with the supplier. All communications on changes *must* go through the buyer. Firms which have gone from from the "looser" approach of engineering being able to make changes at will to communication through the buyer, report a significant improvement in supplier quality along with numerous other benefits.

Many waivers of specification requirements are made on a "one-time" basis to accommodate materials which are urgently required, but which do not meet spec. Acceptance of nonconforming material trains suppliers not to conform. Buyers and their colleagues in quality are teaming up at progressive firms to say, "no more off-specs." At such firms, if the responsible engineer is willing to accept a nonconforming item twice, then the specification must be revised to reflect the change before the material is accepted. As a result, more realistic specifications are being developed, frequently with more realistic tolerances. Purchasing and quality make the firm's suppliers aware that there will be no more off-specs. The net result is improved incoming quality at lower prices.[14]

Assistance

The professional buyer will ensure that any contract provides a reasonable degree of protection in the form of the right to terminate for quality and/or scheduling problems. But before exercising such contractual rights, professional buyers provide assistance to a supplier who is experiencing difficulties with the objective of developing the supplier into a dependable source of quality supplies. Frequently the purchaser's quality assurance, industrial engineering, and/or production departments can locate the source of the problem and recommend remedial action. As long as suppliers are willing and able to take necessary action, they may develop into viable sources.

---

14. W. E. Closer, "Objective: Zero Defect Suppliers," *Quality Progress,* November 1984: 20-22.

Climbing the Quality Mountain.[15] Buyers at Polaroid view the development of a "quality" supplier as a task equivalent to climbing a mountain. They may begin their climb at one of several levels, depending on the circumstances. But their objective is to have their suppliers achieve the quality necessary to eliminate incoming inspections with certification as the ultimate goal. (See Figure 15.2.)

Two examples of Polaroid's collaborative efforts that have resulted in higher quality and lower cost follow. Troy Manufacturing makes millions of rollers a year for Polaroid's instant film cameras. Troy, which is the single source of supply for this item, has contributed ideas and suggestions for process and product changes such as elimination of a costly coating step, standardization of the rolls, development of a knurled journal substitution of a plastic gear in place of a metal gear, and the use of reusable packaging. The last two changes alone accounted for annual savings of over $580,000. These changes, which Polaroid agreed to, lowered the manufacturing cost, and Troy and Polaroid shared the benefits.

Troy, one of the first suppliers to be certified under Polaroid's tough supplier certification program, had developed its process controls so well that Polaroid did not have to perform incoming inspection on the precision-made rollers. Moreover, Troy's high quality has made it feasible to use JIT delivery. The cost of storage, incoming inspection, rework, scrap, and warranty work—all of which add significantly to acquisition cost—are negligible with this supplier.

Another supplier which manufactures flexible electronic circuits adopted Polaroid's suggestions for statistical process control, although the general manager had told purchasing that such controls would raise the cost and the price of the circuits. After installing these manufacturing controls, the general manager discovered that his costs on Polaroid and other similar business fell to below what he believed was possible, and a price reduction of 11 percent was passed on to Polaroid.

---

15. W. E. Norquist, "The What, Why and How of Zero Base Pricing™," in *Purchasing and Technology, 1986 and Beyond* (Oradell, NJ: NAPM, 1986).

Figure 15.2 Climbing the Quality Mountain

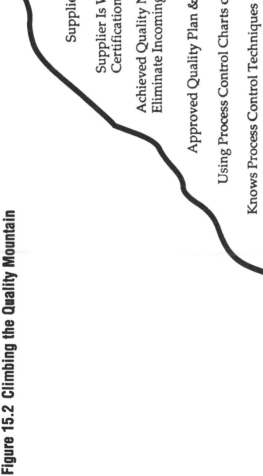

Supplier Has Been Certified

Supplier Is Working to Meet Certification Requirements

Achieved Quality Necessary to Eliminate Incoming Inspection

Approved Quality Plan & Approved Specs

Using Process Control Charts on Our Product

Knows Process Control Techniques

Using Statistical Sampling Techniques

Realistic Specification Being Discussed

Pilot or Pre-Production Stage

Quality Requirements Communicated

CONCLUDING REMARKS

We have described several critical activities that, when properly performed, drastically reduce quality problems in incoming material. Perhaps of equal or greater importance is the buyer's attitude toward quality. Professional buyers do the following:

- Know that their ideas are wanted by others
- Avoid the "buck-passing syndrome"
- Are not satisfied with the status quo
- Do not blame others for problems
- Look for problems constantly
- Avoid unsupported hunches
- Are sure of their facts
- Listen to others
- Organize their findings
- Share their discoveries with others
- Think of ways to do things better
- Correct problems permanently

RECOMMENDED READING

Keki R. Bhote, *World Class Quality*, an AMA Management Briefing (New York: American Management Association, 1988). An excellent review of traditional statistical process control techniques and readable coverage of the design of experiments, including the classical, Taguchi, and Shainin approaches. The best little book on the market.

Philip B. Crosby, *Quality Is Free: The Art of Making Quality Certain*, (New York: McGraw-Hill, 1979). A most readable book.

Philip B. Crosby, *Quality Without Tears: The Art of Hassle Free Management*, (New York: McGraw-Hill, 1984).

W. Edwards Deming, *Quality, Productivity, and Competitive Position*, (Cambridge: Center for Advanced Engineering Studies, M.I.T., 1983).

Masaaki Imai, *Kaizen*, (New York: Random House, 1986). An excellent work describing the keys to Japan's competitive success.

David A. Garvin, *Managing Quality: The Strategic and Competitive Edge,* (New York: The Free Press, 1988).

Donald W. Dobler, David N. Burt, and Lamar Lee, Jr., *Purchasing and Materials Management: Text and Cases,* especially Chapters 9, 10, 18, and 19 (New York: McGraw-Hill, 1990).

Armand Vallin Feigenbaum, *Total Quality Control,* 3rd. ed. (New York: McGraw-Hill, 1983).

J.M. Juran, *Juran on Planning for Quality,* (New York: The Free Press, 1988).

Robert M. Monczka and Steven J. Trecha, "Cost-Based Supplier Performance Evaluation," *Journal of Purchasing and Materials Management,* Spring 1988: 2-7.

Richard G. Newman, "Single Source Qualification," *Journal of Purchasing and Materials Management,* Summer 1988: 10-17.

Richard L. Pinkerton, "Finding, Selecting, and Evaluating Vendors," *Pacific Purchaser,* July-August, 1987: 8-11.

Robert R. Williams and V. Sagar Bakhshi, "Competitive Bidding: Department of Defense and Private Sector Practices," *Journal of Purchasing and Materials Management,* Fall 1988: 29-35.

Chapter 16

How to Implement Zero Base Pricing

To implement Zero Base Pricing successfully, you must win the support of many groups within your company. This requires the commitment of the purchasing organization, obviously, and also of top management, whose demonstrated interest is necessary for winning the full cooperation of other functions such as engineering, manufacturing, and marketing.

But where is the starting point? Is it top management? Or is it the purchasing organization? Success has been achieved with each approach.

ZBP can start as a program initiated by purchasing management. By achieving a continuing series of cost reductions and quality improvements, measuring them in dollars, and publicizing them, purchasing can win recognition from the rest of the firm for its contribution to profitability. Top management's commitment to ZBP can then be won, leading to more opportunities for purchasing to contribute and be recognized. This approach is consistent with the growing organizational trend to decentralization, which delegates decision-making responsibilities and initiatives to the appropriate levels of management within the firm. Besides, increased profitability is the surest way to win the hearts and minds of top management.

In some organizations, top management may take the initiative to sponsor or direct changes. For these situations, the Procurement

System Review (discussed later in the chapter) is a proven systematic approach to identify, motivate, and implement the needed changes, such as ZBP, in the firm's procurement system.

Purchasing Initiative

The Zero Base Pricing concept evolved in 1983 as Polaroid's purchasing worked to develop strategies for the coming years—strategies that would remain valid whether economic conditions were inflationary, stable, or deflationary. The objective was to help buyers work with suppliers to examine *all* the costs making up the current price and see how, together, they could lower the costs to their mutual benefit.

A CASE STUDY: HOW IT WAS DONE AT POLAROID

First, Polaroid purchasing developed a simplified description of ZBP to help Polaroid buyers understand the program and explain it to existing and potential suppliers. Price was divided into five cost elements: material, labor, factory overhead, general and administrative costs, and supplier profit. (See Chapter 1, pages 3–5.)

All buyers participated in a case study course in cost analysis which emphasized understanding overhead allocations. Buyers also participated in ZBP strategy discussions, where they were encouraged to identify what help they needed to be better prepared for negotiations. The purchasing administrative staff worked to see that the buyers received the requested assistance.

Kickoff

ZBP was formally introduced to Polaroid purchasing groups with a companywide kickoff meeting in September 1983. This meeting was conducted with the zeal and enthusiasm normally associated with corporate sales motivation sessions and included a full display of the multimedia material created for the fall sales meeting. Buyers were given manuals outlining the ZBP program to help them explain the program to their suppliers. Promotional items, such as pens with Polaroid and Zero Base Pricing logos, allowed buyers to turn the tables on salespeople by giving them a premium.

The kickoff session emphasized purchasing's ability to contribute to fighting inflation costs. It was evident that purchasing was poised to play a major role in reducing costs:

> Not questioning price increases is unpatriotic. It only feeds inflation and makes our country less competitive in the world economy.
>
> .... Warren Norquist, Vice President of Purchasing and Materials

> I am not talking about resisting price increase requests and just holding the line. I am asking you to work in concert with our vendors to roll back prices.
>
> .... Owen Gaffney, Group Vice President

Intense Training and Support

Through a series of courses, Polaroid trained its buyers in negotiations, use of indexes, overhead allocation, the actual cost of overtime, and other subjects. (See tool kit, page 17 in Chapter 1.) In fact, some managers were sent to sales training and pricing seminars in order to understand how salespeople think. They then taught probable approaches by salespeople as well as selling skills to purchasing personnel.

A purchasing research department with a staff of two concentrated on helping buyers gather pertinent data and apply tools such as price indexing, cost analysis, and cost modeling. Buyers became much better prepared for negotiations than previously.

Maximizing Value Inside the Company

As progress was made with suppliers, it became obvious that additional savings could come from using ZBP inside the company and working to reduce the all-in-cost of any purchase. Buyers started implementing ZBP with their "internal customers" to maximize the value of what they requisitioned. The buyer would work with his or her Polaroid customer to clarify the real needs. Polaroid found that "maximizing value" requires purchasing to question as well as help when people are deciding what to specify—whether secretaries ordering stationery supplies or engineers seeking sophisticated equipment.

Also contributing to ZBP's success and the standing of the purchasing group was the hiring of more technical specialists into purchasing from elsewhere in Polaroid. These scientists and engineers provided the knowledge to help define material requirements and specifications between research and engineering and suppliers—and do it effectively.

Buyers learned to sell their customers (the requisitioners) on the benefits of trying alternate, lower cost methods to meet their needs. The buyer often had to prove that brand preference and value are not necessarily related. For example, a buyer who knows who actually manufactures various branded computer supplies can sell requisitioners on not buying the more expensive brand name.

Maximizing Value from Suppliers

Zero Base Pricing also emphasizes early supplier involvement and the many benefits which flow to both Polaroid and the supplier. As suppliers understood the benefits resulting from a closer relationship, they became more willing to share appropriate cost data with the buyer. The sharing of cost data had a synergistic effect. Program managers at Polaroid became more willing to choose suppliers earlier in the design process.

At Polaroid, the development of closer relationships with existing suppliers may be viewed as a series of steps which ultimately results in more open cost negotiations. Polaroid buyers began to employ a "staircase of cost knowledge" (Chapter 8, Figure 8.1) to identify a buyer's knowledge relative to eight graduated steps. In this way, buyers readily identify how far they have traveled toward a complete understanding of a supplier's costs.

Sharing/Learning Throughout Purchasing

After working with ZBP for a few months, buyer groups participated in negotiation sharing sessions where they told of numerous real-world experiences and learned about new tools and techniques. These sharing sessions have become an annual event as buyers learn by sharing experiences on a wide variety of products and services.

Winning Management Support

To win management support, purchasing should document the dollar savings it brings to the bottom line. The latest 1988 version of the rules Polaroid purchasing developed with corporate finance for a Cost Reduction/Cost Avoidance reporting system is outlined in Appendix I.

The reporting rules were developed two years before ZBP and gave purchasing a way to show its contribution to profit. The yearly savings being documented built support for the ZBP program. Since there are over 300 projects under the program, Polaroid purchasing offered management proof of accuracy by the use of random sampling. A company officer was invited to select projects at random during a meeting of purchasing managers. The purchasing manager responsible explained how the savings were calculated. Although some savings were considered overstated, the overall impression of such reviews was that the purchasing people, on average, *understated* their contribution to profits. In fact, one of the major obstacles to publicizing purchasing's contribution was the belief of many buyers that "making savings is just part of my job and such savings should not be reported."

Documenting quality improvements was more challenging than the documentation of cost reductions and cost avoidances. Both the number of defects and the cost of defects must be tracked. Polaroid bills its suppliers for the costs of scrap and rework resulting from defective incoming materials. Tracking the reduction in "bill-backs" helps monitor the progress in improving incoming quality.

The need to publicize cost reduction and qualify efforts stems from common sense: "There is no job security unless the importance of your work is understood."

Several major firms have dropped recently adopted corporate-wide systems that produced large savings (10 to 20 percent) through the consolidated purchase of widely used items. Why were these programs dropped? Purchasing had failed to keep upper management informed on how high the return on this investment was. It is too late to sell top management on the benefits of such programs after cutback decisions have been made.

A year after the kickoff, the savings generated and the forward thinking involved in the Zero Base Pricing program led to recognition by Polaroid President I. M. "Mac" Booth, who presented purchasing professionals with special certificates of appreciation.

Publicity is an essential part of ZBP and serves many purposes:

- It gains recognition of contributions made by individual personnel in purchasing, engineering, and other areas. A vital part of any recognition program is to share credit with other functional groups involved in a cost reduction or cost avoidance project.
- It fosters teamwork among the members of the procurement system in seeking further reductions.
- It gains top management's attention and awareness of the significant contributions by the procurement team.
- It maintains the momentum required to ensure that the procurement team continues to enhance the firm's success.
- Ideas for savings generate additional projects in other areas.

TOP MANAGEMENT SPONSORSHIP

Many Chief Operating Officers (COO) and business managers have the uneasy feeling that the procurement system—the one which spends over half of their sales dollar, which affects their productivity, and which plays a major role in the quality of their firm's products and market share—should operate more effectively. At the same time, many professional buyers and purchasing managers are frustrated in their efforts to maximize their department's contributions to the firm's success.

They are seeing an increasing number of American companies embrace modern procurement concepts and techniques such as Zero Base Pricing. These firms enjoy the following benefits over the more traditional approach to purchasing:

- Reductions in expenditures for materials, equipment, and services of 5 percent to 30 percent
- Elimination of approximately 50 percent of their former incoming quality problems

- Reduction in purchased material inventory reductions of 50 percent and more
- Significant increases in manufacturing productivity
- Shortening of new product development time
- Greatly reduced cycle times
- Significantly increased profits
- Major increases in ROI

Figure 1.6 on page 14 shows the effect of Zero Base Pricing techniques on a typical firm's ROI. Such benefits win top management's attention.

Proactive procurement evolved at this handful of firms for one of two reasons:

- Firms such as Xerox, the Ford Motor Company, and Harley Davidson were faced with threats to their survival.
- Management at firms such as G. E., Apple, and Polaroid recognized the critical role which procurement must play if the firm were to achieve and maintain world-class stature.

Many a company embracing proactive procurement invested much time and effort and went through many trials and errors in the evolution of its procurement system from the traditional mode to its present status as a major contributor to the firm's success.[1]

The Procurement System Review

The Procurement System Review (PSR) was developed to be a more effective and efficient means of enhancing the procurement system's contribution to the organization's success.

The PSR has five basic characteristics. First it is *comprehensive* rather than narrow in focus. It cuts across organizational boundaries and investigates the effectiveness of the procurement process throughout the organization. In contrast, a purchasing audit checks for compliance with established procedures. The narrow focus of the

---

1. See D. N. Burt, "Managing Suppliers Up to Speed," *Harvard Business Review*, July-August 1989: 127-135.

audit overlooks most of the benefits gained from proactive procurement concepts and techniques such as Zero Base Pricing.

Second, the procurement system review is conducted by someone who is *independent* of the operation which is being studied. Self-audits may be useful, but they lack objectivity and independence. The review can be conducted by a person or group from within the firm but outside of the organizations being evaluated, or by an outside entity.

Third, the procurement system review is *systematic* in the questions it addresses. In contrast, the reviewer who randomly selects and interviews individuals within the firm and its key suppliers, asking questions as they occur to him or her is a "visceral" practitioner. Though not methodical, such an effort may develop some significant findings. However, the thoroughness of the procurement system review normally will increase the number of opportunities for improvement identified.

Fourth, the review should be *conducted periodically*. Typically, senior management calls for such evaluations only after profits have taken a nosedive or severe shortages have occurred. In most cases, companies are in such crises because they failed to take appropriate and timely actions during good times. A review conducted during good times often can prevent such serious problems.

The final (and perhaps most crucial) characteristic of the review is that *the reviewing team works with the firm's staff to implement the agreed upon changes*. Generally, if the review team is not explicitly charged with facilitating implementation, few of the potential benefits of the review will be realized.

These five principles can be joined together into a working definition:

> A procurement system review is a comprehensive, independent, systematic, and periodic review of an organization's procurement system, including procedures and operations, with the objective of identifying opportunities and recommending and implementing a plan of action to improve the organization's procurement performance.

Where to Begin

In most organizations, the various members of the procurement team have only one supervisor in common: the COO. This individual must provide the necessary direction and support to the procurement team to ensure that sound practices are observed by *all* members of the procurement system. When the involved departments function as a team with interdependent components, a synergism results and the desired competitive benefits are enjoyed.

The PSR consists of three principal phases: (1) benchmarking, (2) the establishment of objectives and development of an implementation plan, and (3) implementation. Key PSR activities are shown in Figure 16.1.

Benchmarking

The review's first step calls for a meeting between the COO or business unit manager, the procurement or materials manager, and the senior reviewer to discuss the procurement operations and the firm's present and future requirements in this area. It is essential that the COO, or, in the case of a business unit, the business unit manager be part of these meetings, since his or her support will be essential during the development and implementation of agreed enhancements. Experience indicates that many of the recommendations resulting from the review will be at the interface level involving purchasing and engineering (for early purchasing involvement in the design process); purchasing, marketing, and production planning (on forecasts); engineering, quality, and marketing (on the ability of engineering's design to meet the quality requirements of the marketplace); purchasing and finance (cash flow issues); and purchasing and operations (make-or-buy). A good review that benchmarks how the operation compares with world-class ones lays the foundation for the implementation of recommendations required to effect necessary changes throughout the procurement system.

During benchmarking, the reviewers have two major objectives: (1) to gather relevant and useful data and (2) to lay the foundation for improved practices, procedures, and strategies. As an example,

Figure 16.1 Mechanics: Procurement System Review

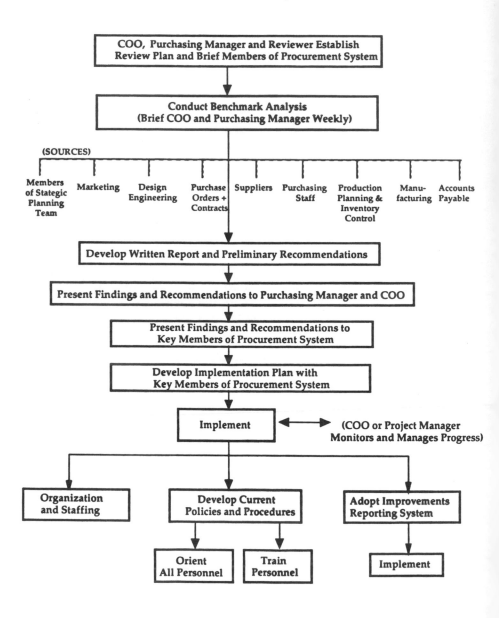

assume that a reviewer is interviewing a member of the engineering department with the objective of reaching conclusions on purchasing's involvement in the design process.

In addition to gaining insight into purchasing's involvement, the discussion leads to the conclusion that the engineer feels that it is his or her responsibility to select potential suppliers and discuss engineering requirements and commercial issues with the potential suppliers. The engineer then selects the supplier and issues a single source requirement or designs the specification so that the chosen supplier is the only one whose resulting bid will be responsive. While gaining essential data, the reviewer has an opportunity to note this practice and find out how often the practice occurs. For example, does it always relate to certain technology? If so, what are the technical drivers that encourage this practice? Are the components strategic? Is the technology strategic? Should a strategy be developed to identify the most competitive technology, sourcing, quality, and "all-in-cost" advantages?

Developing Objectives and the Implementation Plan

During the benchmarking phase, the review team chief has kept the COO and the procurement manager aware of significant findings. On completion of this phase, the COO and procurement manager are briefed on all key findings and preliminary recommendations.

Next, a meeting of all involved should be conducted off site. *This meeting is the most critical phase of the review.* Findings and preliminary recommendations are discussed, reviewed, rediscussed, and refined until they are acceptable to all members of the procurement system. During this process, objectives are agreed to and a commitment to achieving these objectives is made by all.

The most valuable aspect of the PSR is not the reviewer's preliminary recommendations but rather the process that key personnel go through as they digest and assimilate the facts and opportunities identified by the review and develop their own concept of needed change. The outcome of this process is an implementation plan containing key actions, responsibilities, a schedule, measurement reports, and closed loop feedback on progress and improvements.

Implementation

By now it should be apparent that the PSR may result in a significant degree of change in how the procurement system operates. This
change will have a major impact on the organization's bottom line,
its global competitiveness, and on its ability to survive and grow. A
systematic implementation program must be developed and executed. Such a program commonly has five major components: (1)
organization and staffing, (2) policies and procedures, (3) orientation, (4) training, and (5) reporting.

Organization and Staffing. Procurement is every bit as important to
the firm's competitiveness as are design, marketing, and conversion.
Accordingly, it normally is desirable to have the individual with primary responsibility for procurement be at an organizational level
parallel with his or her counterparts in engineering, marketing, and
operations.

Policies and Procedures. During the course of the PSR, it is very
likely that outdated policies and procedures will have been identified. Appropriate assistance should be provided by the review team
to update these documents.

Orientation. Once revised policies and procedures have been developed, a briefing or a series of briefings should be conducted to reori-
ent all levels of personnel involved in the procurement system. Use
of persuasion and direction will ensure that all members of the system understand and accept the firm's objectives, policies, and procedures in this area and their responsibilities as members of this team.

Training. Selected members of the procurement system frequently
require training on relevant modern procedures. Frequently, a systematic training program must be developed and conducted for
members of the purchasing department and others involved in design, sourcing, pricing, and supplier relations. The training program
must include an "applications" module where participants solve a
few of their day-to-day problems using the new techniques learned
in training.

Reporting Improvements. Introduction of conservative quality and
reliability improvement and profit enhancement reporting systems

play a key role in implementing an upgraded procurement system. Data for the quality and reliability improvement reports normally are readily available. The profit enhancement reporting system must be tailored to the firm's operation. As discussed earlier in the chapter, it is essential that this system be conservative to the point that any manager may review any claim and agree that yes, the specified number of dollars or more were contributed to the bottom line!

These reports give recognition to those whose efforts are improving quality and/or profitability. They may be the basis of an incentives program tailored to the firm. The resulting recognition causes others to want to receive similar recognition. The reporting systems create a momentum which drives the continuous improvement concept, practice, and results.

Experience. The PSR has been tested in the following settings: high-tech and low-tech manufacturers, institutions, and firms in the service industry. Our experience demonstrates that the PSR is an extremely effective means of implementing the philosophy, the tools, and the techniques described in this book!

CONCLUDING REMARKS

The survival and success of American industry depends on our competitiveness in the world marketplace. No function has greater impact on the competitiveness of our firms than that of procurement. The cost and quality of the goods sold and the time required to bring new products to market are all greatly influenced by the firm's procurement team.

You now have some of the most powerful concepts and tools ever available. Use them and remember,

YOU CAN MAKE IT HAPPEN!

Appendix A

Relevant Publications by the Authors

DAVID N. BURT

Books

Proactive Procurement: The Key to Increased Profits, Productivity and Quality. Prentice-Hall, NJ, 1984.

Purchasing and Materials Management, 5th ed. Co-authored with Donald Dobler, and Lamar Lee, Jr., McGraw-Hill Book Co., NY, 1990.

Articles

"Managing Product Quality Through Strategic Purchasing," *Sloan Management Review,* Spring 1989 (Vol. 30, No. 3).

"Managing Suppliers Up to Speed," *Harvard Business Review,* Jul-August 1989, 127-135.

"Purchasing's Role in New Product Development," *Harvard Business Review,* September-October 1985. (Co-author.)

"The Nuances of Negotiation Overseas," *Journal of Purchasing and Materials Management,* Winter 1984 (Vol. XX, No. 4); reprinted in the 25th Anniversary, 1989 issue.

"The Effect of Award Fees on Supplier Performance," *Journal of Purchasing and Materials Management*, Spring 1984 (Vol. XX, No. 1).

"Simulated Negotiations: The Way to Prepare for Actual Negotiations?," *Journal of Purchasing and Materials Management*, Summer 1982.

"Reduction in Selling Price After the Introduction of Competition," *Journal of Marketing Research*, May 1979. (Co-author.)

"The Award Fee Contract: A New Approach to Governmental and Industry Marketing," *Michigan Business Review*, January 1977.

"The Right Type of Contract for Every Procurement Situation," *Management Review*, May 1976.

"Acquisition: A Dynamic Process," *Air University Review*, March 1975.

"Stretching Your Building Dollar," *California Management Review*, Summer 1973 (Vol. XV/No. 4).

"Understanding Quality Control," *Journal of Purchasing*, May 1973 (Vol. 9, No. 2).

"Builder-Design Concept Offers Economies in Municipal Construction," *The American City*, April 1973.

"Should Cost—A Multimillion Dollar Savings," *Air University Review*, September-October 1972 (Vol XXIII, No. 6).

"Selecting and Compensating Your Next Architect-Engineer," *Michigan Business Review*, January 1972.

"The Effect of the Number of Competitors on Cost," *Journal of Purchasing*, November 1971.

WARREN E. NORQUIST

Book

Creative Countertrade: A Guide to Doing Business Worldwide. Co-authored with Kenneth W. Elderkin, Ballinger subsidiary, Harper & Row, NY, 1987.

Articles

"Purchasing" Chapter in *Manufacturing Manager's Handbook,* Prentice Hall, NJ, 1990.

"Information, Please Now," co-authored with Martin Helsmoortel, *Purchasing Management,* January 8, 1990.

"Zero Base Pricing™": Achieving Competitiveness through Reduced All-in-Cost." In *Revolution in Purchasing and Materials Management.* Presentation from the 75th Annual International Purchasing Conference, Tempe, AZ: National Association of Purchasing Management, 1990.

"Purchasing's Role in Countertrade." In *Revolution in Purchasing and Materials Management.* 74th Annual International Purchasing Conference, Tempe, AZ: NAPM, 1989.

"Countertrade Strategies," *Purchasing Management,* February 20, 1989.

"The Ultimate in Negotiation Preparation: On-Line Data Bases." In *Purchasing's New Frontiers.* 73rd Annual International Purchasing Conference, Tempe, AZ: NAPM, 1988.

"Countertrade: Another Purchasing Horizon," *Journal of Purchasing and Materials Management,* Summer 1987 (Vol. 23, No. 2).

"The What, Why and How of Zero Base Pricing™." In *Purchasing and Technology—1986 & Beyond.* 71st Annual International Purchasing Conference, Oradell, NJ; NAPM, 1986.

"Zero Base Pricing™." In *Purchasing: A Productivity Resource.* 69th Annual International Purchasing Conference, Oradell, NJ: NAPM, 1984.

"Improving Quality/Purchasing Teamwork," *37th Annual Quality Congress Transactions,* American Society for Quality Control, 1983.

Contributor to *Productivity: Problems and Prospects,* Work in America Institute, October 1981.

"Quality Assurance in the Photographic Industry," *Journal of Applied Photographic Engineering,* August 1981.

"Quality: How Well Are You Communicating It?," *Quality Progress,* June 1981.

"Quality of Life in the Workplace," *Engineering,* American Society for Engineering Education, 1981.

"How to Increase Reliability of Consumer Products," *Mechanical Engineering,* January 1973.

"Polaroid's Quality Data System," *A.S.Q.C. National Convention Transactions,* 1963.

"Evaluating the Quality Data System," *The Tool and Manufacturing Engineer,* November 1962.

"Improve Material Utilization—Engineer Your Scrap Accounts," Industrial Quality Control, May 1962.

JIMMY ANKLESARIA

Articles

"Financial Analysis: A Critical Tool for Supplier Management." Presentation from the 75th Annual International Purchasing Conference, New Orleans, LA: National Association of Purchasing Management, 1990.

"Using Incremental Analysis to Buy Capacity." 75th Annual International Purchasing Conference, New Orleans, LA: NAPM, 1990.

"Personal Factors in the Purchasing/Engineering Interface," co-authored with David N. Burt, *Journal of Purchasing and Materials Management,* Winter 1987.

"The Importance of a Divestment Policy," co-authored with Daniel Rivetti, *Journal of Buyouts and Acquisitions,* January 1987.

Appendix B*

VA/VE Checklists

1. A checklist for substitution:
   A. Have some items been included simply because they were handy when the breadboard or model was constructed?
   B. Have suppliers been consulted about alternatives or modifications?
   C. Has a special look been taken at components such as transistors, semiconductors, magnetic and high power devices, motors and gear trains?
   D. Has coax cable been specified when hookup wire or shielded cable will do the job?
   E. Are obsolete or obsolescent electronic devices specified?
   F. Could plastics be used instead of ceramic packaging of semiconductors?
   G. Could sealant be used in place of lock washers?
   H. Has tubing been analyzed? Could steel be replaced by copper, aluminum or magnesium?
   I. Could aluminum be used in place of zinc in large die cast parts?
   J. Have unusual forms of raw material been considered?
   K. How about epoxies, nylon, fiberglass—or even wood?

*Referred to on page 58.

L. Have in-house specialists been consulted about alternative test processes?

M. Could different tooling be used for production runs?

N. Could new or different processes be used: castings, forgings, weldments, molded plastic, heat treatments?

O. Would paint dipping rather than spraying be possible?

P. Could barrel plating replace dipping in a still tank?

Q. How about lithographing plates instead of etching them?

R. Have all possible fabrication methods such as die casting, extruding, permanent mold casting, stamping, rolling and welding, roll forming, investment casting, powder metallurgy, plastic molding, and structural foam been considered?

2. A checklist for elimination (if it's not necessary, get rid of it):

A. Have changing technical developments made parts, processes or circuitry unnecessary?

B. Could circuitry be eliminated by having one circuit do the job of two or more?

C. Is every part absolutely necessary?

D. Have accessory items and features been checked to make sure the need for them still exists?

E. Could tapping be eliminated by the use of standard commercial fasteners?

F. Could fastening devices be eliminated by stamping a nut impression into the part?

G. Could roll-pins eliminate reaming?

H. Can any test specification be eliminated or relaxed?

I. Have interacting controls been eliminated or adjusted so that factory personnel can align the circuit?

J. Has tooling been studied to eliminate the need for labor?

K. Are all manual welding operations absolutely necessary?

L. Is all masking from finishing materials—such as plating solutions and paint—necessary?

3. A checklist for standardization (this is one of the most important tools of value analysis because it reduces cost by reducing prices, improving availability, reducing order frequency, and reducing inventory levels):

   A. Can a standard vendor item do the job?

   B. Have standard "preferred circuits" been reviewed to see how many can be used?

   C. Have nearly identical parts been made identical?

   D. Are mechanical tolerances within the limits of standard shop practice?

   E. Are the surface finishes the coarsest that will do the job?

   F. Will standard components and hardware supply the minimum-required characteristics?

   G. Do control drawings leave no doubt that a standard vendor part is being specified when such is the case?

   H. Have standard alloys, grades and sizes of stock been specified for all material?

   I. Has standardization been carried too far, so that the cost of the excess function outweighs other gains?

   J. Can the design be altered in any way to avoid the use of non-standard tooling?

4. A checklist for combination:

   A. Can adjacent parts purchased from one supplier be pre-assembled?

   B. Can the same conductor be used for warm-up and operational conditions?

   C. Could a single part provide multiple functions?

   D. Is the combination of material and protective finish the best one?

   E. Could sub-assemblies be combined to make the final assembly self-supporting?

F. Are the quantities to be built known? Have future orders been considered for combination of requirements?

G. Could model shop tooling be combined for production runs?

H. Could processes be combined through automation?

I. Would a combination design avoid unnecessary handling such as riveting and spot welding on the same sub-assembly?

J. Could small parts be drilled and tapped in strips before cutting apart?

K. How about resistance welding in one operation rather than spot welding one at a time?

L. Is there adequate clearance between parts to allow for each assembly? (Parts have become smaller but hands have not.)

5. Keep it simple—avoid over-design or complexity. Consider the dictum, "Dimensions will always be expressed in the least usable term. Velocity, for example, will be expressed in furlongs per fortnight." This certainly requires simplification.

A checklist for simplification:

A. Has the effect of contract required over design been discussed with the customer?

B. Does the design give the customer what he requires—performance, reliability and maintainability—and no more?

C. Have specifications been reviewed to make sure they are not overspecified on subcontracts?

D. Is the circuitry overly complex?

E. Could all the tapped holes be put into one part?

F. Could making a part straight instead of curved reduce the need for elbows?

G. Can through holes be used instead of blind holes?

H. When blind holes are necessary, couldn't the specs show minimum depth—with a note, "don't drill through,"—rather than exact limits?

I. Is bending necessary?

J. Could a casting or molded part be used in place of several small stampings?

K. Could a higher cost material afford simpler designs or easier assembly? (Examples: heat treated beryllium copper in place of phosphur bronze to eliminate adjusting labor; special materials in flux paths to save laminations; brass instead of steel on very small screw machine parts to save labor.)

L. Can test processes be simplified and still meet the design requirement?

Each question, when applicable, should be analyzed completely. If the answer to any question is not satisfactory, it should become the starting point for more detailed investigation.

Procedures and checklists are important, but in the end, value management depends on the analyst and on teamwork and requires the acceptance and support by management. Teamwork is critical. Engineering, Production, Quality Control and Purchasing all have a mutual interest and responsibility for the success of the program, and must be dedicated to its success. In today's technical and economic climate, involvement is the only key to success. Reduced purchased material costs, increased profits, and improved competitive position in the marketplace are the benefits.

Appendix C*

Price Indexes

In Chapter 7, the reader saw that the price analyst must adjust for changes in the general price level in order to use historic cost information to facilitate price or cost comparisons. Price index numbers indicate price changes for a commodity or service over time. Price index numbers are price relatives, usually expressed as percentages. As price relatives, they relate prices paid in one time period to prices paid in some base time period. To provide comparability, a series of index numbers representing some commodity, product, or service is usually constructed using the same base period, thus reflecting a percentage increase or decrease in prices relative to that base period.

The selection of a base period is usually an arbitrary process. With a short series of data, say five to ten years, the analyst often chooses the first (earliest) year as the base year.** Under ideal conditions, it is best to choose as a base year one in which prices did not change erratically. Finding such a year is difficult when hundreds of items are included in an aggregative index number. So, again, one may be led to an arbitrary choice of a base year.

The U.S. Department of Labor's Bureau of Labor Statistics (BLS), a widely recognized constructor and publisher of general index numbers, currently uses a base year of 1977 for most of its index numbers.

---

*Referred to on page 132.
**It should be noted that price indexes can use monthly or quarterly data.

In constructing price index numbers, it is important to express a price in dollars per measure of quantity (for example, $/#, $/person, or $/feet). One should not express the price in terms of dollars per period, such as found in accounting data. Accounting data must be edited to dollars per measure of quantity before they can be used in price index number construction.

A simple price index involves a single commodity or service over time. There are four steps to be followed in constructing a simple price index.

Table C.1 Price Index Electronic Relays (1982 = 100)

Year	March Price	Index Calculation	Relative Price	Relative Price Index	BLS Producer Price Index
1982	$105.60	$\frac{105.6}{105.6}$ =	1.000	100.0	100.0
1983	$104.50	$\frac{104.5}{105.6}$ =	.989	98.9	112.3
1984	$145.90	$\frac{145.9}{105.6}$ =	1.382	138.2	132.1
1985	$140.00	$\frac{140.0}{105.6}$ =	1.325	132.5	131.9
1986	$144.50	$\frac{144.5}{105.6}$ =	1.368	136.8	132.5
1987	$149.70	$\frac{149.7}{105.6}$ =	1.412	141.2	132.0
1988	$148.00	$\frac{148.0}{105.6}$ =	1.401	140.1	135.7

Steps to Develop Table C.1

1. **Collect Data.** For each index period, collect average data for the product, commodity, or service. For example, assume the March prices

Year	1982	1983	1984	1985	1986	1987	1988
Price	$105.6	$104.5	$145.9	$140.0	$144.5	$149.7	$148.0

2. **Select Base Year.** Select a base year appropriate for the data available. In this case we will use 1982 for calculating the relative price.

3. **Calculate Relative Price.** Calculate a time series relative price for each year by dividing each yearly price by the base year price.

4. **Convert to Index.** Convert an index number or percentage by multiplying each price relative by 100. Normally, we round indexes to the nearest tenth.

5. **Compare to Producer Price Index.** Use the Producer Price Index for the particular item/commodity as a reference to compare against. This comparison will show whether the item is better than (lower) or worse than (higher) the PPI index value.

Seldom will a single simple index number suffice for pricing purposes. Many items purchased are made up of many different materials and types of labor, the prices of which vary at different rates over a period of time. Therefore, it often pays to construct composite index numbers that reflect aggregative changes in the prices of the components, assemblies, and types of labor that make up an item. This need has been satisfied by the development of a number of different methods for constructing aggregative indexes. A discussion of these methods is beyond the scope of this text. However, there are several good texts that discuss construction of index numbers if one desires to pursue the subject.

Often one will not have enough data or time to construct needed index numbers. Many sources exist for previously constructed price index numbers that are general in scope but may be used to approximate price changes of a particular product or service.

Probably the best known and most frequently used source of price index numbers is the *Producer Prices Index* published monthly by the Bureau of Labor Statistics (BLS). Economic indicators can also be found in the BLS publication entitled *Monthly Labor Review*, as well as other similar publications.

The producer price indexes are a series of price indexes of specific commodities and products. Each series is successively arranged in homogeneous categories of items and commodities to form a general aggregation of wholesale prices for all U.S. production. Accordingly, one may choose an index that best fits a specific product from the indexes of many different commodities or services and many different levels of aggregation.

Another widely used source of price index numbers is the *Survey of Current Business, National Income Issue,* which is published each July by the U.S. Department of Commerce, Bureau of Economic Analysis. A series of "Gross National Product Implicit Price Deflators" are included in this publication.

A source of data useful for constructing labor price index numbers is the BLS periodical, *Employment and Earnings,* which sets forth average wage rates segregated by skill and geographical categories. These rates are useful in tailoring an index to fit a specific product or company. Another source of wage data useful to the price analyst as an economic indicator is the annual *National Survey of Professional Administrative, Technical and Clerical Pay,* a BLS publication. This survey is useful as a source of data concerning indirect labor pay rate changes.

The *Economic Report of the President,* an annual publication of the executive branch, sets forth extensive summaries of economic indicators. This publication is useful for evaluating long-range trends of data.

These sources are only a sample of the many index numbers and economic series available to the buyer. Remember when using them that a general index series must be used carefully since it usually will not exactly fit the cost pattern of the product or service being analyzed. Sources of error include the fact that the data is not from a specific supplier, and it usually represents national or regional averages. Another source of error stems from the fact that the sample of items that make up an index probably will not fit a specific product or supplier effort. Nevertheless, preconstructed index numbers offer a practical alternative to the costly and time-consuming task of building index number series from basic cost data.

Index numbers indicate the percentage change in price with respect to the base year only. The index we constructed in Table C.1 for 1987 of 132 indicates that the average price of electronic relays went up 32 percent with respect to 1982. It does not indicate that prices rose 20 percent (132.5 − 112.3) between 1983 and 1986. To calculate the percentage increases in price for 1986 with respect to 1983, one divides the 1983 index into the 1986 index, multiplies the dividend by 100, and subtracts 100.00. In this case, the price level rose 18 percent between 1983 and 1986.

$$\left(\frac{132.5}{112.3}\right) \times 100 - 100 = 18\%$$

How to Adjust Forward or Back

Prices can be inflated or deflated to adjust for general price level changes. Consider the problem of analyzing a supplier's proposed price of $1500.00 for a metal cutting tool to be delivered in 1988. A procurement history file reveals that the same tool was purchased in 1982 at a price of $1100.00. The task is to determine if the 1988 proposed price is fair and reasonable. (We will assume that the two tools are identical in features and capacity.)

Select Index. To determine if the price is fair and reasonable, we would first select or construct an appropriate index series. The Metal Cutting Tools Subindex of the Producer Price Index (BLS) might be selected as a reasonable indicator of price movement for metal cutting tools. We could extract the data from a publication, such as the appropriate issues of the *Producer Price Index.*

| | *Metal Cutting Tools* |
Year	*(1967=100)*
1982	365.6
1983	374.7
1984	381.9
1985	395.9
1986	399.1
1987	413.8
1988 (est.)	428.0

Adjust for Inflation. After we have selected an index, we can adjust prices to a common dollar value level. In this case, we might adjust the historical 1982 price to the 1988 dollar value level. We alternately might adjust the current price to the 1982 dollar value level. It really makes no difference as long as we get both prices to comparable dollar value levels. To make the adjustment, we simply find the percentage of dollar value change between the periods and multiply that change by the price in the period. This can be shown in the following information.

$$\frac{\text{Projection Period Index}}{\text{Price Data Period Index}} \times \text{Price Data} = \text{Projected Price}$$

1. To adjust the 1982 price to 1988 dollars, (1988 constant $) this could be written as follows:

$$\frac{1988 \text{ Index}}{1982 \text{ Index}} \times 1982 \text{ Price} = \text{Comparable 1988 Price}$$

$$\frac{428.0}{365.6} \times \$1100 = \$1,287.75$$

Our calculations show that the suppliers' quoted price of $1500 is $212.25 greater than the historic price adjusted for inflation.

2. To adjust the 1988 quoted price to 1982 dollars, (1982 constant $) we could do the following:

$$\frac{1982 \text{ Index}}{1988 \text{ Index}} \times 1988 \text{ Price} = \text{Comparable } 1982 \text{ Price}$$

$$\frac{365.6}{428.0} \times \$1500 = \$1281.31$$

These calculations indicate that the suppliers' quoted price, when adjusted back to 1982, is $181.31 higher than the price paid at that time.

Once the adjustment for inflation is made, we can compare the quoted and historical prices in comparable dollar values. If we want to compare using 1988 dollar values, we must compare the 1982 historical prices adjusted to 1988 price levels with the unadjusted 1988 price quote. The quoted price is $1500 (16.5 percent) higher than what we would expect it to be, based on the historical price, adjusted by the index.

Based on the 16.5 percent difference between the historical price and quoted price, the buyer should question the reasonableness of the price quoted.

Appendix D*

Index Data for a Specific Product

EXAMPLE 1

To: Polyethylene Products Buyer   cc:
From: Purchasing Research
Date: May, 1988
Subject: Low Density Polyethylene Bags

This report updates my memo of February 22, 1988 to you. The current situation with _____ and its requested increase for a 35% price change highlights some of the pricing pressure in the market place.

Item	*Comments*
Low Density Polyethylene Resins PPI 066203 CC 066203	There has been a significant fall back during the 1986-1987 period. The latest period of April 1988 is 10.8% above the 1984-1985 previous high, while the first quarter of 1988 was 15.1% higher. See Figure D.1.

*Referred to on pages 136 and 290.

Figure D.1   Low Density Polyethylene Resins—WPU066203

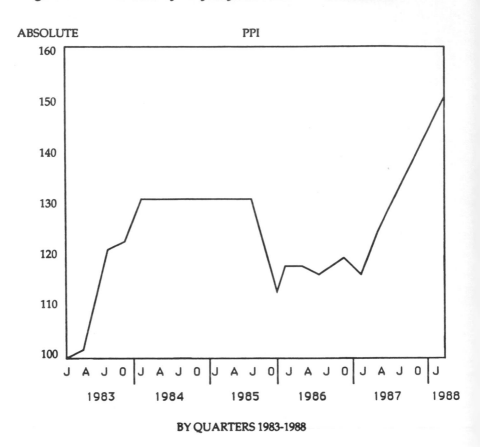

ABSOLUTE   PPI

BY QUARTERS 1983-1988

PE Resin, Low Density
Film and Sheeting
PPI 06620301

This index also demonstrates the dramatic fall back during 1986-1987. April 1988 is 5.0% above the 1984-1985 previous high while the first quarter of 1988 was 8.3% higher. Even though there has been a significant rate of increase recently, we cannot ignore the low area of 1986-1987, and we must indirectly ask what benefit, if any, was seen in this period. See Figure D.2.

Average Hourly
Earnings (for specific
plant location)

While the graphical data depicts a steady
rise in hourly earnings, the period from the
first quarter of 1987 to the first quarter of
1988 represents a 2.3% increase.

Figure D.2 PE Resin, Low Density Film and Sheeting— WPU06620301

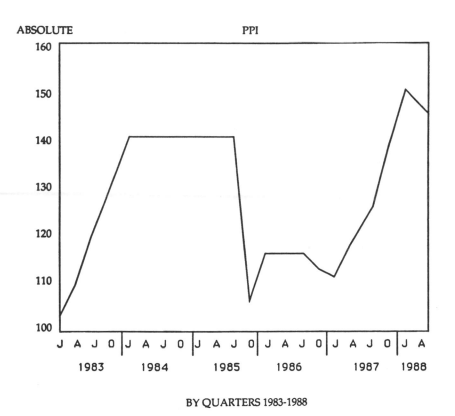

BY QUARTERS 1983-1988

Other Comments

- Resin output rose in March. Low density polyethylene output increased 6.4% on a year to year basis.

  Journal of Commerce, June 1, 1988

- Materials' shifts escalate. Converters and users are actively seeking alternative materials to reduce price increases of various polymers.

  Plastics World, May 1988

SUMMARY

The apparent message from management is that they not only wish to catch up with their pricing but they also wish to get ahead. As noted in my February memo we should avoid the future potential increase element of the present request and we must focus heavily on what is reasonable.

Strong emphasis has to be placed on the material cost fall back during 1986-1987. Since the vendor points out that there have been no price increases since 1984—when the raw material was stable—we must ask what benefit we derived during the reduction of material costs.

Some additional information on the vendor's material costs relative to his total costs of material, labor, factory overhead, G&A costs and profit would definitely help us in determining what is fair and reasonable. Certainly a 35% price increase request is not only excessive but appears on the surface unreasonable.

EXAMPLE 2

To: Fiber Drum Buyer   cc:
From: Purchasing Research
Date: May, 1988
Subject: Polyethylene Lined Fiber Drum Prices

Based on our discussion and review of polyethylene lined fiber drums additional producer price information for the various major components is supplied. Graphs for the producer price information are presented for both the absolute index and percent change. All information is for quarterly data.

Item	*Comments*
Paper Board Fiber Drums PPI 09150337	Following the initial increase at the beginning of 1987 the producer price was flat for two quarters but in the last quarter of 1987 and the first quarter of 1988 there has been a 7.1% increase.
Polyethylene Resin Low Density—All Other Uses PPI 06620303	This index shows a major period of relative stability from 1984 to 1987. From late 1987 through the first quarter of 1988 there has been a 13% increase in this item.
Low Density Polyethylene Resins PPI 066203	This general category item is showing a steady and major rate of increase. From the third quarter of 1987 through the first quarter of 1988 this index has increased 11.4%. However there was a major fall back during late 1985 which lasted through mid-1987.
Cold Rolled Sheets and Strips PPI 101702	This general category shows a major fall back during 1986 with recovery during 1987. Even with this the index is only 1.0% above the 1984 high point.
Sheets, C.R. Carbon PPI 10170711	This specific index shows the same major pattern as Cold Rolled Sheets and Strips

Energy Mid-Atlantic
PPI 05431204

but is more exaggerated and the present period—first quarter of 1988—is only 0.8% greater than the 1984-1985 high.

General trends of softening of electric power rates are apparent. The Orange & Rockland Utilities is the probable supplier of power, analysts' reports are attached.

Additional producer price index data strongly supports falling power rates in the mid-Atlantic area.

Labor

Labor dollars for New Jersey are available only for the entire state. The change from the third quarter of 1987 to the first quarter of 1988 is 3.3%.

Massachusetts data for the Springfield area shows a 2.5% increase over this same period.

SUMMARY

The major items of kraft paper, polyethylene, and steel are all under heavy supply-demand pressures. These items are not likely to abate in the near future.

Our target should be no greater than one-half of the "general" price increase. I base this position on the following:

1. Our growing business volume with them.

2. Their ability to increase efficiency as noted in their 1986 annual report.

3. The various producer price index charts while showing recent increases in prices also show major drops in prices in the near past.

These two memos are examples of the support provided buyers by Polaroid's Purchasing Research Manager, Martin Helsmoortel.

PRODUCER PRICE INDEX

For those interested in being able to work with the Producer Price Index, the following information is provided on getting the index.

The PPI tapes come in three different formats:

Magnetic Tapes
1. 9 track, 1600 BPI $60
2. 9 track, 6250 BPI $60

Floppy Disk
1. 5 1/4 Diskette $38
2. 3 1/4 Diskette $38

NOTE: Information on diskettes only includes last and this year's data, and the data itself is greatly abbreviated.

Source: Office of Financial Planning Mgmt.
(202) 523-1324 (Christine)

To Order: Cannot be done over the phone because they require advance payment. Write a letter stating the tapes desired to:

Bureau of Labor Statistics
Division of Financial Planning Mgmt.
Room 2115
Washington, DC 20212

Include check for amount of tapes ordered.

Appendix E*

Should Cost

SIC CODE	INDUSTRY GROUP AND INDUSTRY	Ratio Materials/ Labor
STATISTICS FOR INDUSTRY GROUPS AND INDUSTRIES:1986		
	Ratio of Materials to Labor	
	ALL INDUSTRIES	5.16
20	Food and kindred products	11.04
21	Tobacco products	6.95
22	Textile mill products	4.18
23	Apparel and other textile products	3.30
24	Lumber and wood products	4.30
25	Furniture and fixtures	2.79
26	Paper and allied products	4.78
27	Printing and publishing	2.88
28	Chemicals and allied products	8.21
29	Petroleum and coal products	39.93
30	Rubber and miscellaneous plastics products	3.56
31	Leather and leather products	3.43
32	Stone, clay, and glass products	3.18
33	Primary metal industries	4.93
34	Fabricated metal products	3.17
35	Machinery, except electrical	3.85
36	Electric and electronic equipment	3.60
37	Transportation equipment	5.59
38	Instruments and related products	3.26
39	Miscellaneous manufacturing industries	3.59
20	FOOD AND KINDRED PRODUCTS	11.04
201	Meat products	14.41
2011	Meat packing plants	22.08
2013	Sausages & other prepared meats	10.49
2016	Poultry dressing plants	7.13
2017	Poultry & egg processing	8.78
202	Dairy products	18.93
2021	Creamery butter	50.00
2022	Cheese, natural & processed	20.91
2023	Condensed & evaporated milk	18.25

SIC CODE	Ratio of Materials to Labor INDUSTRY GROUP AND INDUSTRY	Ratio Materials/ Labor
2024	Ice cream & frozen desserts	10.90
2026	Fluid milk	19.07
203	Canned and preserved fruits & vegetables	6.79
2032	Canned specialties	6.86
2033	Canned fruits & vegatables	7.31
2034	Dehydrated fruits, vegetables & soups	6.01
2035	Pickles, sauces & salad dressings	8.85
2037	Frozen fruits & vegetables	6.11
2038	Frozen specialties	5.67
204	Grain mill products	12.42
2041	Flour & other grain mill products	15.10
2043	Cereal breakfast foods	3.62
2044	Rice milling	15.53
2045	Blended & prepared flour	8.92
2046	Wet corn milling	16.58
2047	Dog, cat & other pet food	8.84
2048	Prepared feeds, not elsewhere classified (n.e.c.)	25.57
205	Bakery products	3.30
2051	Bread, cake & related products	3.35
2052	Cookies & crackers	3.19
206	Sugar & confectionery products	7.30
2061	Raw cane sugar	7.48
2062	Cane sugar refining	15.53
2063	Beet sugar	7.88
2065	Confectionery products	5.77
2066	Chocolate & cocoa products	8.37
2067	Chewing gum	3.88
207	Fats & oils	28.70
2074	Cottonseed oil mills	12.10
2075	Soybean oil mills	66.77
2076	Vegetable oil mills, n.e.c.	34.11
2077	Animal & marine fats & oils	8.66
2079	Shortening & cooking oils	21.76
208	Beverages	11.67
2082	Malt beverages	7.30
2083	Malt	12.44

SIC CODE	Ratio of Materials to Labor INDUSTRY GROUP AND INDUSTRY	Ratio Materials/ Labor
2084	Wines, brandy & brandy spirits	12.99
2085	Distilled liquor, except brandy	10.00
2086	Bottled & canned soft drinks	17.39
2087	Flavoring extracts & syrups, n.e.c.	10.85
209	Miscellaneous foods & kindred products	9.71
2091	Canned & cured seafoods	7.16
2092	Fresh or frozen packaged fish	9.80
2095	Roasted coffee	28.64
2097	Manufactured ice	2.05
2098	Macaroni & spaghetti	5.30
2099	Food preparations, n.e.c.	6.81
21	TOBACCO PRODUCTS	6.95
2111	Cigarettes	5.55
2121	Cigars	2.75
2131	Chewing & smoking tobacco	6.99
2141	Tobacco stemming & redrying	24.58
22	TEXTILE MILL PRODUCTS	4.18
2211	Weaving mills, cotton	2.48
2221	Weaving mills, manmade fiber & silk	3.24
2231	Weaving & finishing mills, wool	2.90
2241	Narrow fabric mills	2.48
225	Knitting mills	3.31
2251	Women's full-length & knee-length hosiery	2.39
2252	Hosiery, n.e.c.	2.76
2253	Knit outerwear mills	2.89
2254	Knit underwear mills	2.80
2257	Circular knit fabric mills	5.08
2258	Warp knit fabric mills	4.95
2259	Knitting mills, n.e.c.	2.40

SIC CODE	Ratio of Materials to Labor / INDUSTRY GROUP AND INDUSTRY	Ratio Materials/ Labor
226	Textile finishing, except wool	5.91
2261	Finishing plants, cotton	4.68
2262	Finishing plants, manmade	6.49
2269	Finishing plants, n.e.c.	5.06
227	Floor covering mills	10.04
2271	Woven carpets & rugs	4.16
2272	Tufted carpets & rugs	10.83
2279	Carpets & rugs, n.e.c.	
228	Yarn & thread mills	4.23
2281	Yarn mills, except wool	3.67
2282	Texturizing, throwing & winding mills	6.63
2283	Wool yarn mills	4.14
2284	Thread mills	9.04
229	Miscellaneous textile goods	4.43
2291	Felt goods, except woven felts & hats	2.52
2292	Lace goods	1.17
2293	Paddings & upholstery filling	3.20
2294	Processed textile waste	5.55
2295	Coated fabrics, not rubberized	5.12
2296	Tire cord & fabric	8.85
2297	Nonwoven fabrics	4.53
2298	Cordage & twine	2.92
2299	Textile goods, n.e.c.	2.01
23	APPAREL & OTHER TEXTILE PRODUCTS	3.30
2311	Men's & boys' suits & coats	2.17
232	Men's & boys' furnishings, incl. work clothes	2.74
2321	Men's & boys' shirts & nightwear	2.94
2322	Men's & boys' underwear	1.96
2323	Men's & boys' neckwear	3.25
2327	Men's & boys' separate trousers	2.77
2328	Men's & boys' work clothing	2.97
2329	Men's & boys' clothing, n.e.c.	2.11
233	Women's, misses' & juniors' outerwear	3.73
2331	Women's, misses' & juniors' blouses	3.43
2335	Women's, misses' & juniors' dresses	7.88

SIC CODE	Ratio of Materials to Labor INDUSTRY GROUP AND INDUSTRY	Ratio Materials/ Labor
2337	Women's, misses' & juniors' suits & coats	5.92
2339	Women's, misses' & juniors' outerwear, n.e.c.	3.29
234	Women's, children's & infants' undergarments	2.78
2341	Women's, children's & infants' underwear	2.50
2342	Brassieres & allied garments	4.03
235	Hats, caps & millinery	2.52
2351	Millinery	2.90
2352	Hats & caps except millinery	2.47
236	Children's outerwear	2.87
2361	Children's dresses & blouses	2.79
2363	Children's coats & suits	2.06
2369	Children's outerwear, n.e.c.	3.07
2371	Fur goods	8.43
238	Miscellaneous apparel & accessories	3.07
2381	Fabric dress & work gloves	0.92
2384	Robes & dressing gowns	4.08
2385	Waterproof outergarments	1.93
2386	Leather & sheep lined clothing	5.23
2387	Apparel belts	3.26
2389	Apparel & accessories n.e.c.	2.37
239	Miscellaneous fabricated textile products	4.03
2391	Curtains & draperies	3.77
2392	House furnishings n.e.c.	5.80
2393	Textile bags	5.23
2394	Canvas & related products	2.97
2395	Pleating, stitching & tucking	3.31
2396	Automotive & apparel trimmings	2.95
2397	Schiffi machine embroideries	1.74
2399	Fabricated textile products n.e.c.	4.77
24	LUMBER & WOOD PRODUCTS	4.30
2411	Logging camps & logging contractors	5.19
242	Sawmills & planing mills	4.18

SIC CODE	Ratio of Materials to Labor INDUSTRY GROUP AND INDUSTRY	Ratio Materials/ Labor
2426	Hardwood dimension & flooring	2.60
2429	Special product sawmills, n.e.c.	2.68
243	Millwork, plywood, & structural members	3.87
2431	Millwork	4.45
2434	Wood kitchen cabinets	2.41
2435	Hardwood veneer & plywood	4.80
2436	Softwood veneer & plywood	3.83
2439	Structural wood members, n.e.c.	4.63
244	Wood containers	3.89
2441	Nailed wood boxes & shook	3.32
2448	Wood pallets & skids	4.20
2449	Wood containers, n.e.c.	3.27
245	Wood buildings & mobile homes	5.45
2451	Mobile homes	5.31
2452	Prefabricated wood buildings & components	5.77
249	Miscellaneous wood products	4.17
2491	Wood preserving	9.92
2492	Particleboard	4.31
2499	Wood products, n.e.c.	3.02
25	FURNITURE & FIXTURES	2.79
251	Household furniture	2.85
2511	Wood housefold furniture	2.45
2512	Upholstered household furniture	2.75
2514	Metal household furniture	3.38
2515	Mattresses & bedsprings	5.13
2517	Wood TV & radio cabinets	2.59
2519	Household furniture, n.e.c.	3.15
252	Office furniture	2.55
2521	Wood office furniture	2.11
2522	Metal office furniture	2.74
2531	Public building & related furniture	3.23

SIC CODE	Ratio of Materials to Labor INDUSTRY GROUP AND INDUSTRY	Ratio Materials/ Labor
254	Partitions & fixtures	2.43
2541	Wood partitions & fixtures	2.04
2542	Metal partitions & fixtures	2.90
259	Miscellaneous furniture & fixtures	3.34
2591	Drapery hardware & binds & shades	4.36
2599	Furniture & fixtures, n.e.c.	2.63
26	PAPER & ALLIED PRODUCTS	4.78
2611	Pulp mills	4.93
2621	Paper mills, except building paper	4.15
2631	Paperboard mills	4.79
264	Miscellaneous converted paper products	5.29
2641	Paper coating & glazing	6.17
2642	Envelopes	3.49
2643	Bags, except textile bags	4.82
2645	Die-cut paper & board	4.64
2646	Pressed & molded pulp goods	1.97
2647	Sanitary paper products	6.30
2648	Stationery products	4.98
2649	Converted paper products, n.e.c.	5.07
265	Paperboard containers & boxes	4.87
2651	Folding paperboard boxes	3.46
2652	Set-up paperboard boxes	3.08
2653	Corrugated & solid fiber boxes	5.91
2654	Sanitary food containers	4.04
2655	Fiber cans, drums & similar products	4.82
2661	Building paper & board mills	3.85
27	PRINTING & PUBLISHING	2.88
2711	Newspapers	2.41
2721	Periodicals	19.24

SIC CODE	Ratio of Materials to Labor INDUSTRY GROUP AND INDUSTRY	Ratio Materials/ Labor
273	Books	4.77
2731	Book publishing	11.95
2732	Book printing	1.90
2741	Miscellaneous publishing	4.53
275	Commercial printing	2.39
2751	Commercial printing, letterpress	2.45
2752	Commercial printing, lithographic	2.37
2753	Evgraving & plate printing	1.18
2754	Commercial printing, gravure	2.85
2761	Manifold business forms	4.04
2771	Greeting card publishing	3.56
278	Blankbooks & bookbinding	1.40
2782	Blankbooks & looseleaf binders	1.88
2789	Bookbinding & related work	0.74
279	Printing trade services	0.84
2791	Typesetting	0.65
2793	Photoengraving	
2794	Electrotyping & stereotyping	0.89
2795	Lithographic platemaking services	1.03
28	CHEMICALS & ALLIED PRODUCTS	8.21
281	Industrial inorganic chemicals	5.44
2812	Alkalies & chlorine	6.98
2813	Industrial gases	8.95
2816	Inorganic pigments	6.66
2819	Industrial inorganic chemicals, n.e.c.	4.75
282	Plastics materials & synthetics	8.67
2821	Plastics materials & resins	12.17
2822	Synthetic rubber	7.98
2823	Cellulosic manmade fibers	3.56
2824	Organic fibers, noncellulosic	5.81
283	Drugs	5.58
2831	Biological products	5.44

SIC CODE	Ratio of Materials to Labor INDUSTRY GROUP AND INDUSTRY	Ratio Materials/ Labor
2833	Medicinals & botanicals	5.47
2834	Phamaceutical preparations	5.63
284	Soaps, cleaners & toilet goods	8.41
2841	Soap & other detergents	10.50
2842	Polishes & sanitation goods	7.16
2843	Surface active agents	15.31
2844	Toilet preparations	5.93
2851	Paints & allied products	10.31
286	Industrial organic chemicals	10.46
2861	Gum & wood chemicals	6.42
2865	Cyclic crudes & intermediates	10.72
2869	Industrial organic chemicals, n.e.c.	10.50
287	Agricultural chemicals	12.49
2873	Nitrogenous fertilizers	12.56
2874	Phosphatic fertilizers	14.17
2875	Fertilizers, mixing only	16.20
2879	Agricultural chemicals, n.e.c.	9.94
289	Miscellaneous chemical products	7.25
2891	Adhesives & sealants	10.55
2892	Explosives	1.90
2893	Printing ink	9.51
2895	Carbon black	7.04
2899	Chemical preparations, n.e.c.	7.24
29	PETROLEUM & COAL PRODUCTS	39.93
2911	Petroleum refining	48.79
295	Paving & roofing materials	10.34
2951	Paving mixtures & blocks	10.35
2952	Asphalt felts & coatings	10.32
299	Miscellaneous petroleum & coal products	18.26
2992	Lubricating oils & greases	19.59
2999	Petroleum & coal products, n.e.c.	13.73

SIC CODE	Ratio of Materials to Labor INDUSTRY GROUP AND INDUSTRY	Ratio Materials/ Labor
30	RUBBER & MISC. PLASTICS PRODUCTS	3.56
3011	Tires & inner tubes	2.95
3021	Rubber & plastics footwear	3.19
3031	Reclaimed rubber	2.58
3041	Rubber & plastics hose & belting	3.18
3069	Fabricated rubber products, n.e.c.	3.17
3079	Miscellaneous plastics products	3.79
31	LEATHER & LEATHER PRODUCTS	3.43
3111	Leather tanning & finishing	6.14
3131	Boot & shoe cut stock & findings	3.63
314	Footwear, except rubber	2.75
3142	House slippers	2.88
3143	Men's footwear, except athletic	3.07
3144	Women's footwear, except athletic	2.22
3149	Footwear, except rubber, n.e.c.	3.21
3151	Leather gloves & mittens	5.10
3161	Luggage	3.49
317	Handbags & other personal leather goods	3.08
3171	Women's handbags & purses	3.11
3172	Personal leather goods, n.e.c.	3.03
3199	Leather goods, n.e.c.	2.80
32	STONE, CLAY & GLASS PRODUCTS	3.18
3211	Flat glass	2.44
322	Glass & glassware, pressed or blown	2.02
3221	Glass containers	2.18

SIC CODE	Ratio of Materials to Labor INDUSTRY GROUP AND INDUSTRY	Ratio Materials/ Labor
3229	Pressed & blown glass, n.e.c.	1.81
3231	Products of purchased glass	3.43
3241	Cement, hydraulic	4.52
325	Structural clay products	2.41
3251	Brick & structural clay tile	2.14
3253	Ceramic wall & floor tile	1.86
3255	Clay refractories	3.80
3259	Structural clay products, n.e.c.	2.07
326	Pottery & related products	1.37
3261	Vitreous plumbing fixtures	1.48
3262	Vitreous china food utensils	0.65
3263	Fine earthenware food utensils	0.85
3264	Porcelain electrical supplies	1.49
3269	Pottery products, n.e.c.	1.73
327	Concrete, gypsum & plaster products	4.15
3271	Concrete block & brick	6.24
3272	Concrete products, except block & brick	2.79
3273	Ready-mixed concrete	4.51
3274	Lime	3.46
3275	Gypsum products	5.57
3281	Cut stone & stone products	2.15
329	Miscellaneous nonmetallic mineral products	3.27
3291	Abrasive products	4.85
3292	Asbestos products	2.65
3293	Gaskets, packing, & sealing devices	2.68
3295	Minerals, ground or treated	3.97
3296	Mineral wool	2.70
3297	Nonclay refractories	3.62
3299	Nonmetallic mineral products, n.e.c.	1.96
33	PRIMARY METAL INDUSTRIES	4.93
331	Blast furnace & basic steel products	4.92
3312	Blast furnaces & steel mills	4.61
3313	Electrometallurgical products	6.49

SIC CODE	Ratio of Materials to Labor INDUSTRY GROUP AND INDUSTRY	Ratio Materials/ Labor
3315	Steel wire & related products	4.81
3316	Cold finishing of steel shapes	8.77
3317	Steel pipe & tubes	5.98
332	Iron & steel foundries	1.86
3321	Gray iron foundries	1.85
3322	Malleable iron foundries	1.76
3324	Steel investment foundries	1.77
3325	Steel foundries, n.e.c.	2.00
333	Primary smelting & refining of nonferrous metals	9.66
3331	Primary copper	20.71
3333	Primary zinc	8.82
3334	Primary aluminum	7.43
3341	Secondary nonferrous metals	15.83
335	Nonferrous rolling & drawing	7.23
3351	Copper rolling & drawing	6.96
3353	Aluminum sheet, plate, foil & welded tube prod	9.74
3354	Aluminum extruded products	5.46
3355	Aluminum rolling & drawing, n.e.c.	13.60
3356	Nonferrous rolling & drawing, n.e.c.	6.37
3357	Nonferrous wire drawing & insulating	6.39
336	Nonferrous foundries	2.21
3361	Aluminum foundries	2.14
3362	Brass, bronze & copper foundries	2.14
3369	Nonferrous foundries, n.e.c.	2.53
339	Miscellaneous primary metal products	2.62
3398	Metal heat treating	1.49
3399	Primary metal products, n.e.c.	4.29
34	FABRICATED METAL PRODUCTS (except machinery and transportation equip.)	3.17
341	Metal cans & shipping containers	6.52
3411	Metal cans	6.67
3412	Metal barrels, drums & pails	4.98

SIC CODE	Ratio of Materials to Labor INDUSTRY GROUP AND INDUSTRY	Ratio Materials/ Labor
342	Cutlery, hand tools & hardware	2.40
3421	Cutlery	1.58
3423	Hand & edge tools, n.e.c.	2.32
3425	Hand saws & saw blades	2.34
3429	Hardware, n.e.c.	2.54
343	Plumbing & heating except electric	3.76
3431	Metal sanitary ware	2.66
3432	Plumbing fittings & brass goods	4.19
3433	Heating equipment, except electric	3.98
344	Fabricated structural metal products	4.02
3441	Fabricated structural metal	4.30
3442	Metal doors, sash & trim	4.25
3443	Fabricated plate work (boiler shops)	2.94
3444	Sheet metal work	3.77
3446	Architectural metal work	3.17
3448	Prefabricated metal buildings	5.87
3449	Miscellaneous metal work	6.32
345	Screw machine products, bolts, etc.	2.21
3451	Screw machine products	1.76
3452	Bolts, nuts, rivets & washers	2.58
346	Metal forgings & stampings	2.74
3462	Iron & steel forgings	3.05
3463	Nonferrous forgings	3.63
3465	Automotive stampings	2.63
3466	Crowns & closures	4.57
3469	Metal stampings, n.e.c.	2.63
347	Metal, casting, engraving & allied services	2.24
3471	Metal plating & polishing	1.47
3479	Metal coating & allied services	3.34
348	Ordnance & asccessories, n.e.c.	1.84
3482	Small arms ammunition	1.85
3483	Ammunition, except for small arms, n.e.c.	2.64
3484	Small arms	1.64
3489	Ordnance & accessories, n.e.c.	0.96
349	Miscellaneous fabricated metal products	3.06

SIC CODE	Ratio of Materials to Labor INDUSTRY GROUP AND INDUSTRY	Ratio Materials/ Labor
3493	Steel springs, except wire	2.68
3494	Valves & pipe fittings	2.71
3495	Wire springs	2.16
3496	Miscellaneous fabricated wire products	3.11
3497	Metal foil & leaf	7.10
3498	Fabricated pipe & fittings	3.69
3499	Fabricated metal products, n.e.c.	2.88
35	Machinery, except electrical	3.46
351	Engines and turbines	4.15
3511	Turbines and Turbine generator sets	3.45
3519	Internal combustion engines, n.e.c.	4.37
352	Farm and garden machinery	5.10
3523	Farm machinery and equipment	4.14
3524	Lawn and garden equipment	7.70
353	Construction and related machinery	4.55
3531	Construction machinery	4.71
3532	Mining machinery	4.00
3533	Oil field & gas field machinery & equipment	3.77
3534	Elevators and moving stairways	4.23
3535	Conveyors and conveying equipment	4.50
3536	Hoists, cranes, and monorails	4.14
3537	Industrial trucks and tractors	5.81
354	Metalworking machinery & equipment	1.75
3541	Machine tools, metal cutting types	2.76
3542	Machine tools, metal forming types	2.77
3544	Special dies, tools, jigs, and fixtures	1.00
3545	Machine tool accessories	1.39
3546	Power driven hand tools	4.35
3547	Rolling mill machinery	4.47
3549	Metalworking machinery, n.e.c.	2.99
355	Special industry machinery except metalworking	3.19
3551	Food products machinery	2.89
3552	Textile machinery	2.45
3553	Woodworking machinery	3.84
3554	Paper industries machinery	3.99
3555	Printing trades machinery	3.91

SIC CODE	Ratio of Materials to Labor INDUSTRY GROUP AND INDUSTRY	Ratio Materials/ Labor
3559	Special industry machinery, n.e.c.	3.13
356	General industrial machinery	2.96
3561	Pumps and pumping equipment	3.51
3562	Ball and roller bearings	1.98
3563	Air and gas compressors	4.90
3564	Blowers and fans	3.18
3565	Industrial patterns	1.40
3566	Speed changes, drives, and gears	1.86
3567	Industrial furnaces and ovens	3.62
3568	Power transmission equipment, n.e.c.	2.55
3569	General industrial machinery, n.e.c.	3.37
357	Office and computing machines	10.36
3573	Electronic computing equipment	11.31
3574	Calculating and accounting machines	5.40
3576	Scales and balances, except laboratory	3.61
3579	Office machines, n.e.c., and typewriters	5.92
358	Refrigeration and service machinery	4.15
3581	Automatic merchandising machines	3.68
3582	Commercial laundry equipment	3.09
3585	Refrigeration and heating equipment	4.10
3586	Measuring and dispensing pumps	4.54
3589	Service industry machinery, n.e.c.	4.66
359	Miscellaneous machinery, except electrical	1.46
3592	Carburetors, pistons, rings, valves	2.02
3599	Macinery, except electrical, n.e.c.	1.36
36	Electric and electronic machinery, equipment and supplies	3.60
361	Electric transmission & distribution equipment	3.17
3612	Transformers	3.39
3613	Switchgear and switchboard apparatus	3.02
362	Electrical industrial apparatus	3.10
3621	Motors and generators	2.70
3622	Industrial controls	3.56
3623	Welding apparatus, electric	3.37

SIC CODE	Ratio of Materials to Labor / INDUSTRY GROUP AND INDUSTRY	Ratio Materials/ Labor
3624	Carbon and graphite products	3.87
3629	Electrical industrial apparatus, n.e.c.	3.05
363	Household appliances	4.82
3631	Household cooking equipment	6.74
3632	Household refrigerators and freezers	4.24
3633	Household laundry equipment	4.34
3634	Electric housewares and fans	5.36
3635	Household vacuum cleaners	4.11
3636	Sewing machines	1.91
3639	Household appliances, n.e.c.	4.37
364	Electric lighting and wiring equipment	3.23
3641	Electric lamps	2,34
3643	Current-carrying wiring devices	2.63
3644	Noncurrent-carrying wiring devices	3.46
3645	Residential lighting fixtures	3.40
3646	Commercial lighting fixtures	4.97
3647	Vehicular lighting equipment	2,81
3648	Lighting equipment, n.e.c.	4.54
365	Radio and TV receiving equipment	9.17
3651	Radio and TV receiving sets	10.18
3652	Phonograph records and prerecorded tape	4.89
366	Communication equipment	3.53
3661	Telephone and telegraph apparatus	5.31
3662	Radio and TV communication equipment	3.11
367	Electronic components and accesories	2.86
3671	Electron tubes, all types	2.31
3674	Semiconductors and related devices	2.84
3675	Electronic capacitors	1.99
3676	Electronic resistors	1.77
3677	Electronic coils and transformers	1.97
3678	Electronic connectors	2.11
3679	Electronic components,n.e.c.	3.40
369	Miscellaneous electrical equipment	3.59
3691	Storage batteries	3.03
3692	Primary batteries, dry and wet	5.47
3693	X-ray and electromedical apparatus	4.22

SIC CODE	Ratio of Materials to Labor INDUSTRY GROUP AND INDUSTRY	Ratio Materials/ Labor
3694	Electrical equip. for internal combustion engine	3.40
3699	Electrical equipment and supplies,n.e.c.	3.27
37	Transportation equipment	5.59
371	Motor vehicles & motor vehicle equipment	7.35
3711	Motor vehicles and car bodies	11.38
3713	Truck and bus bodies	4.19
3714	Motor vehicle parts and accesories	3.77
3715	Truck trailers	5.46
3716	Motor homes produced on purchased chassis	8.98
372	Aircraft and parts	4.01
3721	Aircraft	5.59
3724	Aircraft engine and engine parts	3.66
3728	Aircraft equipment,n.e.c.	2.14
373	Ship and boat building and repair	2.03
3731	Ship building and repairing	1.59
3732	Boat building and repairing	3.48
3743	Railroad equipment	2.98
3751	Motorcycles, bicycles, and parts	5.00
376	Guided missiles, space vehicles, parts	3.49
3761	Guided missiles and space vehicles	3.74
3764	Space propulsion units and parts	3.53
3769	Space vehicle equipment,n.e.c.	1.79
379	Miscellaneous transportation equipment	4.45
3792	Travel trailers and campers	5.51
3795	Tanks and tank components	3.29
3799	Transportation equipment,n.e.c.	6.18
38	Instruments and related products	3.26
3811	Engineering and scientific instruments	2.36
382	Measuring and controlling devices	2.56
3822	Environmental controls	1.96
3823	Process control instruments	2.97

SIC CODE	Ratio of Materials to Labor INDUSTRY GROUP AND INDUSTRY	Ratio Materials/ Labor
3824	Fluid meters and counting devices	2.62
3825	Instruments to measure electricity	2.44
3829	Measuring and controlling devices,n.e.c.	2.85
3832	Optical instruments and lenses	3.64
384	Medical instruments and supplies	3.21
3841	Surgical and medical instruments	2.64
3842	Surgical appliances ans supplies	3.70
3843	Dental equipment and supplies	3.22
3851	Opthalmic goods	2.28
3861	Photographic equipment and supplies	4.95
3873	Watches, clocks, and watchcases	4.97
39	Miscellaneous manufacturing industries	3.59
391	Jewelry, silverware, and plated ware	5.69
3911	Jewelry, precious metal	5.96
3914	Silverware and plated ware	3.20
3915	Jeweler's materials and lapidary work	6.81
3931	Musical instruments	2.15
394	Toys and sporting goods	4.73
3942	Dolls	10.20
3944	Games, toys, and children's vehicles	5.24
3949	Sporting and athletic goods,n.e.c.	4.10
395	Pens, pencils, and office and art equipment	3.42
3951	Pens and mechanical pencils	3.13
3952	Lead pencils and art goods	3.87
3953	Marking devices	1.70
3955	Carbon paper and inked ribbons	4.55
396	Costume jewelry and notions	2.94
3961	Costume jewelry	3.03
3962	Artificial flowers	3.20
3963	Buttons	3.84
3964	Needles, pins, and fasteners	2.54

SIC CODE	Ratio of Materials to Labor INDUSTRY GROUP AND INDUSTRY	Ratio Materials/ Labor
399	Miscellaneous manufacturers	2.66
3991	Brooms and brushes	3.25
3993	Signs and advertising displays	2.26
3995	Burial caskets	3.22
3996	Hard surface floor coverings	3.18
3999	Manufacturing industries, n.e.c.	2.77
	These ratios were developed from data	
	contained in the U.S. Department of Commerce	
	Publication, "Annual Survey of Manufacturers:	
	1986" using column 'g' divided by column 'e'.	

Note: n.e.c. means not elsewhere classified.

	OVERHEAD AS A PERCENT OF DIRECT LABOR		
	Manual Hand Type Operations One Stage Machine Operations	Semi-Automated Process Operations & Techniques Multi-Stage Machine Operations	Automated Facilities Processes N.C.M. Computer Systems
Piece Parts	100%	175 to 200%	250 to 300%
Sheet Metal Stamping Forming Blanking Drilling Other	125%	150 to 200%	250 to 350%
Casting	125%	150 to 250%	275 to 400%
Assembly (Apparatus)	100%	100 to 200%	225 to 400%
Components	-	175 to 200%	250 to 300%
Equipment	125%	175 to 225%	250 to 500%
Plastic Molding	-	150 to 200%	225 to 300%

		OPERATING EXPENSES AND OTHER EXPENSES*			
		(as a percent of factory cost - for selected industries)			
			$1MM-$10MM	$10MM-$50MM	ALL
SIC CODE		INDUSTRY	IN ASSETS	IN ASSETS	SIZES
	2394	Canvas Products	28.1	-	45.3
2621,	2631	Pulp Paper and Paperboard	24.1	19.4	25.5
2652	2653	Paper Board, Containers, Boxes	28.6	20.8	28.7
2655	2656				
	2752	Commercial Printing (Lithographic)	39.3	26.7	46.8
	2759	Commercial Printing , Letterpress & Screen	38.0	-	47.1
	2821	Plastic Materials & Synthetic Resins	25.7	27.2	29.7
	2851	Paint, Varnish, Lacquer & Allied Products	41.8	40.0	45.1
2861,	2865	Industrial Chemicals	39.4	26.9	41.2
	2869				
	3089	Misc. Plastic Products	28.6	24.6	30.9
3321,	3322	Iron & Steel Foundries	26.1	15.7	26.0
3324,	3325				
3363 -	3366	Non-Ferrous Foundries	22.5	15.7	24.9
	3369				
	3398	Metal Heat Treating	37.4	-	41.0
	3411	Metal Cans	22.5	-	18.3
3421,	3423	Cutlery, Hand Tools &	40.2	34.6	41.3
3425	3429	General Hardware			
	3441	Fabricated Structural Metal	23.3	19.4	27.9
	3443	Fabricated Plate Work	25.6	15.8	29.4
	3444	Sheet Metal Work	28.6	25.5	33.9
3451,	3452	Screw Machine Products	28.0	21.4	30.4
	3462	Iron & Steel Forgings	23.1	23.8	23.9
3465,	3466	Metal Stampings	23.1	18.5	25.7
	3469				

		OPERATING EXPENSES AND OTHER EXPENSES*			
		(as a percent of factory cost - for selected industries)			
			$1MM-$10MM	$10MM-$50MM	ALL
SIC CODE		INDUSTRY	IN ASSETS	IN ASSETS	SIZES
	3496	Miscellaneous Fabricated Wire Products	25.3	22.1	28.6
	3499	Miscellandous Fabricated Metal Products	30.8	27.8	37.1
	3544	Special Dies & Tools, Die Sets,	31.5	21.1	36.9
		Jigs & Fixtures, & Industrial Molds			
3552 -	3556	Special Industry Machinery	40.4	33.9	41.7
	3559				
3561,	3564	General Industrial	39.2	33.1	39.7
3566,	3567	Machinery & Equipment			
	3569				
	3562	Ball and Roller Bearings	32.4	-	31.7
	3571	Electronic Computers	58.6	71.5	62.6
	3599	Machine Shops - Jobbing & Repair	32.9	29.0	42.7
3612,	3613	Equip. for Public Utilities & Industrial Use	36.9	33.1	38.2
	3621				
	3663	Radio & TV Broadcasting &	48.8	51.6	51.2
		Communications Equipment			
3671,	3672	Electronic Components	43.6	40.7	45.2
3674 -	3679	& Accessories			
	3823	Industrial Instruments for	59.4	59.9	64.1
		Measurement Display & Control			
	3825	Instruments for Measuring of	78.6	65.5	75.4
		Electricity & Electrical Signals			
	3861	Photographic Equipment & Supplies	51.2	41.6	50.6
		Tables Adapted From: "Annual Statement Studies" - Robert Morris Associates - 1989,			
		using the formula:			
		((Operating Expense + Other Expense)/(100 - Gross Profit)) x 100			
		* Operating expenses include GS & A, R&D, interest, amortization and other charges.			

		PROFIT BEFORE TAXES			
		(as a percent of total cost - for selected industries)			
			$1MM-$10MM	$10MM-$50MM	ALL
SIC CODE		INDUSTRY	IN ASSETS	IN ASSETS	SIZES
	2394	Canvas Products	1.1	-	4.1
2621,	2631	Pulp Paper and Paperboard	4.5	5.4	5.3
2652	2653	Paper Board, Containers, Boxes	3.5	4.6	3.6
2655	2656				
	2752	Commercial Printing (Lithographic)	3.6	4.9	3.5
	2759	Commercial Printing , Letterpress & Screen	3.8	-	3.3
	2821	Plastic Materials & Synthetic Resins	3.2	4.7	3.2
	2851	Paint, Varnish, Lacquer & Allied Products	3.1	3.5	3.2
2861,	2865	Industrial Chemicals	4.7	8.8	5.7
	2869				
	3089	Misc. Plastic Products	4.3	4.9	4.1
3321,	3322	Iron & Steel Foundries	4.3	3.7	3.7
3324,	3325				
3363 -	3366	Non-Ferrous Foundries	4.9	5.4	4.8
	3369				
	3398	Metal Heat Treating	7.1	-	8.6
	3411	Metal Cans	-0.4	-	2.2
3421,	3423	Cutlery, Hand Tools &	5.7	6.2	5.7
3425	3429	General Hardware			
	3441	Fabricated Structural Metal	3.7	2.9	3.8
	3443	Fabricated Plate Work	5.0	5.2	5.4
	3444	Sheet Metal Work	3.1	5.8	3.5
3451,	3452	Screw Machine Products	5.0	7.4	4.9
	3462	Iron & Steel Forgings	4.2	4.1	4.9
3465,	3466	Metal Stampings	4.4	6.7	4.9
	3469				

SIC CODE		INDUSTRY	$1MM-$10MM IN ASSETS	$10MM-$50MM IN ASSETS	ALL SIZES
		PROFIT BEFORE TAXES (as a percent of total cost - for selected industries)			
	3496	Miscellaneous Fabricated Wire Products	4.5	5.3	4.0
	3499	Miscellandous Fabricated Metal Products	3.7	7.1	4.1
	3544	Special Dies & Tools, Die Sets, Jigs & Fixtures, & Industrial Molds	3.2	5.4	4.2
3552 -	3556 3559	Special Industry Machinery	3.8	4.5	4.0
3561, 3566,	3564 3567 3569	General Industrial Machinery & Equipment	4.4	6.2	4.3
	3562	Ball and Roller Bearings	5.6	-	4.7
	3571	Electronic Computers	3.1	1.4	4.4
	3599	Machine Shops - Jobbing & Repair	5.4	5.5	4.9
3612,	3613 3621	Equip. for Public Utilities & Industrial Use	3.2	1.8	3.5
	3663	Radio & TV Broadcasting & Communications Equipment	5.8	7.8	4.7
3671, 3674 -	3672 3679	Electronic Components & Accessories	4.6	4.1	4.5
	3823	Industrial Instruments for Measurement Display & Control	5.8	5.5	5.3
	3825	Instruments for Measuring of Electricity & Electrical Signals	1.6	11.4	4.6
	3861	Photographic Equipment & Supplies	1.3	2.0	1.8

Tables Adapted From: "Annual Statement Studies" - Robert Morris Associates - 1989, using the formula:

{(Profit before taxes)/(100 - Profit before taxes)} x 100

Appendix F*

Price Adjustment Clauses Based on Cost Indices**

Price adjustment (PA) clauses can be used effectively as tools for mitigating price-escalation risks in long-term contracting. This approach provides for the negotiation of a mechanism that can automatically adjust contract recoveries in response to fluctuations in price levels in specific sectors of the economy. PA clauses result not only in risk reduction for the supplier but also, if used wisely, in lower prices for the buyer.

PA clauses are included in contracts to protect both the buyer and the seller from significant cost changes caused by fluctuations in price levels in the general economy. These fluctuations, which are beyond the control of either party, may introduce substantial risk into contract negotiations. This is particularly true if the negotiators are required to agree on firm prices for materials or services to be

---

*Referred to on pages 132, 263, and 278.

**This material is based on the article "Price Adjustment Clauses Based on Cost Indices" by James M. Caltrider of the University of San Diego which appeared in the April 1987 issue of the *Journal of Purchasing and Materials Management*. The article is copyrighted by the National Association of Purchasing Management and used with its permission.

delivered over an extended period of performance. The PA clause limits the risks associated with these price changes by automatically adjusting the costs recovered in response to changes actually occurring in the economy.

If no price adjustment mechanism is included in a contract, the seller will often include an escalation contingency pad in its price to cover most possible cost escalations. To the extent that escalation contingencies are included in sellers' prices, buyers' costs are increased by escalation uncertainty even if firm-fixed-price contracts are used.

If a PA clause is used, the buyer accepts the risk of cost escalations, but is immediately rewarded by removal of the escalation contingency pad from the seller's price. In reality, the buyer receives a guaranteed, immediate price reduction in return for accepting the risk of possible cost escalation of uncertain magnitude at some point in the future. In most cases the escalation actually experienced is less than the contingency a risk-averse seller would have included to cover most possible cost escalations. Roles and risks are reversed if a decrease in price levels is expected.

This concept is illustrated by the following example. Assume the seller expects cost escalation ranging from 3 to 17 percent, with an average of 10 percent. To cover itself against most probable escalation rates, the seller may include an escalation contingency of 15 percent in its price. This escalation-adjusted price must be paid regardless of what actual escalation develops.

The use of a PA clause would shift the escalation uncertainty to the buyer and allow the seller to remove the escalation contingency pad from its price. The buyer now pays for the escalation that actually occurs. That actual inflation level will likely be less than the amount of the escalation contingency.

Application of PA clauses involves the use of projected escalation factors to adjust estimated constant dollar costs for price increases expected during the future period of performance. Anticipated future recoveries for the seller are based on these escalation-adjusted cost estimates. These projected escalation rates then are compared periodically with the actual escalation experienced. Contractor recovery is adjusted if actual escalation varies outside of a defined range bracketing the projected escalation rate.

BASIC COMPONENTS OF PA CLAUSES

The mechanics of the recovery adjustment are prenegotiated as part of the original contract. Although the provisions negotiated in any individual contract may vary, PA clauses usually require agreement on the following components:

1. The costs that would be incurred if all materials or services were delivered instantaneously instead of over an extended period of performance. These costs are sometimes called "constant dollar" or "today's dollar" costs because the impact of cost escalations, inflation, deflation, etc., have purposely been omitted.

2. Specific definition of which contract costs will be subject to escalation and which will be excluded. Typically, only portions of contractor labor and material, but no other cost elements, are covered.

3. An assumed or projected rate of cost or price increase or decrease. In other words, what rate of cost escalation is anticipated in each period of the contract?

4. A means of retrospectively measuring the actual rate of cost escalation experienced in each period. This measure would quantify the actual cost increases and decreases caused by changes in the general economy as a whole. Because these changes result from fluctuations in general economic conditions, such as inflation and deflation, they lie beyond the control of either of the contracting parties.

5. An adjustment process to correct the contractor's recovery, based on the difference between the actual change in the selected index and the projected escalation rates negotiated in the original contract. This adjustment may take place monthly, quarterly, annually, or at any other time interval written into the contract.

Many different adjustment methodologies are utilized in developing economic price adjustment clauses. However, the following discussion develops the logic and mechanics of adjustment based on cost indices.

BUREAU OF LABOR STATISTICS INDICES

Bureau of Labor Statistics (BLS) data lie at the heart of escalation based on cost index calculations. The BLS is the federal agency charged with gathering labor and related economic data. It obtains data primarily from voluntary responses to surveys of businesses and households. This data is then compiled, analyzed, and published by the BLS on a regular basis; much of it is published monthly. BLS statistics often are used as an input for price adjustment clauses because they represent an independent, impartial, published evaluation of price changes in the national economy or in specific sectors of the economy.

BLS statistics include thousands of different cost indices which measure the changes in cost that have occurred since a given historical reference point. For example, an average index figure of 322.5 in January 1985 and a corresponding index of 100 for January 1967 would indicate that the price of this material increased 222.5 percentage points between 1966 and 1985. This data makes it possible to quantify price or cost changes through time. BLS statistics include thousands of different cost indices, including the Producer Price Index (PPI) and the Consumer Price Index (CPI).

The Producer Price Index (PPI) measures changes in prices received in primary U.S. markets by producers of commodities in all stages of processing. Indices are reported monthly in stage of processing and commodity formats. Indices are also reported for selected industries by industry and product code.

The Consumer Price Index (CPI) measures price changes for a weighted combination (market basket) of 382 items representing the goods and services purchased by urban residents.

PA BASED ON COST INDICES

The use of BLS indices in PA activities requires identification of the specific indices that best track the costs subject to escalation. The values of these selected indices are then projected for each contract year by the negotiating parties. Contract prices for goods and services to be delivered in each year are defined by these projected index levels. Finally, the variation between actual and projected levels is used to retroactively adjust contract prices. For example, if actual indices are lower than those projected, then cost escalation has not been as high as was anticipated at the time the contract was negotiated. In this case, the seller owes the buyer for the difference between the price paid, which included projected escalation, and the total cost determined by the escalation that actually occurred. If the actual index is greater than the projected index, the seller would receive a larger payment than was included in the initial negotiation.

The structure of BLS indices makes it possible to select the most representative index which indices will be projected and used to measure the escalation actually experienced for a specific component of cost in a given sector of the economy. Figure F.1 illustrates this concept. SIC 37 includes costs for all transportation equipment, including the costs of aircraft (and parts) and guided missile and space vehicle parts. SIC 372 segregates the costs of aircraft and parts from the broader coverage of SIC 37. Similarly, SIC 376 captures the costs of guided missile and space vehicle parts only.

Figure F.1 Standard Industrial Classification Structure

SIC 37   Transportation Equipment

SIC 372   Aircraft and Parts

SIC 376   Guided Missile and Space Vehicle Parts

When developing a PA clause based on cost indices, negotiators attempt to identify those BLS indices which most accurately isolate the relevant components of cost within the specific industry involved. If a contractor's total costs are determined by both wage and material costs, separate indices may be identified to forecast and measure escalation for labor and material. The following hypothetical example illustrates this process.

AN ILLUSTRATION OF THE PROCESS

PA Clause Negotiation

Assume that two aerospace firms are in the process of negotiating a contract that will be executed over a five year period of performance. Representatives of both firms believe that there is substantial uncertainty regarding cost escalation over that period. Price levels in the economy may decline, remain stable, or climb if inflation develops. Therefore, a PA clause based on cost indices is being negotiated as part of the contact.

This negotiation will require agreement on the following points:

1. A constant dollar cost for contracted goods and services.

2. An explicit definition of which costs are subject to escalation.

3. Definition of the published indices that will be used to measure the escalation occurring in the time interval between the base year and each year in the period of performance.

4. Projection of the selected indices for each year during the period of performance.

5. A mechanism for adjusting payments if actual escalation indicated by the indices varies significantly from the levels projected at the time the contract is negotiated.

The negotiators ultimately develop a PA clause with the following provisions. The product to be delivered in each of the five contract years will have a $40 million cost in constant 1986 dollars. Of this total, $30 million is subject to escalation.

Contract labor costs account for $10 million of the total annual cost subject to escalation. Material purchased by the contractor makes up the $20 million balance. SIC 372, which measures the changes in wage costs for workers in aircraft and aircraft parts manufacturing, will be used to escalate and adjust the $10 million labor cost component.

The negotiators have agreed that the $20 million in projected material cost will be escalated and adjusted using a combination of PPI-IC (Producer's Price Index-Industrial Commodities) and SIC 372. This composite index is used because contractor material costs are influenced by changes in supplier's labor costs as well as by the obvious impact of cost changes in raw materials, parts, and assemblies purchased by the contractor and its suppliers. Because the contractor often has PA clauses negotiated with its suppliers, cost increases subject to escalation experienced by suppliers will probably be passed through to the contractor and finally to the buyer, the contractor's customer. In this hypothetical case, the contractor has surveyed its suppliers to determine which indices best track supplier cost increases. These surveys revealed that approximately 30 percent of the contractor's material cost was determined by supplier labor cost, which could be tracked using SIC 372. The remaining 70 percent of the material cost was determined by supplier material costs, best tracked with PPI-IC. These percentages, or weighting factors, must explicitly be included in the adjustment mechanism negotiated.

Once a constant dollar cost has been negotiated and appropriate cost indices identified, the selected indices must be projected for each period of contract performance. Forecasts may be obtained from a forecasting service or may be developed internally, based on the firm's procurement history and experience. In this case, the negotiators settle on a projected first-year index of 349.70 for PPI- IC and 15.5 for SIC 372. Table F.1 summarizes these results.

Table F.1   Negotiated PA Clause Provisions

	Labor	Material
1. Costs Subject to Escalation (Constant 1986 Dollars	$10mm	$20mm
2. Index Composition	100% SIC-Wages 372	30% SIC-Wages 372 70% PPI-IC
3. Base Year (1986) Indices		
A. SIC-WAGES 372	15.0	15.0
B. PPI-IC	N/A	323.8
4. Projected 1987 Index		
A. SIC-Wages 372	15.5	15.5
B. PPI-IC	N/A	349.70

Finally, the negotiators must define an adjustment mechanism. The mechanism to be used is shown in Figure F.2. It is agreed in this hypothetical case that prices will be adjusted if the actual index varies from the projected index by 1 percent or more.

Sample Adjustment Calculation

A year has passed since the initial negotiation, and actual indices have become available for PPI-IC and SIC 372. The current indices are 356.18 and 16.0 respectively. Prices or costs recovered in the first year of the contract can now be adjusted for the difference between actual and projected escalation rates. These adjustment calculations are shown in Figures F.3 and F.4.

In this illustration the actual escalation incurred exceeded the rates projected during the original contract negotiation, so the contractor will receive an additional $776,036 to compensate for the additional cost increases—a $323,236 labor adjustment shown in Figure F.3 and a $452,800 material-related adjustment detailed in Figure F.4. On the other hand, if the escalation rates actually experienced had been lower than those included in the original contract, the contractor would owe the buyer the difference between the actual and the projected figures.

A supplier will often negotiate PA clauses with its vendors as well as with the buyer's organization. In this situation it may be important to coordinate the projected escalation rates used in these clauses to ensure consistency throughout the entire agreement.

Figure F.2   Negotiated Adjustment Calculation Mechanism

A. Indices used   A. <u>SIC-WAGES 372 PPI-IC</u>

B. Average Actual 1987 Index   B. _____
    (from published BLS indices)

C. Average 1986 (base year)   C. _____
    Index

D. Line B/Line C = Normalized   D. _____
    Actual Index (average actual
    escalation rate since base year)

E. 1987 Index Projected in Origi-   E. _____
    nal Contract Negotiation

F. Average Base Year Index   F. _____
    (1986 index in this case)

G. Line E/Line F = Line G   G. _____
    (expected escalation rate built
    into the original contract)

H. Line D – Line G = Line H   H. _____
    (difference between actual and
    expected escalation rates)

I. Line H/Line G = Line I   I. _____
    (percentage change in
    escalation from the rate built
    into original contract)

J. Costs Subject to Escalation (as   J. _____
    identified in original contract)

K. Weighting Factor(s) (negoti-   K. _____
    ated in original contract)

L. [(Line I) x (Line J) x   L. _____
    (Line K)] = Line L:
    Total Adjustment in Dollars

Figure F.3   Negotiated Adjustment Calculation Mechanism

Cost Category: Labor

A.	Indices used	A.	SIC-WAGES 372
B.	Average Actual 1987 Index (from published BLS indices)	B.	16.0
C.	Average 1986 (base year) Index	C.	15.0
D.	Line B/Line C = Normalized Actual Index (average actual escalation rate since base year)	D.	1.0667
E.	1987 Index Projected in Original Contract Negotiation	E.	15.5
F.	Average Base Year Index (1986 index in this case)	F.	15.0
G.	Line E/Line F = Line G (expected escalation rate built into the original contract)	G.	1.0333
H.	Line D – Line G = Line H (difference between actual and expected escalation rates)	H.	.0334
I.	Line H/Line G = Line I (percentage change in escalation from the rate built into original contract)	I.	.0323
J.	Costs Subject to Escalation (as identified in original contract)	J.	$10mm
K.	Weighting Factor(s) (negotiated in original contract)	K.	100%
L.	[(Line I) x (Line J) x (Line K)] = Line L: Total Labor Adjustment	L.	$323,236

Figure F.4 Negotiated Adjustment Calculation Mechanism

Cost Category: Material

A.	Indices used	A.	<u>SIC-WAGES 372 PPI-IC</u>
B.	Average Actual 1987 Index (from published BLS indices)	B.	<u>16.0</u> <u>356.18</u>
C.	Average 1986 (base year) Index	C.	<u>15.0</u> <u>323.8</u>
D.	Line B/Line C = Normalized Actual Index (average actual escalation rate since base year)	D.	<u>1.0667</u> <u>1.10</u>
E.	1987 Index Projected in Original Contract Negotiation	E.	<u>15.5</u> <u>349.7</u>
F.	Average Base Year Index (1986 index in this case)	F.	<u>15.0</u> <u>323.8</u>
G.	Line E/Line F = Line G (expected escalation rate built into the original contract)	G.	<u>1.0333</u> <u>1.08</u>
H.	Line D - Line G = Line H (difference between actual and expected escalation rates)	H.	<u>.0334</u> <u>.02</u>
I.	Line H/Line G = Line I (percentage change in escalation from the rate built into original contract)	I.	<u>.0323</u> <u>.0185</u>
J.	Costs Subject to Escalation (as identified in original contract)	J.	<u>$20mm</u> <u>$20mm</u>
K.	Weighting Factor(s) (negotiated in original contract)	K.	<u>.30</u> <u>.70</u>
L.	[(Line I) x (Line J) x (Line K)] = Line L: Total Material Adjustment	L.	<u>193,800</u> <u>$259,000</u> $452,800

CONCLUDING REMARKS

This presentation has shown how PA clauses can mitigate some of the risks involved in long-term contracting. PA clauses protect both buyer and seller from cost fluctuations caused by changes in general economic conditions. The use of these clauses can also result in lower prices for the buyer. PA clauses are not designed, however, to protect contracting parties from cost changes owing to poor management, procurement, and the like.

Price adjustment clauses based on cost indices provide a means of impartially assessing fluctuations in general price levels based on regularly published government statistics. The structure of the Bureau of Labor Statistics indices allows negotiators to define precisely which indices will be used to evaluate the cost changes relevant in a particular situation. Generally speaking, the use of PA clauses can be expected to increase with the growing volatility in materials and labor markets and the continued escalation of international competition.

Appendix G*

The Ultimate in Negotiation Preparation: On-Line Data Bases**

Using electronic data bases is not an all-or-nothing situation. The occasional user can employ one of the local libraries that will search for a fee, or he/she can use a gateway service such as "Easynet" which helps the buyer to focus the search topic and then does the search for the buyer, at a cost.

The regular user should look for a data base company that incorporates the data bases that meet the organization's particular requirements. Then each candidate's costs and user friendliness of its search techniques should be compared. The buyer or researcher should not confuse the data base with the company selling the service. Many data bases can be reached through a number of suppliers.

To get started the purchasing professional needs:

- An on-line supplies subscription and password
- Communications software
- A personal computer terminal

*Referred to on page 292.

**Much of this appendix is adapted from W. E. Norquist's paper "The Ultimate in Negotiation Preparation: On-Line Data Bases," *Purchasing's New Frontiers*, National Association of Purchasing Management, Tempe, Arizona, 1988.

- A modem, preferably high speed
- A telephone line
- A printer

MECHANICS

Search Strategy

The first skill required for the use of on-line data bases is that of searching for pertinent information. This involves identifying the relevant data base and developing key words to use so that the search will be narrow, brief, and to the point. Searches can be expensive if one cannot get in and out of the data base quickly.

The buyer or purchasing researcher can become skilled by taking a course or workshop, joining a local users' group, and of course, by reading as well as working with others in the department who are more skilled in information search. Polaroid has two people in Purchasing Research who do data base searches as a significant part of their overall responsibilities. These individuals also teach others how to conduct efficient searches.

Communications Software

Communications software packages such as "Pro-search" or "Cross-talk" are meant to help the researcher, whether novice or expert. "Pro-search," for the IBM-PC and its compatibles, is designed to make it easy to access Dialog and BRS on-line and offers the following benefits:

- Knows the data bases and helps locate the right one.
- Lets the user formulate search strategy on his or her own computer screen before the expense of going on-line.
- Dials the data wholesaler and sends the search request that the user has already organized on the screen almost instantaneously at the touch of a key.
- Provides the user with the charge at the end of each response.

Both packages give the researcher the ability to perform complex operations routinely; i.e., the PC to dial an on-line service, log on, submit search requests, collect and save responses on a disk, then log off. Such searches also can be set to run off-hours when rates are lower.

Data Base Training Files

Lockheed's "Dialog" data base file selection offers "partial standard files" which are prefixed ONTAP. They are priced reasonably. The buyer can use them while learning the skill of searching economically. Picking key words, using the right combination of key words and evaluating an article's potential from titles and abstracts, are all skills that develop with practice.

Some of Our Most Searched Data Base Files

Experience has shown that a department tends to use certain data bases more than others. Polaroid's purchasing professionals have found the following data bases particularly useful.

Dialindex (Dialog) — A file created to help dialog searchers determine what data bases are best to search on a given topic. This file provides the number of postings for each search statement in each of the specified data bases—useful in determining which files would be the most productive. (Provider: Dialog Information Services, Inc., Palo Alto, CA.)

Investext (Dialog) — Provides financial research reports from financial analysts containing sales and earnings forecasts, market share projections, R&D expenditures, etc. (Provider: Business Research Corp., Boston, MA.)

Newsearch (Dialog) — Daily index of more than 2,000 news stories, articles and book reviews from over 1,700 newspapers, magazines and periodicals. (Provider: Information Access Co., Belmont, CA.)

ABI Inform (Dialog/ BRS/Orbit)	Stresses general management and administrative information applicable to many types of businesses and industries. Has lengthy, in-depth articles on many business subjects. (Provider: Data Courier, Louisville, KY.)
PTS Prompt (Dialog/ BRS/Orbit)	Predicasts Overview of Markets and Technology—Provides broad international coverage of companies, products, markets and technologies for all industries (market share hard numbers, percentage, etc.). The only system that provides a seven digit product code enabling the searcher to go beyond the four digit SIC code for more specific data. (Provider: Predicasts, Cleveland, OH.)
PTS U.S. Forecasts	Contains abstracts of published forecasts for the U.S. including historical base, period data, a short-term forecast and a long-term forecast. The scope can be seen from the fact that this data base has 501,912 records.
Standard & Poor's Register Corporate	Provides facts on over 450,000 companies including financial and marketing records and biographical information on officers and major executives.

As discussed in Chapter 14, a new class of services has emerged which provides customized and proactive searches of up-to-the-minute news (as opposed to historical sources) and delivers the information to the buyer's desk on a regular basis.

Polaroid has also been using an individualized research service called *First!* (from Individual, Inc., 84 Sherman Street, Cambridge, MA), which uses new technology to analyze the concepts and topics in an article, thereby identifying news items of greatest relevance to the buyer. This requires plain English input from the buyer and simple feedback at regular intervals: the buyer checks off the stories that proved to be of greatest relevance. *First!* learns from this feedback and becomes more intelligent at identifying stories that truly match the buyer's evolving interests.

First! is delivered by fax to the buyer's desk by 8:00 AM or can be delivered by electronic mail for internal redistribution to groups which are tracking the same issues or companies. Redistribution rights allow the purchasing executives to keep all their buyers up to date on critical issues affecting their markets and vendors.

First! analyzes business stories from regional, national, and international wire services including Reuters, UPI, Business Wire, and various European and Japanese services.

BENEFITS

The benefits of using electronic data base searches include:

- The actual and psychological advantages that result from knowing all about the supplier and the supplier's industry.
- Speed in gaining data.
- Access to information on a 24-hour-a-day basis.
- Speed in learning that further searching is not warranted.

BUYERS THAT DO WELL ARE MORE THAN LUCKY. They know the value of resources and know how to acquire the background intelligence for doing their job well. They also are the people who know the value of information. This is the most critical part of the job—getting and using information intelligently. The result of extensive preparation is a buyer with confidence.

Following is a form (Figure G.1) that a company with a purchasing research department could use to have buyers request specific information that he/she feels will be of possible value in an upcoming negotiation.

Alternately, the buyer who needs more help can ask for assistance and meet with the researcher. The researcher can, by asking incisive questions, set the scope for a series of data base searches that can enhance the buyer's negotiation leverage and clout.

The potential user of on-line data bases is encouraged to obtain NAPM's Publication, 3.22, On-Line Databases. It can be ordered from the N.A.P.M., 2055 East Centennial Circle, Post Office Box 22160, Tempe, Arizona 85282-0960 (602-752-6276).

Figure G.1

Purchasing Research
Negotiation Information Request Checklist

BUYER'S NAME:

COMPANY/NEGOTIATION:

REASON FOR REQUEST:

INFORMATION DUE DATE:

Financial

☐ Financial Information
☐ Balance Sheet
☐ Income Statement
☐ Annual Report Statement
☐ Efficiency Improvement
☐ Overhead Rate
☐ Change in Cost of Goods Sold
☐ Change in Market Share of Products
☐ Amount of Debt vs. Equity
☐ Sources and Uses of Funds
☐ Cash Flow
☐ Dun & Bradstreet
☐ 10-k Report

General Business

☐ Our purchases relative to supplier's annual sales
☐ Supplier's sales as a function of industry
☐ Supplier's product announcements

- Changes in capacity
- Personnel changes (at supplier)
- EPA considerations; lawsuits, pollution control investments
- Change in union contract
- Long-term contracts
- Changes in lead time
- Suppliers available in this field
- Sales for cash
- Acquisition and divestiture by supplier
- Joint ventures of supplier
- Business news files
- Who owns what

Cost Model

- Price & Cost Changes
- National
- Regional
- Specific material (list materials)
- Wage rates
- Power-energy rates
- Producer price index (state items)
- Industry model

Appendix H*

Certification Letter

Dear

Congratulations! This letter is to inform you that XXXXXXXXXXX has been qualified as a Certified Component. This selection has been based upon the criteria on the attached check list, as well as the individual judgment and recommendation of the engineers and managers on the material procurement team.

We at Polaroid want you to know how much we appreciate the organizational strengths and attention to detail that made this certification possible. In addition to the satisfaction your organization should feel in this new status, it also carries with it a new and added responsibility. With a certified component, Polaroid places the decision to accept and ship to stock in the hands of the organization manufacturing this material rather than an acceptance inspection in our Incoming Inspection Department. Our Supplier Relations Quality Engineering involvement will now shift to a monitoring mode only and an occasional inspection of selected samples for the purpose of maintaining interlaboratory correlation. In addition, our Supplier Engineer will continue to include Process Improvement as an agenda item in our periodic Quality Reviews, in order to quantitatively measure and to discuss the status and progress of your Process Improve-

---

*Referred to on page 326.

ment Program. The focus of your program is to continue to control the process around aim point and decrease the variation.

Components and products which are certified may be shipped, based upon the process control data and consistent with the terms of the Polaroid Purchase Order. However, the Supplier Relations and Incoming Inspection departments still would like the receipt of the required data in advance of the shipment. This is necessary to insure proper identification and physical release in our Materials organization.

To help with this we have supplied a computer software program to use for these purposes. Our goal is to move towards the implementation of a system which will allow for electronic submittal of your data on an ongoing basis, in order to monitor your SPC system. However, the real benefit of this software will be as an analytical tool for monitoring your own process:

1. If you enter the appropriate data as it is being generated, the system may be used as a real-time process monitor, using statistical comparison to expected results with more statistical power than simple X-Bars and R-Charts. In addition, there are options to test interrelationships between process and product parameters which may be used in a problem-solving situation.

2. Once the data is entered, it may be used to monitor both compliance to specification and relationships to expected results, based upon your capability studies.

   It is strongly recommended that you monitor these results prior to transmittal to Polaroid, as this exercise is what we will be doing upon receipt.

   At this point, this software may be useful to your organization as a post-run performance review, as a Quality Circle activity, or as a prevention aid *before* actual defective product is produced on subsequent runs due to deteriorating equipment. In this regard, it could also be used to determine optimized preventive maintenance or equipment calibration schedules.

3. Through the selective use of data before and after a process improvement or cost reduction project, a *quantitative* evaluation of the project can be prepared. These analyses could be the basis of your presentation of your Process Improvement Program within the Quality Reviews.

4. At Polaroid, we will be using your data to monitor the quality of the component and in our own Specification Refinement and Fit-for-Use Programs in our film assembly plants. The outcome of these programs are realistic specifications for component materials which optimize both the productivity of our manufacturing facilities as well as the quality of the products we ship to our customers.

This effort is expected to be an incremental series of steps over the coming years which move an Aim or Target Value, modify specification tolerance limits, eliminate some currently specified parameters, or add new ones with the overall objective of providing specifications for *key controlling* parameters which the person actually manufacturing the component can monitor *and control* on a real-time basis.

All of us here at Polaroid look forward to working with you in this new status. We know that this new status will prove profitable to both our companies.

Sincerely yours,

Vendor Relations Manager
Film Division

Purchasing Manager
Film Division

Supplier Certification Requirement Status

SUPPLIER: XXXXXXXXXXXX

DATE: 11/03/87

MATERIAL: XXXXXXXXX

PREPARED BY: XXXXXX

CERTIFICATION REQUIREMENTS

Status	No	Yes	Date
1. Approved specifications - no exceptions		x	7/1/87
2. Capability study approved and on file		x	1/21/87
3. Parameters 75% of specification limit		x	11/03/87

Name	Spec.	Process Control Index
XXXXX	_____	.55
XXXXXXXXXX	_____	.66
XXXX	_____	.69
XXXXXXX	_____	.74
XXXXXXXX	_____	.50
XXXXXXXXXX	_____	.60

	No	Yes	Date
4. Process Control Plan approved and on file (1)		x	1/88
5. Methodology to summarize & analyze data (ongoing)		x	1/87
6. Electronic Data Submission-Product & Process Data		x	9/87
7. Ongoing system of continuous improvement		x	1/87

EXCEPTIONS AND PLAN TO RESOLVE _____
_____
_____

APPROVAL LIST

_____
_____
_____

Appendix I*

Polaroid Ground Rules—1988 Update for Cost Reduction/Cost Avoidance** Reporting

---

*Referred to on page 341.

**Cost avoidance savings generally are not known and therefore cannot be estimated ahead of time. However, circumstances arise where to not count these actual savings would be unrealistic. The object of this program is to motivate and recognize the personnel making these contributions.

I. DEFINITIONS

Savings

The savings to be achieved during the first full year at the planned volumes, including yield allowances. Savings are counted for the first twelve months they become effective.

Planned Volume

Budget plan for the year or part of two years involved.

Target Date

The quarter of the year in which the savings will become effective. (invoice payment, not orders).

Incremental Savings

Savings achieved by purchasing incremental volumes at the same price or lower unit prices should *not* be included in cost reduction reports. They should be tracked and reported in purchase price variance reports.

General Price Reductions

Industrywide price reductions granted by suppliers as a result of deflationary or competitive factors should *not* be added to or qualify as cost reduction or avoidance projects.

Quarterly Reporting

After the annual cost reduction/cost avoidance plan is developed for the calendar year by each division there are quarterly reports of actual savings performance. If projects have changed during a quarter, the necessary report adjustment is made. Since this report notes your cost reduction/cost avoidance activity, it is important that accuracy be maintained and backup calculations be available and readily understandable.

I.A. RATIONALE FOR DEFINITIONS

Savings

The intent is to state firmly, but with a degree of conservatism, the savings of cost reduction and cost avoidance efforts. Some contracts or purchase agreements will produce multi-year savings; these rules recognize and report only the first twelve months' savings.

Planned Volume

The volume element for the cost savings calculations. The savings calculations are not adjusted unless there is a major change in volume to minimize paperwork.

Target Date

The reporting is on a quarterly basis. Since our schedules are on a monthly accounting basis, the single element of cost savings calculations deals with monthly activity.

Incremental Savings

Price/volume effects are a normal function of the supply/demand principle and therefore do not qualify for cost savings. An unusual volume discount could qualify as a cost avoidance.

General Price Reductions

These market force effects are generally available and do not reflect the efforts of the buyer but are rather the result of supply and demand.

Quarterly Reporting

Maintaining confidence through credibility is a major element of the cost reduction/cost avoidance report activity.

II. COST REDUCTION CALCULATIONS

A. Material substitutions

B. Design or specification change

C. Supplier process improvement

D. Materials movement/handling improvements:
    The difference between the current cost (or projected cost) and the proposed cost for the coming year times the planned volume.

E. Alternate supplier selection
    The difference between the price charged by the old and new supplier items and the planned volumes allocated to the new supplier.

F. Competitive bids—*old items*
    The difference between the median bid price, the arithmetic mean bid price or the independent industry forecasted price, whichever is lower, and the accepted price times the planned volumes. Include any further savings produced from negotiations.

G. Negotiations—*Polaroid initiated*
    The difference between the current or independently forecasted price and the newly negotiated price times the planned volumes.

H. Procurement systems or cycle efficiencies
    1) The total savings in labor and systems costs or improvement of quality achieved by simplification or elimination of functions.
    2) Inventory reduction program-supplier location, quality, performance, etc., which influences the reduction of safety stock.

I. Other savings—to be analyzed on an individual basis until rules can be formulated.
    1) Make/buy decision
    2) Negotiation of a new escalator clause
    3) By-product sales

J.   Ongoing lease converted to a buyout. Calculate remaining savings and claim up to one year's savings.

K.   Learning curve improvement savings resulting from performance in excess of original learning curve calculation. Note: increased capital to change/lower learning curve does not qualify as a cost reduction for reporting.

II.A.   RATIONALE BEHIND COST REDUCTION CALCULATIONS

A.   Cost reduction - new material costs less.

B.   Cost reduction - new design costs less.

C.   Cost reduction - new process costs less.

D.   Cost reduction - of handling cost. If the old method would cost more because of wage increases, then the savings can be against the projected cost.

E.   Cost reduction - from prior purchase cost.

F.   Cost reduction - using the lower of three alternatives against the accepted bid. Experience shows that bidding pays and the buyer should get credit for the time expended.

G.   Cost reduction - in inflationary periods an independent forecast (or later, the PPI actual) is used to give credit for actual savings that inflation would otherwise obscure.

H.   Cost reduction - based on a more efficient materials function.

I.   1) Savings depend on whether the company is at or near capacity.

2) Hard to tell escalator clause savings except by hindsight.

3) Savings should be against the previous practices. If by-product was wasted, savings would be selling price and previous cost of disposal.

J.   Cost reduction - in money paid out, savings should be reduced by interest lost on early buyout.

K.   Cost reduction - if original learning curve goals are exceeded and buyer gets a further savings in price.

III. COST AVOIDANCE CALCULATIONS - SAVINGS THAT DON'T MEET COST REDUCTION CRITERIA

A. Negotiations - *supplier initiated*

The difference between the supplier's asking price and the negotiated price times the planned volumes. If the supplier's asking price is higher than an independent industry estimate, the latter should be used.

B. Negotiation - *Polaroid initiated*

The difference between the weighted index factors and the negotiated price times the planned volumes.

C. Negotiation - *increase postponed*

The difference between the new price and the old price times the volume involved in the delay.

D. Negotiation - *new way vs. old way*

The purchase is restructured in some way (consolidation, is now competitively bid, schedule changed to eliminate overtime and rush shipments, or it was not previously handled by purchasing). The action results in savings in addition to those counted under the cost reduction rules.

E. Lease/buy

Requisitioner wants to lease or buy an item. Purchasing takes action to apply alternative (buy changed to lease or lease changed to buy) which produces savings.

F. Competitive bids - *new items*

The difference between the median bid price, the arithmetic mean bid price or the recognized market (not list) price, whichever is lower, and the accepted bid price times the planning volumes.

G. Capital items

Savings obtained on capital item purchases from what might have been paid without purchasing's skills. For items with future delivery times beyond one year, the savings are reported when the purchase order is issued.

H. Duty exemptions

Savings obtained by avoiding duty payments; e.g., application of G.S.P.

III.A. RATIONALE BEHIND COST AVOIDANCE CALCULATIONS

A. An obvious overstatement will undermine the credibility of this report. Use of a government index (over the time involved) will avoid such overstatement.

B. This category falls within the avoidance area and gives the buyer credit based on buying below the change in the appropriate government index.

C. This is an avoidance that a buyer should be encouraged to make when all the other efforts to avoid an increase fail.

D. This incremental element of cost savings fits the cost avoidance definition because the price was definitely less than it would have been. Example: someone began buying furniture for full price without involving purchasing. Purchasing became aware of the situation. The buyer immediately was able to get a 25% discount and, with time, got 10% more. The 10% is a cost reduction, the 25% is a cost avoidance.

E. Since this is an item of new involvement, it falls under the cost avoidance structure.

F. New items under competitive bid are by definition, to be counted in the cost avoidance structure of cost savings.

G. Capital items are a unique situation when considering cost savings. Since lead times for capital items are usually in excess of one year, the provision for reporting savings will recognize savings when the purchase order is generated.

H. This is an avoidance of a cost incurred in the past or it may have taken a lot of effort to obtain exemptions. Savings are counted to recognize the contribution involved but are in avoidance.

Index